MUSIC

ITS LAWS AND EVOLUTION

BY

JULES COMBARIEU

PROFESSEUR D'HISTOIRE DE LA MUSIQUE
AU COLLÈGE DE FRANCE

1910

TABLE OF CONTENTS

INTRODUCTION

FIRST PART

MUSICAL THOUGHT AND PSYCHOLOGY

SECOND PART

MUSIC AND SOCIAL LIFE

THIRD PART

MUSICAL THOUGHT AND PHYSIOLOGY

FOURTH PART

MUSICAL THOUGHT AND THE LAWS OF NATURE

ERRATUM

Page 73. Second musical quotation, fourth bar. The second crotchet should have a rest added to it, increasing its value by one-half.

Page 78. Musical quotation, second bar. The same treatment should be applied to the first crotchet.

MUSIC: ITS LAWS AND EVOLUTION

INTRODUCTION

The chief aspects of music—Its place in the history of civilization—
Its connection with the Moral and Natural Sciences—Different
modes of defining music—Plan here adopted.

WE know that the waves rising on the surface
of the sea are not uniform, and that each of them
is made up of independent wavelets, added together
in such a way as to make but one mass and movement. In acoustics this fact is generally used as a
comparison when one wishes to explain the decompo-
sition of a sound-wave; but the æsthete and the
psychologist may also employ it to give an idea of
the very numerous and different phenomena, which,
like an indefinite harmonic series, enter into musical
expression and there find their unity. Music is a
breath which passes away, a wave of the air.

If we only considered the sensation produced,
nothing would be more ephemeral or more deceptive ; but in this breath the soul of a Beethoven
may speak eloquently : it is capable of bringing
before us, with the help of a special *technique* and
the projection forth of itself of a rare personality,
an image of social life, of race, of humanity, and of
certain laws of nature, together with something

B

superior to all these, or at any rate differing from them.

If verbal eloquence and recited poetry were known to us merely by the material ear, even they would be a brief and empty gratification of the senses. Like them, music owes its magical gift of exciting emotion to its extraordinary complexity.

The interpreter and creator of deep psychical conditions, the delicate emanation of the mind, the subtle force of the moral life, it is at once feeling and thought. Into the enchantment of sounds it puts logic for the intelligence, a language of love for the heart—an art of construction and of form for the imagination. It is the meeting-point of the law of numbers which rules the world, and the unfettered fancy which creates the possible. Although hemmed in on every side by its relation to ordinary life, it is yet a glorious example of that spontaneity of the reason which attains " to greater heights than theology or philosophy " (Beethoven). By bringing agreement into these contraries, it represents, and, by widening the small domain of the ego, causes to act upon us, the harmony of different worlds. Great musicians, unlike great poets, do not employ the medium of the word : they understand by direct intuition, and they see farther afield. We might have said that, in comparison with the sublime interior into which they raise us, the sublime exterior of the ocean seems vulgar, and that of the stars icy.

In order to explain this sound-wave formed out of other waves, this aerial and fugitive thing so complex and rich in meaning—the secret of which we must give up the attempt to completely fathom —many sciences must be invoked. I reckon as many as seven. Occupying, as they do, domains with over-lapping frontiers, they divide the work between them, and each endeavours to solve a series of distinct problems. Each of them also opens up a vista of wonders.

In the first place, what is a sound? How are sounds measured? On what do their qualities of force, of *timbre*, and of shrillness depend? What essential difference is there between those produced by the human voice, by strings, and tubes, and those given out by skins, plates, and metal rods? The first special domain to be explored is that of *acoustics*.

How do we perceive the sounds once objectively emitted according to the independent laws of our will? What is the mechanism of the ear? Does our auditory apparatus accommodate itself, as a whole, to the impressions of sound, or is there indeed an organ of perception ready - made for each separate sound? What is the meaning of consonance and dissonance? Here is a second domain, viz. *physiology*.

Can the principles brought to light by these two sciences be explained—as Pythagoras, Descartes, and Euler would have it—by the more or less simple relations of numbers? Must we hold with Leibnitz " that music is an unconscious act of calculation "? Here is a third domain, viz. *mathematics*.

When these impressions of sound have penetrated into us and the consciousness has grasped and reduced them to a unity, what becomes of them?

What does the memory, the sensitiveness, the imagination, and the intelligence do with them ? What mental conditions do they induce ? By what process of abstraction does the musician raise himself to a mode of thought totally different from that of the poet and other artists ? What action unconsciously goes on within him ? Here is a fourth domain, viz. *psychology*.

We have nothing further to do with sounds ; henceforward we shall deal with *syntheses* of sounds, *i.e.*, with a whole work. What do we mean by a work ? Is there any criterion by which its value may be estimated ? Here we find a fifth domain, viz. *æsthetics*.

It is not merely a single work, but the collection of all works, their origin and their connection throughout the ages, that we wish to be acquainted with. How have the many different kinds of compositions been formed ? What part has music played in civilization from its most humble beginnings ? Here comes in *history* with its supplements, archæology and the study of monuments made in primitive times, when written notes were not. *Philology* is here indispensable, because all the treatises on Western music until the sixteenth century, with rare exceptions, are written in Latin or Greek. This leads us to *palæography*, or the art of deciphering the musical writings of antiquity and the Middle Ages.

Finally, what is the part of the common life in the formation of the different types of music ? Do not the elements forming what may be called the grammar of the language of sounds (and, *à fortiori*,

the general character of the works founded on that
basis, with their meaning and ʃ evolution) presuppose a society which imposes upon them provisional forms, and without which technical rules
could not exist ? Such questions come under the
head of *sociology*, which, as a trial of its strength,
could scarcely find better subjects than the following : The primitive incantation, plain-song, counter-
point, the fugue, and the symphony.

Such a programme is somewhat disconcerting by
reason of its fullness, and the necessity of a method
is at once apparent.

If we wish to have an accurate idea of music,
ought we not to formulate a system of study corresponding to what appears to be the natural order
of facts ; that is to say, to interrogate in turn these
different sciences, each of which has the task of
explaining a portion of our subject ? We should,
then, begin with acoustics, and end with what are
called the moral sciences.

This method would be legitimate and fairly safe.
A person who undertakes to speak or write on the
art of music should begin by practising it ; and,
without going into too many details, we shall not
fail to give here the substance of the programmes it
suggests. But this order of research cannot form
the plan of our work without three objections.

If we confine ourselves to tracing the material
basis of music, from the moment when it is constituted outside ourselves to that in which it blossoms
forth within us as a melody or a symphony, and to
characterizing each stage of its evolution, we shall

have at first nothing but juxtaposed ideas. The
bird's-eye view needful to a " scientific philosophy "
would be lacking to us. In the second place, those
ideas would appear contradictory to each other.

Lastly, we should run the risk of establishing
our theory on very unstable foundations, because,
in spite of the authority of the great scholars who
have made so much progress in them since the
eighteenth century, acoustics, and especially physiology, are yet very far from accepting, uncondition-
ally, the principles with which these sciences have
wished to supply the elementary grammar of music.
Our first requirement, therefore, *in music* (and not
in a sister-science such as acoustics) is an experimental basis of certainty.

A second method would be to consider the subject
ject solely on historical lines, and to deviate from
it only to draw conclusions. Beginning at the
period of the earliest known appearance of music,
its development throughout the ages could be described without troubling oneself about philosophic
generalizations. Acoustics and physiology would
be mere episodes in the path traversed ; they would
be introduced in their place in the succession of
facts at the moment when they were formed into
sciences—that is to say, rather late in the day.
This long review once finished, an endeavour would
have to be made to gain therefrom a bird's-eye
view.

This last method is fascinating, because by it, instead of the theorist, the things themselves are, as it
were, made to speak. It is, however, impracticable.
If, before investigating any period of history, we

do not begin by giving as exact an answer as possible to the question, *What is music?* how can we recognize, and, especially, how interpret the facts which interest us?

Our first task, then, must be to give a definition, and this we shall look for from the domain of psychology. Our starting-point can only be from the musical feeling itself, the state of mind, that is, of the average listener at the concert or the theatre during the performance of a symphony by Beethoven, Berlioz, or César Franck, an opera by Bizet or Wagner, one of Schumann's lieder or Chopin's nocturnes, one of those works, in fine, which, to use an old metaphor, " inflicts on the soul a voluptuous wound and leaves the point therein."

A good definition ought to be applicable only to the object defined. If, for example, we attribute to music any quality which may also be affirmed of poetry, our definition is worthless. What we ought to bring to light is the essential originality, or the *specific* difference.

We think that we shall satisfy this rule by stating that music is the art of *thinking in sounds*.

This primary notion, somewhat disconcerting to grammarians and psychologists of the ancient classical school, is arrived at, chiefly by the use of contrasts, or by comparing thoughts expressed by music with those expressed by words. In everyday life, in literary work, or even when communing with ourselves, we use words ; each of these words is the symbol of a concrete object, represented in our minds by an idea, or, as it is called in philosophy, a *concept*. If I say, " the earth turns round the

sun," I utter a thought made up of four concepts :
the two material bodies, rotation on itself and movement round a point.

Our ordinary life is pervaded, filled, and directed
by representations of a similar kind.

The originality of the musician consists in sup-
pressing the concepts in the acts of the intelligence.
Does he thus arrive at a vague formula ? By no
means. The elimination of words and the employment of the activity, pure and simple, of the mind
in the linking together of sounds seems rather to
favour the free exercise of thought, and sometimes
even to allow it to become deeper. To the true
musician music is more intelligible than speech ; in
fact, words may even obscure it. The sense of a
beautiful passage from Bach or Handel can be rendered by no other language except that of sound,
and in such manner only can it be properly grasped.
Composers frequently write above a stave of music,
for the guidance of the player, " with expression " !—
Expression of what ? There is no need for such
minuteness, and only mediocre musicians would
condescend to such directions. Every good melody
carries within itself its sense and its explanation.

To think without concepts, not for the losing sight
of the objects the concepts represent, but rather to
penetrate better their meaning ; to dissolve that
surface personality encumbered with words and
turned outwards, which envelopes and conceals one's
true personality ; to return to the state of nature,
to the free disposal of oneself, to the ingenious and
yet skilful use of our internal energies ; to subtly
intellectualize the sensitiveness and to pour into the

intelligence a diffused emotion, so as to produce, as it were, a delicate emanation from both—such appears to me to be the privilege of music.

It will not be difficult to justify the definition given above, without which the æsthetics of music is an inextricable chaos.

What appears certainly more difficult is, after having chosen such a starting-point, to show the connection of music with the sciences enumerated above—on the one hand, history and sociology ; on the other, physiology and acoustics.

First Objection. What we have just termed " *musical thought* " is found particularly in the great modern symphonists (period of Bach and Handel to Beethoven). But is it not a fault in method to generalize one type of music, recent and, in short, exceptional ? Are we not about, in order to remain faithful to our first declaration, to isolate ourselves in the region, no doubt very exalted, of the pure ether of Beethoven, where we shall nevertheless lose grip, to a certain extent, of the rude realities of history as well as those of social life ? Are we not putting ourselves in the category of those who wish to build by beginning with the roof ?

Second Objection. If we see in music the enfranchisement of thought and the free exercise of the pure activity of the mind, what can we say of the determinism of acoustic laws ? A definition of the art of music, if it is applied only to composers of the first rank, is but the opinion of a dilettante or of a critic on a few points culled from the immense field of facts : it is neither philosophic nor scientific, in

the first place, because it is not general, and, in the
second place, because it isolates the art by cutting
its lines of communication with nature.

(1) As regards the difficulty of covering by our
definition the whole range of the history of music
in time and space, from the melodious stammerings
of an Esquimaux or an Australian to a César Franck,
I might say, first of all, that to understand the
nature of an art such as music, which has passed
through its various phrases slowly (except since the
time of Haydn, after whom its progress has been
extraordinarily rapid), it must perhaps be observed
in its state of maturity and of development, when
it becomes real in a complete way, and not in its
embryonic stage. Before an oriental pulling at
the single string of a toy violoncello, I should
willingly repeat the words of Nietzsche : " Thy true
nature is not in thee : it is infinitely above thee "
(which brings to mind the saying—dangerous, perhaps—of Malebranche, that to know man another
line than direct observation must be taken, and
God must be contemplated). But I need no such
metaphysical " bias," which is absolutely repugnant
to that followed in this work. One very simple
observation will suffice.

Musical thought has as many forms and degrees
as literary thought, although it is very different from
it. It may be sublime, beautiful, modest and
mediocre, feeble, and rudimentary. It may be
applied to a thousand different objects. It may
possess more or less brilliancy, depth, strength,
clearness, etc. The literary author who contem-

plates writing, for example, a history of comedy, first forms for himself a certain idea of his subject, according to Aristophanes, Plautus, Terence, or Molière ; but he considers it essential, and by no means contradictory, to go back to the drunken scenes and obscenities of the Atellanæ, to the farces which preceded and prefaced the masterpieces. In the same way, we shall be in no way embarrassed by speaking of the melodious stammerings which exist at the outset of civilization ; and in the presence of the songs of primitive folk (whether the real primitive folk of history or the existing non-civilized races resembling the primitive) we shall not say " it is musical thought," but " it is *their* thought."

And if a thesis should be found to be implied in such a statement, positive documents to justify it will not be wanting. We shall see that, by the side of their speech, formed of concepts more or less closely connected, primitive folk had a special language with untranslatable formulas, which was attached in their minds to something entirely distinct from the ideas of the current language ; we shall see that the first use they made of song is found in the rites of magic, which presupposes a conception of the expressive power of music, at bottom identical with that possessed by the great German metaphysicians Schelling, Hegel, and Schopenhauer, and the great composers down to Richard Wagner.

Thus it was not solely of the first rank of composers that we think when we define music. The griot of the African negroes is as much worthy of the attention of the observer as the ἀοιδός of the Greeks ; the liturgical mechanism of the strophes and antistrophes which, at the time of Sophocles, were sung round the altar of Dionysos has no deeper meaning than the chanted dances of the Abipones, who, with a priestess wearing little bells on her wrists and ankles, celebrate at midnight the reappearance of the Pleiades in the sky. It is the whole of musical history that we claim to include in our definition when we study the art of thinking in sounds.

(2) In what concerns the relations between music and sociology, far from evading the problem, we shall approach it from its most difficult side. Were we to confine ourselves to the easy task of demonstrating that the state of social life has always exercised an influence on the evolution of music, so that a Lulli working for a court like that of Louis XIV does not write the same operas as a Gustave Charpentier or an Alfred Bruneau, we should misunderstand its true nature. Although it would not be capable of an entirely exact solution, the question puts itself in the following form : What are the elements of the grammar of music which have an individual origin ? What are those furnished and forced upon us by the common life ?

The French or German author writing a book has, in short, only a limited personality ; many of his ideas come from heredity, education, or imitation ; to express them he uses a vocabulary, a syntax, and written symbols which he has not created himself, but the meaning of which has been determined for him by a tacit agreement of the community, which exercises upon him a *constraint*. Is it the same for the composer ? To give an answer to this quite novel question, suggested by studies now fashionable, we must enter into some technical analyses ; from this point we can fit them into a frame of general observations.

Music is neither an exceptional nor an intermittent fact in history, a chance auxiliary to religious ceremonies, a passing expression of joy, or sadness, or dreaminess ; nor yet is it an art of luxury, a pastime invented by men of leisure. It is a fact as natural and universal as language itself, characterized, like it, at first by incoherent efforts, but appearing wherever there are men ; and it can be attached, if the forms in which it manifests itself are considered, to the deep and permanent laws of social life. There are peoples more or less gifted in song, as there are those who are more or less artistic, and others more or less warlike ; but there are none who, savage or civilized, do not know chant and rhythm at the same time as speech, even if they only make use of a few notes of the scale.

The field of musical history stretches beyond our sight. The most ancient document we possess is a Chaldean bas-relief representing a harpist, discovered by M. de Sarzec at the palace of Telloh, on the left bank of the canal which connects the Tigris and the Euphrates. Good judges, like M. Pottier, attribute it to the thirtieth century before the Christian era. There is no paradox in saying that music is more ancient than poetry, and that it has provided poetry with its structural laws. From the most distant ages to the present time the series of

facts is unbroken. It has even happened that in
the modern period music has acquired an exceptionally representative value. Every one knows the
names of Bach, Handel, Mozart, and Beethoven ;
but how many of us know the names of the painters,
sculptors, and architects who were their contemporaries in Germany ?

As it appears in history, music has always been
united to the manifestations of social life, or, more
accurately, to the working of its essential organs.
It has never been, as philosophers put it, " an end
in itself," for we have always subordinated it to
some important act of public life.

Nowadays we betake ourselves to a theatre or
concert-hall with no other object than to hear a
beautiful opera or a fine symphony, and to taste an
entirely disinterested pleasure ; the singers and
players have nothing to do with our public or
private affairs, and we rather ask them to make us
forget them. Music, indeed, frequently accompanies
certain religious ceremonies, but this is either a
survival of ancient customs or in order to lend
them an ornamental and pleasing appearance, like
the objects we put in a drawing-room. Formerly
it was quite different. Music was associated, as an
organic and essential element, with the acts of religious and profane life, of war and of peace. It
was by incantation that primitive man, in his
ignorance and fear in the presence of nature, tried
to defend himself against sickness, death, or the
cruelty of the gods. Now magic, as we shall prove,
presupposes the constitution of a society.

Religion and verbal language are the sociological

phenomena *par excellence*, and music cannot, at first, be separated from them. Music is never represented alone on sculptured monuments; it is always part and parcel of a group, performing a particular ceremony. This custom lasted for a very long time, and must not be lost sight of if we wish to understand certain great composers who flourished in the first half of the eighteenth century. Music was hardly cultivated for its own sake elsewhere than in a few " academies of music " or in certain middle-class circles. A musician like|Bach, with some rare exceptions, has always put his genius at the service of a community; it was the same with Handel; and those *concerti grossi* which they wrote for pure art are an exception. Hence, under the old régime, musical criticism, as we now understand it, did not exist : no one ever dreamt of discussing a mass, a cantata, a motet, or an oratorio, and of characterizing them by an æsthetic judgment, because such works formed part of the acts of a community, and these acts were the principal thing.

For these reasons music is the only popular art. It draws its substance from social life, as a plant draws its substance from the soil into which its roots plunge. There is no popular painting nor popular sculpture. Architecture is too complicated an art, too loaded with technical knowledge and archæology, and too much subjected to the prejudices of luxury or to special needs, to be the spontaneous product of a community. To music alone and to its younger sister, poetry, belongs this privilege.

Such are the principles we shall elucidate when re-

viewing different peoples and ages. Taking as our
basis the first proposition, that *music is the art of
thinking in sounds*, we shall reserve to ourselves the
right of adding this, which is founded on observation : *musical thought is the manifestation of a
general and deep instinct, more or less hidden, but
everywhere recognizable in humanity.*.

If we can come to a satisfactory demonstration
on these two points, the half of our task—but the
half only—will have been accomplished. We shall
have laid down a definition, marking the *specific*
character of the musical art ; we shall have shown
that this definition can cover while it illuminates
the immense variety of historical facts, and that it
does not exclude the sociological point of view at
which we to-day like to place ourselves for the purpose of accounting for things ; and all the connections of our subject with " the moral sciences "
will have been put in evidence. But we shall have
ousted the *physical* sciences from a discussion in
which they have sought to intervene, and of which
they have claimed the direction. How shall we
put ourselves in agreement with physiology, with
acoustics, and with mathematics ? What part shall
we assign to them in our theory of music ?
Between musical thought, the free exercise of the
pure activity of *the ego*, and everything included
under the term determinism, coming from the outer
world, there appears at first sight conflict and irre-
ducible antinomy. On the one hand are physical
instruments, ciphers, and all the apparatus of
science ; on the other, works of art.

One method, which is by no means new and which can rely on very serious testimony, consists in doing away with the difficulty by simply abolishing the first of the two terms to be reconciled. To the scholar who attempts, with the help of mathematics, to formulate the laws of multiple resonance, or to describe the mechanism of the ear in order to deduce therefrom the principles of grammar, we might say : " With what are you meddling, you musician of the laboratory, when you dare to point out the path and to lecture true musicians ? Your labours have, no doubt, the interest which attaches to the observation and explanation of well-ascertained facts, but among all your experiments there is not one which has for its object a *musical* phenomenon. You study a note given by such and such an elastic body, and you arè able to analyse it ; you tell us what happens when two sounds produced at the same time have or have not common harmonies ; you measure and you explain by numerical ratios an interval of an octave, of a fifth, of a fourth, etc., etc. ; *but all this is not music*, any more than the letters of the alphabet are literature, or a few words made up of those letters are poetry. We can do without you. The syren of a Cagniart de la Tour has nothing in common with the syrens of antiquity ! "

To take up this attitude, we might first rely on the almost unanimous evidence of those musicians who hold the interference of " men of science " to be useless or annoying, and are much against listening to them at all. But as their opinion may be considered biassed, we might also claim support for

c

the students of acoustics by taking advantage of their own disagreements. Helmholtz, who in 1863 flattered himself that he had given a scientific foundation to the A B C of musical composition, has been completely confuted by von Öttingen ; and many people consider that Professor Stumpf, of the University of Berlin, gave the decisive blow to his theory.

A French philosopher, M. Guillemin, Professor at the Algiers School of Medicine, thus sums up the matter : " Good cooking was known long before chemistry made its appearance ; and even chemistry, since it has grown up, has not helped much to perfect cooking ; in fact, some people assert that it has destroyed the art. It may be the same with music." Thus the existence of harmonics is denied by M. Guillemin.

Nevertheless, this will not be our attitude. It is an easy matter to seek out oppositions, to draw impassable lines of demarcation between the domain of artistic activity and that of objective nature ; but what is really interesting is to search out the hidden harmony of things which appear as the most opposed to each other, or to see music in thought, thought in mankind, mankind in society, society in universal nature, all with incessant and minute interpenetration, crossings of lines, series of facts forming the transformations of force, and in sum that magnificent and stupendous harmonic whole called life. It appears certain that, before they are organized within us, and take, under the influence of imagination, the shape of a melodious synthesis, sounds receive outside ourselves a primary organization which prepares and conditions the work of the artist. These laws are made visibly manifest by experiments on a vibrating string or a small metal plate covered with fine sand. When a bow is drawn along the edge there appear in the sand nodal lines and curious geometrical figures. Nature is not a musician and yet she *composes :* she has a plan and a method ; and she obeys inflexible laws. A Mozart or a Beethoven are completely ignorant of them, and yet they conform with them unknowingly. This we shall prove by the analysis of certain musical texts. By the production of facts, and not of personal theories, we shall endeavour to prove that the musical composer, standing at the point where two groups of influences meet, obeys instinctively laws which at one and the same time may be referred both to social life and to physics.

If this end is attained our task will, so far, be finished. We shall have brought back to unity all the branches of our subject, dominated by a single principle. Instead of a mere juxtaposition of facts, we shall have an intrinsic and essential co-ordination of the sciences enumerated at the beginning of this introduction : to wit, acoustics, mathematics, psychology, æsthetics, history, and sociology.

There we shall cry halt. As we claim never to stray outside observation and to defend only a thesis that can be verified, we shall not follow certain philosophers who desire to go further still.

In Book VII of his "Republic," Plato laughs at those musicians who limit themselves for the explanation of their art to arithmetic added to physics, and trouble not as to what is above this. To him the relationship of numbers, to which the grammar of music may be reduced, appears to be but the first stage of dialectics, that is to say, of a concatenation of ideas, ascending ever higher and higher, the last of which is that of the Good. According to him, it is this Idea of the Good which radiates through all the domains of life and makes its unity.

According to Schopenhauer, whose opinions are equally bold, it is Force, or, if I rightly understand it, an Idea pre-existent to concrete realities and concepts (*universalia ante rem*). Admirable systems, whose least defect is that they overshoot the mark and escape from all control. To arrive at the supreme solution which such metaphysicians seek, "one must," as Glaucon says, "be a god!"

If we do not venture into this region of clouds, where the mind, thinking it can reach the First Cause which gives the secret of things, only builds up its own dreams, our reason is not merely to exclude from our studies those tendencies to mysticism to which they have often given birth and which are the rocks ahead of them. There is in music something which is and must be inexplicable, under pain of being no longer musical. Such facts are not to be examined by the same disposition of mind which we bring to the exegesis of a printed text or the working out of a theorem of geometry.

The emotion which suddenly and utterly invades us when we hear beautiful voices or a beautiful orchestra renders undefined the trinity of the individual consciousness ; it reveals to us the harmony of different worlds, and founds our powers of egoism in the feeling of this harmony. But part of its charm is due to the mystery which always accompanies it, for we are far from understanding all the causes of what we feel. We enjoy our emotion in a half-conscious state, astonished at having suddenly become the meeting-place of so many reconciled forces.

To obstinately endeavour to reduce such a subject to clear and distinct notions, that is to say, beyond certain analyses, would be to misunderstand the originality of it.·

Let us finally remember that we shall be obliged to touch upon a certain number of subjects, which professional scholars are still investigating with fervour, without being able to arrive at any final doctrine. The musical theorist meets those scholars more than once on his journey, and he is pleased to note that, although their tasks are most dissimilar, their foundation is the same; but his part is not to supersede the specialists in elucidating those weighty problems of which the solution belongs to them alone.

FIRST PART

MUSICAL THOUGHT AND PSYCHOLOGY

CHAPTER I

I WILL give forthwith an example of what I call
musical thought. Below is a popular air, charming
and quite simple ; I intentionally leave out the
words, which, moreover, have nothing to do with
the musical text—

There is one analogy, and only one, between this
combination of sounds and a verbal sentence—
namely, that caused by the rhythm. Our air, taken
as a whole, can be compared to an oratorical period.

22

In the first place, it has a beginning, a middle, and an end. The dropping of the tonic *Fa*— for which the singer substitutes the lower fourth, *Do*, as if retreating for a greater spring—and return to the tonic. Secondly, this period is divided into three propositions; the two first, which are merely the same formula repeated twice, finish in the fourth bar on the mediant (or third) *La*, which forms an imperfect cadence, so that the cæsura, indicated here by a crotchet rest, is equivalent to a *semicolon*; the third and last proposition finishes on the tonic, which is a perfect cadence, after which there is, so to speak, a *full stop*.

In addition, each of these propositions is subdivided into " sections," marked in our score by a little vertical line, indicating a slight cæsura. The first proposition has two sections, the last four, thus forming two symmetrical groups.

If we take a period from Bossuet, Rousseau, or Chateaubriand, we shall see that it is constructed in the same way. The plan is identically the same, and this identity may be traced to a common origin —namely, the necessity for taking breath, and of making these breathings coincide with the logical divisions. We might, perhaps, hesitate as to the punctuation of the sections, but not as to the more important propositions which form the main design of the period. If, for example, instead of inserting the chief cæsura, the semicolon, on the rest, it were placed before the preceding note, we should have a phrase as ridiculous as the following—

Oui, je viens dans son temple adorer l'Eter ;
nel je viens selon l'usage, etc. . . .

Hence there is, so far, a perfect analogy between the construction of the sounds and that of the words. But let us not push our search for resemblances further. Here are facts which lead us further and further from the literary point of view.

1st. In the first place there is something here which, in verbal—that is to say, artistic—language, would be considered a serious fault or, at least, a blunder, but which in music is perfectly allowable—namely, the repetition of the first part of the period, consisting of four bars. If a philologist, in reading a manuscript of Demosthenes, Cicero, or Bossuet, were to come across a part of a sentence repeated twice, without any intermediate expression, he would simply ascribe the repetition to an error on the part of the copyist, such as may happen to any transcriber, and would pay no further attention to it. In music, on the contrary, not only is repetition allowable, but it is of normal and constant occurrence, and the artistic method *par excellence.*

2nd. This air has a basis of construction. This is the scale of *Fa* and the two essential chords arising from it—namely, the tonic chord *Fa, La, Do,* and the dominant *Do, Mi, Sol,* which, augmented by a minor third, *Si♭*, forms the chord of the seventh, *Do, Mi, Sol, Si♭*, the mainspring of movement and modulation, because it is a dissonance which calls for a solution. Another third, *Ré♮*, added will give the chord of the ninth, which is in the same case. All the notes figuring in our period are understood by us harmonically, that is to say, in conjunction with the chord of the tonic or that of the dominant

(excepting certain notes occurring on a weak
beat, which may be a simple *passing note*, like the
Si♭ in the first bar, or the *Ré♮* in the second bar,
which is an *embroidery*).

Even when not figuring on the stave, this tonic
Fa, with its satellite *Do*, placed a fifth higher, is the
centre of attraction round which the whole revolves,
and which gives its uniformity to the whole.

3rd. Consequently, the notes are perceived not
directly and in themselves, but according to their
relations with each other and with the tonic.
Melody is a system of relations; now a ratio is not
conveyed by a sensation (especially when one of the
two terms of the ratio is understood or suggested,
as here). A ratio is an *abstraction ;* it is the work
of him who hears, the creation of the intelligence
which steps in to compare and appreciate. Therein
lies the fact, to my mind, which renders a musical
thought *possible*, since philosophers teach that to
think we must abstract and unite.

But we have, so far, analysed only modalities.
We have the skeleton of a body ; it still lacks flesh,
and blood, physiognomy, and life !

4th. This *life* of the melody is that musical meaning which it bears within itself. All those ratios of
sound which go to make up our period are presented
to us in the form of a synthesis ; and a special act
of the composer's mind has endowed this synthesis
with a value not found in any of its component
parts. He has given it a signification which we
should seek in vain to express by words, and which,
although only to be reached through the musical
sense, has for it perfect clearness.

It is not any subtle metaphysics of the art which allows us to speak thus ; it is observation and experience. Indeed, no musician can fail to see this. Hearing this popular song, he distinguishes it from an unmeaning formula ; a non-specialist would make this distinction as well as he.

The following will prove that we are not the dupes of illusion when we attribute a positive content to a work of this kind. We can very well suppose a concatenation of sounds—such as every pianist is accustomed to improvise mechanically— in which the tonic and dominant chords are associated in conformity with the rules of musical theory, and which yet have no signification ; that would form, to borrow an expression from Leibnitz, " regular sequences," and nothing more. There exists, consequently, an essential difference between the formula which is simply correct and one which says something.

In order to make intelligible the impossibility of translating this *proprium quid* into words, we will call to mind the following remarks on literary thought. Music is like the last term of a series. A business letter or a report may be without difficulty translated from one language into another ; a page from Plato or Virgil lends itself much less easily to an operation of this kind because the thought is of a higher quality ; a poem of Lamartine would render still more difficult the translator's work, and can only very imperfectly and with serious loss of meaning be rendered into German or Swedish. As for the sense of a musical phrase, it is impossible to describe it by verbal formulas, because here the thought, though not necessarily superior, is of a different order.

To ask the meaning of a melody is impertinent, inartistic, and beside the question, like the tourist who, on seeing a beautiful statue of Parian marble, inquired how many pounds sterling it was worth.

If, instead of examining a very simple specimen of popular music, we examine an air of Schubert, Mozart, or Handel, we should find new *meanings*, differing greatly from each other, but all possessing the characteristic just mentioned. By pushing our investigations further, and running through the dazzling variety of works in which the musical phrase is enriched by the inexhaustible resources of rhythm and orchestral *timbre*, we should find that the musician treats all kinds of subjects. He has written on coffee, on toothache, on the declension of *hic, hæc, hoc*, on children's games, and on the Passion—in fine, on all matters which observation, history, or fancy is able to supply. He is a landscape painter ; he depicts at will light and shade or *chiaroscuro*. The orchestra, to him, is a palette whence he obtains combinations of undefined colours appropriate to a given theme. In such cases it is perfectly legitimate to translate into ordinary language the ideas which guided him and the success with which he has realized them ; but these descriptive feats at his service only represent an optional use of his art ; while, at all times, and under all circumstances, whatever the realistic tendency to which he yields, he is compelled, unless he would produce a vain and unmusical work, to give to his sonorous constructions a meaning intelligible in itself and by itself alone, to the exclusion of any specified object.

This is what Schumann wished to imply when he said to a young man who was explaining the programme of his symphony : " Play your music first ; your programme will add to my pleasure if the music is good."

I cannot point out too forcibly the confusion existing in the minds of some eminent philosophers regarding two orders of facts.

| 1st. Among the numerous characteristics of music a certain number are to be found *otherwhere than in music*. We shall study these later on ; but, though recognizing their importance, we shall take care not to seek in them the elements of the exact definition we require. " If, after having given a definition of life," says M. le Dantec,* " there should be discovered in material substances some of the peculiarities hitherto considered to be the appanage of living beings, it will simply prove that we have made a mistake, and the work will have to be done over again." A good definition should, in fact, mark the specific difference of the object defined. If, for example, I am told that music is a " game " which absorbs a " surplus of energy," or a " language of the sentiments," or an " unconscious arithmetic," or a means of " pleasing the ear," I shall without difficulty recognize that each of these formulas contains a part of the truth ; but I should not accept them as definitions, and if they are forced on me as such, I can only attribute them to an incorrect and deceptive use of the word " music."

* *La Lutte universelle*.   Paris, 1906.

There exists in music one characteristic which can be found *nowhere else.* It is neither the use of intervals, nor consonance and dissonance, nor *timbre,* nor bar, nor rhythm : it is the untranslatable *sense,* which yet is acknowledged by every one (even if its value be disputed) in certain combinations of sounds. It is this "something," this *proprium quid,* which renders the musical text given above neither a casual sequence nor even a simply regular sequence of sounds and values of duration, but a melody. This forms the principle of our definition. I simplify it by saying : music is the art of thinking in sounds.

Let us not be told that " to think " is, according to Descartes, Kant, and all the standard philosophers, " to unite *concepts.*" The philosophers of the old school were not musicians ; if they were, they erred in giving an exclusive character to their statement. It is also needless to object that it is impossible for us to define musical thought by indicating its *content.* In the first place, this impossibility results from the very nature of the fact in question ; in the second, we are sufficiently explicit when we state that the thought of the musician, while *sui generis,* is as variable and has as many degrees as that of the literary man.

Finally, there must not be demanded from psychologists definitions more precise than those current in all sciences save mathematics and geometry.

Do we know what electricity is ? We are told, " It is produced by atoms called *electrons.*" A great step forward, indeed ! The term to be defined is reproduced in the definition, as formerly in the case

of light. In biology, as Claude Bernard has proclaimed it, nothing is defined. A few years ago
M. Dastre published in the *Revue des Deux Mondes*
a very fine study on foods ; and, after examining a
certain number of hypotheses, he wound up by
declaring himself incapable of defining a food.
Nevertheless, there exists an art or a science of
nutrition and living, just as there is a science of
electricity.

Does " to think without concepts " appear a contradiction in terms ? What, then, shall we say of
the physicists who define the ether as " a solid without density or weight, yet more rigid than steel "
(Lord Kelvin) ? And yet this ether is indispensable ;
on it, we are informed, depend light, heat, radiant
electricity, gravitation, and the course of the stars.
Here we have a decided superiority : we do not
arrive at our principle by a logical conclusion ;
we simply found it on observation.

No doubt, after we have isolated the musical
phenomenon, we shall demonstrate in the second and
other parts of this book that it is in harmony with
social life as well as with the laws of physiology and
those of objective nature ; but there will here be
no contradiction. A harmony is an adaptation ;
it does not exclude real differentiations.

Before we start on the analysis of a subject which
it is easier to write round than to describe, let us
strengthen our point of view and clear the ground
by examining rapidly a few celebrated definitions
of music. Of those, I take three.

CHAPTER II

EXAMINATION OF SOME OPINIONS

§ 1. Music and Sensation—The Pleasure to the Ear

In J. J. Rousseau's time, music was defined as " the art of combining sounds so as to please the ear." Some modern scholars have endeavoured to give this saying a formal character and to justify it by scientific demonstrations. They maintain that consonance and dissonance act on our organism quite independently of all æsthetic judgment, in the same way as a burn or the contact of ice, a sweet or a bitter taste, a sting or a caress.

The little concert given in the Jardin des Plantes, on the 10th Prairial in the Year VI of the Republic, to two elephants whose names history has handed down—Hans and Marguerite—seemed to prove that animals are susceptible to the influence of music in the sense that they are affected by it as by a series of impressions from which it is not possible to escape.

In 1863, Helmholtz built up his musical theory on the study of *sound-sensations*, by dwelling on this point, that they act the chief part and determine all the other effects ; and, twelve years later, Wundt set forth clearly the principle of the same thesis : " The first condition of a sound method of research in these matters," he wrote, "is to consider consonance and dissonance as phenomena of sensation, and to separate them from the feelings which are linked with them."

Since then interesting experiments have been made in Russia, in Italy, and in France. M. Féré, not to quote others, has made researches on the influence of sounds on persons without artistic intelligence, incapable even of perceiving the differences of musical intervals—in fact, persons afflicted with musical deafness—and he has noted certain effects.

From all this it appears to us that a well-established but partial truth may be drawn, and that we must abstain from any general deduction.

If physiology brings us, on our way, supplementary information and clear views, so much the better ; but if, at our first step, it proposes to bar our progress and subject us to its laws, it is an impossible aid.

It is plain that sensation pure and simple plays, or may play, an important part in music. Certain combinations of sounds draw from us, instinctively, a cry of impatience or of pain ; I prefer to hear a piece played on a Stradivarius rather than on a poor violin, etc. . . . But if we adopt the conclusion that sensation is the principle of pleasure from music, what a number of objections can be raised. I will mention a few of them.

1st. Why have not the sensations of smell, in themselves as independent as those of hearing, given birth, like the latter, to a liberal art ? Why does not perfumery rank as high as music ?

2nd. Any sensation of the touch always has its own value, even when isolated and resulting from a single impression of the external object on the periphery; the contact of a hot coal always causes pain; an iced beverage always gives pleasure to a thirsty person, etc. . . . . On the contrary, one single consonance heard by itself leaves a musician, in most cases, perfectly indifferent. It has no appreciable value; to give it one it must be attached to something else, to what precedes or what follows it. In music everything is done by comparison. It is only relations which count. The perception of sounds is at once memory and expectation.

Admitting that a fifth is an agreeable consonance, if preceded by two other fifths having a similar movement it will be very unpleasant. Conversely, a group of notes in itself dissonant and painful may be admirable thanks to the context. In one of Schumann's finest melodies, *Mondnacht*, we meet with a *Mi* ♮ under a *Mi* ♯; now this conjunction, extremely harsh by itself, becomes, by reason of the plan of the phrase, an exquisitely sentimental and poetical feature. In such a case the thought dominates the sensation.

3rd. If music were solely the art of flattering the ear in the physiological sense of the word, it would never make use of anything but consonances. Now, there are no compositions for parts, vocal or instrumental, which are in this case. This would infer that one could never experience pleasure from music in a pure and complete state, which is contrary to common experience. The pleasure would

always be thwarted ; if we kept solely to consonances, the most we could say would be, with the
scholar of old, that our keenest joys are but
griefs appeased.

4th. Why do the impressions produced by music
vary in different persons ? Why do they vary in
one and the same person ? Is not a sting painful
to every one under all circumstances ? Why did
Berlioz declare that he did not understand the prelude to *Tristan and Iseult ?* Does any one ever
hesitate to acknowledge a burn after putting one's
hand in the fire ? Why have we to listen several
times to certain symphonies of the present day in
order to understand them ? . . .

When physiologists, in order to show the effects
of the sensations caused by sound, take graphs
of the respiration, the capillary pulse, or the
motions of the heart ; when a particular case
enables them to note the rush of blood which,
under the influence of sounds, increases the volume
of the brain ; or when they register, by the aid of
Mosso's ergogram, the muscular energy expended
by a person receiving acoustic impressions, they
are effecting useful work, from which, however, it is
impossible to frame general conclusions and laws,
because the facts observed would not perhaps
be the same with all persons. Now, musicians
never disagree as to the fact that an air has a
meaning.

Physiology has a part to play in the theory of
music, but it is not within its province to frame a
definition of the art. It must be limited to a contribution in aid. The nature of this we shall specify

later in a special chapter of this book (Part III). Arrived at a certain degree of culture—that, precisely, when real problems are put before it—the ear no longer creates music by a kind of passive receptivity, just as a mould impresses its shape on the liquid poured into it ; the intellect intervenes to judge, to undo and remake, in a certain measure, the work of the auditory organ, and to give it, by a secondary creation, a definite meaning or one provisional and variable, like the mind itself. There is here a transformation of the acoustic phenomenon into a musical phenomenon, in which the activity of the mind plays sometimes a part more important than that of the ear. The mistake made by certain scholars arises from their not rising to this, but remaining on the threshold of the question. They think they have grasped music, while they have but touched the fringe of her garment.

§ 2. Music and Formalism—The Arabesques of Sound

There exists a doctrine akin to the above called Formalism. According to this, the characteristics and the beauty of a work of art should be sought for, not in the sentiments, thoughts, and ideas it may contain, but solely, and as if dealing with an architectural construction, in the relations of the respective parts of this work of art. In literature, for instance, one must take account of the plot, the style, the choice of expressions, the syntax (in the widest acceptation of the word), the rhythm, the imagery, the sonority of the period or of the verse ; but the meaning expressed may be ignored in accordance with the dictum of Herbert : " The beauty of a temple cannot be enhanced by the furniture placed in it."

Very paradoxical when applied to the works of Æschylus, of Dante, of Shakespeare, this doctrine jars less on common sense when applied to the musical art, which, not being associated with concepts, never possesses the analytical clearness of verbal language.

This application was made by the Viennese critic, Hanslick, in 1854, in a celebrated little work abounding in extremely good ideas,—without attaining the conclusions one would have wished,—but promulgating an inadmissible definition of music.

In the mind of Hanslick there is an ornamental art which may help us to understand how it is possible for music to create forms which, while of great value, contain no exact sentiment : it is *the art of the arabesque.* Let us imagine arabesques, which, instead of being inert and without life, like those of the delineator, should form themselves before our eyes, the work of a mind endeavouring to depict, by the movement of lines, an endless phantasy. This would be an exact image of music.

When, after having pulverized sentimentalism, Hanslick discourses, with infinite good sense, of *musical ideas,* of *specifically* musical beauty, one would expect to find him showing exactly the part played by the mind, asserting the existence of a thought *sui generis,* special to the language of sound, and thus giving compensation, in the domain of reason, to an art, the traditional rights of which he had contested in the domain of emotion. Nothing of the kind. To his mind the word "idea" (musical) is synonymous with image, form, and nothing more. So that, according to the doctrine of the Viennese æsthete, the art of music is thrust back on itself on two sides at once—that of intelligence and that of sensibility; it has no more hold on thought than on sentiment. This "arabesque," to which it is reduced, resembles a frontier line subsisting all alone after the vanishing of the two great empires which it formerly separated—that of intelligence and that of sentiment. Certainly there is a plastic art of sounds; but to assert that formalism defines the whole art of music is strange.

1st. What arabesques could Hanslick have had in mind when applying such a word to music? It was not, evidently, those so well-known and so admired works of the decorative painters of the sixteenth century, whose arabesques are so largely drawn from natural models:—twining vines, laurel branches, ivy leaves, flowers, fruits, panthers, leopards, lions, and, lastly, human figures. Nor can he have had in mind the arabesques of the Alhambra, or the mural decorations of Herculaneum and Pompeii! It is evidently a question, in his theory, of some *particular* arabesque which could only have been suggested by the association of several simultaneous melodious movements.* But an arabesque of this kind (I refer only to the design which would embody it) exists neither in nature nor in art. What light can we expect from

---

* Nicomaque de Gérase (*Manuel d'Harmonique*, chap. IV.) defined sound as "a degree, without breadth, of the melodious voice." As M. Ch.-E. Ruelle points out. this metaphor is borrowed from geometry, and tends towards discovering in music a system of lines forming arabesques.

a chimerical fact as the explanation of an actual one ? *Obscurum per obscurius.*

2nd. The three or four parts, in different movements, of which is composed, for instance, a fugue, might call to mind flexible lines sometimes superposed, and sometimes interlaced ; but the language of an orator, with its multiple inflexions, might likewise have as a diagram a line of this kind ; this diagram, however, would be a long way from representing the eloquence of the speaker ! We should be informed according to what laws the arabesques are organized :

3rd. I took a piece of music, the adagio of the *Pathetic Sonata,* and on thin paper I traced the arabesque resulting from following the lines of the melody. It is difficult to imagine anything more displeasing, more incoherent and absurd. The experiment seems to me interesting, for, however much Hanslick may harp on his " *sonorous lines,*" we can only figure them as lines situated in space. Now, such lines are only a worthless *grimoire.*

4th. An arabesque is always an ornament accessory to a whole ; it may add to the splendour of a monument (the Baths of Titus, the galleries of the Vatican, Hadrian's Villa, etc.), but it is never an independent work complete in itself. Is this the case with a symphony ?

5th. An arabesque is subject to no physical law ; the art of music, on the contrary, cannot free itself from the determinism of the laws of acoustics nor from those of respiration (rhythm).

6th. There are, in music, many essential things which a linear arabesque could not reproduce, even as a distant analogy: the tonality, mode, time, scale, modulations, and register employed. How is it possible to reproduce, in drawing, an enharmonic modulation? or a dramatic accompaniment like that of Schubert's *Erl King*? A note long repeated is the opposite of an arabesque, yet it can produce a very musical effect.

7th. One of the most interesting things to use in a symphony is the development of an idea. Is there anything of this in an arabesque?

8th. Even were music but a system of arabesques, would it be necessarily void of all psychological value? Is not writing itself a system of lines? Yet do not graphologists, not wholly wrongly, discover therein an appreciable reflection of the writer's character? Why should we not admit that in time, and by the aid of certain genius-gifted artists, the most arid forms have become capable of expressing life and conveying a meaning? Quatremère de Quincy said of Raphael: "He has made the arabesque a *figurative language* of which the hieroglyphics, known to all, still give the spectator the pleasure of guessing them." And Hittorf affirms that in the arabesque there must be sought, above all, "unity of thought."

If an art is neither thought nor sentiment, if it resembles that game which consists in tracing in darkness, lines in space with the point of a burning stick, in what way can it interest us? There are oriental carpets of which the designs are meaningless, yet the effect is charming; but do they affect us as does music? For these reasons we are unable to adopt the theory of Hanslick.

§ 3. MUSIC AND SENTIMENT

A theory partly founded on truth, more seductive than but quite as inadmissible as the foregoing, because it ignores some essential facts, perceives in music " the adequate language of sentiment." This was Aristotle's opinion. To his mind, music is not an expression of psychical states obtained by the aid of more or less conventional signs (σημεῖα), but an absolute and direct reproduction (μίμησις) of these states ; hence it should be a great factor in education, for by expressing certain *habits* of the soul it may communicate them to the young listeners, and even incite them to practise the actions which are the consequences of these *habits*. The Germans have often recurred to this theory ; to convey the fact that music expresses the affective states they have a word (*Nachahmung*) which is a literal translation of Aristotle's μίμησις.

That sentiment is at the origin and at the basis of all music cannot be doubted. Beethoven affirmed that all emotions, *even anger*, could be sources of musical inspiration ; he was rallied for this statement, and it was said that, in that case, his housekeeper, who had a bad temper, ought to share the composer's fees ! With good reason we regard a great musician as a very passionate man, endowed with keener sensitiveness than an ordinary man. But from the fact that emotion is a necessary starting-point, it by no means follows that it should find its *adequate* expression, by a kind of law, in sonorous combinations, and that, in order to create " a work," it should have no need of anything quite different to itself ; in the second place, the sentiment expressed in music is not one which can be translated into verbal language. Music comes from far greater depths than those superficial emotions which are defined by an ordinary type, and it requires something more than sensitiveness to be what it is. The theory of *pure* sentimentalism must be rejected on account of certain inexact assertions, and, above all, because it is as incomplete as the physiological theory.

We only know sentiment, in a direct way, by the consciousness. Without the consciousness we are only cognizant of its effects or of its representation by images and symbols, of which the accuracy, entirely relative, depends upon the association of ideas. An imitation, in the antique sense of the word, of love or jealousy is a chimæra. The impossibility one experiences of showing any real resemblance between a sentiment and a sound-formula musically constructed has given rise to a vague and contradictory terminology which the best writers use without concern and as if they understood themselves, but which betrays a manifest gap. In French we say that music *expresses*, and *translates*, and these words require elucidation, for there is nothing more vague than the word " expression " in art.

Among the Germans it is far worse. Music is the *language of emotions* (Kant) ; it is the *art of sentiment* (Hegel) ; music represents (*darstellt*) the passional life ; it embraces it (*erfasst*) ; reveals it (*kundthuet*) ; proclaims it (*verkündet*) ; calls it forth (*hervorruft*) ; expresses it (*sie drücktaus*) ; reflects it (*wiederspiegelt*) ; echoes it (*wieder-*

klingt) ; traces its images (*abbildet*) ; draws attention to it (*zeichnet*) ; publishes it (*offenbart*) ; relates
it (*erzählt*). . . . Nor is Helmholtz himself any clearer.
According to him and to a doctrine which we shall
discuss later on, music expresses not the sentiment,
but the state into which the soul is brought and the
tone which it gives to it (*Gemüthsstimmung*). This
equivocal term of *Gemüthsstimmung* Helmholtz
hastens to explain : " By this I mean," he says,
"those properties of the psychical states which
music is able to reproduce ; that is to say, the
general character presented at any given moment
by the *course* of our ideas. . . ." And, for lack of
a clearness which he here seeks with evident
trouble, Helmholtz further defines what he understands by "*course* of ideas" (*Fortbewegung der
Vorstellungen*) : " Our thoughts can move rapidly
or slowly ; they can *wander here and there*, without
rest and without object, in anxious agitation, or
follow, with precision and energy, a fixed end ;
they can let themselves be drawn, with ease and
without effort, into pleasant musing, or else, linked
with sad remembrances, change their subject but
slowly, painfully, without energy, and *step by step*.
All this can be imitated and expressed by the
melodious movement of sound." It will be granted
that this materialism of images, quite natural in a
literary man, is a little singular from the pen of a
physiologist and physicist who asserts the close
connection of music with the exact sciences. At all
events, it is not clear.

We have come to one of the knotty points of the
problem. Sentiment is the life of music ; it is as

necessary to it as sap to the plant ; but it is strange
that we should have so much difficulty in explaining ourselves in that regard, and that what is most
alive in us cannot be expressed ! " Everything individual is ineffable," was the profound remark of
Leibnitz. In any case, we cannot define music by
sentiment alone.

One simple question : all part music is based
on the art of counter-point, and all the forms of
counter-point are gathered together in the fugue.
What relation of *real* resemblance exists between
any given emotion and the setting forth of a
fugue or of a motet ? Unless we are to be satisfied with mere words, we must put the problem in
that way. No doubt, the writer of a fugue is an
accomplished musician, and it will be granted that
he would not have become a musician had he not
had a sensitive character and obeyed the movements
of his sensitiveness. But if that is all he is, and
all he can do, we can affirm positively, with the
authority of history added to that of evidence, that
he will never do any good.

A critic (Ferdinand Hand, 1837) has gone to the
point of saying that the laws of sentiment are
likewise those of music. Nobody knows this,
for the *laws* of sentiment are very imperfectly
known, which is by no means the case with
musical composition ; if the two are identical, why
has not music arrived, at one bound, at the bringing into play of all its resources ? Every musical
work is a *construction*, and every construction
presupposes a plan, a logic, and a method, reached
by slow degrees as the fruit of long experiment.

Now, pure sentiment, if considered apart from the thought which intervenes and regulates it, is repugnant by nature to all this. Logic is foreign to it. As regards method and the idea of a plan, it is an element of incoherence and a solvent.

Music is a special act of the intelligence, intervening in the chaos of the emotional life to bring into it order and beauty. Instead of saying that it reflects certain sentiments, we might just as well maintain that it *creates* sentiments which without it would not exist, or of which we should have no knowledge. To measure the distance which separates an art of imitation from an art which dominates imitation, compare the attitude of the public in a picture gallery and in a concert hall. Before the pictures —portraits, landscapes, scenes from middle-class and low life—the public is quite at its ease and feels at home ; it perceives without any effort the effect the artist intended to produce ; it discusses with a perfect competence the resemblance of the images, the truth of the physiognomies, the dresses, attitudes, and furniture, and the correctness of the drawing and colours.

How does it behave when listening to a quartet or a symphony ? Its attitude should be the same if it be true that music *imitates*, repeats, echoes, represents outwardly, etc., sentiments already felt. Now this is not the case. The public only perceives in a vague and very confused way the relations between what it hears and what it habitually feels ; it is touched, but is far from recognizing its own personality in what is said to it. It tries to establish a connection between the melody, or the tones of the orchestra, and its own anterior psychical conditions, but only succeeds imperfectly and intermittently; even then it only succeeds by a variable act of its own fancy, and not by virtue of a law of perception. It wonders; it *admires*.

It drifts about in a shadowy world of sensations, of sympathetic tendencies, of memories, of associations of ideas, in which the curiosity of the intelligence, anxious to understand, acts a greater part than does memory. It feels itself in the presence of an enigma to be solved.

This arises from the fact that music brings to it something new which goes beyond and troubles its experience. One can hardly conceive its being otherwise. The composer himself is often astonished at what he has written. He may happen to take as the starting-point of his work the idea of some possible æsthetic effect, and to only perceive afterwards the exact relation of the formula he discovers to the sentiment chosen. It was thus that in many of the scenes in his operas Wagner composed the air before the words.

As noticed by Darwin, who studied the question with admirable impartiality, the sentiments " expressible " in music clearly and unmistakably are, in reality, very restricted in number. They are all reduced to a few rather indistinct types. The formula used at the beginning of the second act of *Lohengrin* to " translate " the shame and despair of two detected criminals is almost the same as that used by Berlioz to " translate " the boredom of Faust in his study. Yet what a differ-

ence between the two conditions. Take the charming overture to the *Magic Flute* : what sentiment
are we to recognize in the fugue it contains ?   The
irritation of the merchants who are quarrelling ?   A
wild outburst of joy ?   The chattering of old
women all speaking at once ?   Does it even deal
with any certain sentiment ?   Is it simply a display of skill ?   And in the very improbable case
of our being able to express in words what it is
about, do we really think that this would sufficiently
explain such a composition ?

There are some who have gone so far as to assert
that to each sentiment there corresponds a sound
of the voice peculiar to it which music makes its
own.   In the first place, music only begins when
there is a synthesis of sounds ;   and, in this synthesis, each element loses its own peculiar value to
take that imposed on it by its relations to the whole.
But let us admit that the composer puts in juxtaposition, as in a kind of mosaic, exact representations of sentiment.   Then would there be a sort
of " ear-deception " for the expression of the
emotional states, as there is an " eye-deception " for
material objects.   Would this " ear-deception " be
music ?   Would the musician possess in his art
an exactness and precision analogous to those of
the photographer ?   This far from artistic conception, does away, in melodious constructions, with
everything invented, original, and interesting.   It
renders the art both useless and displeasing.   Two
remarks out of a hundred !   At the theatre, singers
who desire to give the illusion of real emotion use
means (attack of the note from below, slurring the

voice, liberties with the time, shricks in lieu of the
musical note, hiccough, catching of the breath, etc.),
which, plainly, have an anti-musical character. Yet
these artifices bring them closer to the real emotional
state ; the *bel canto*, the " style," removes them
further from it. There have been imitative styles
—the pantomimic, the *atellan*, the farcical ; they
were only able to become works of art by an
evolution which essentially transformed them and
kept them at a distance from the type supplied by
reality.

Some æsthetes have taken a bias, and have
attributed to music the power of expressing not
real emotion, but its " analogues " (Riemann,
Wundt) ; they have said it translates fictitious sentiments (Ed. de Hartmann), or sentiments of imitation (Karl Groos). What they mean to say is this.
You read a novel which provokes certain emotions
in your mind ; these emotions are abstract ; they
have neither the depth, the intensity, nor the duration of those you would feel in actual life, in face of
corresponding objects. Here are the fictitious passions, the *Scheingefühle* (Hegel, de Hartmann), which
constitute the domain of music. . . . Notwithstanding the great authority of the principal philosopher
who has developed this theory, I do not think it is
more acceptable than the former, or that it avoids
the same objections. Between the two categories
of emotions, fictitious and real, there is but a difference of degree ; whether it is a question of one or
the other, the difficulty of passing thence into
musical art is the same. There is an abyss to be
got over.

§ 4. MUSIC AND THE ABSTRACT EMOTIONS

Thought does not subject itself to ready-made.
means of expression which come to it from without ;
it creates the language itself requires, and its
resources are infinite. It can project itself into any
system of signs whatever and can make it its own.
As Montaigne says, the human mind is a great
worker of miracles. We need not therefore be
astonished at the idea of being able to think in
sounds. Kant and Descartes, who were not
musicians, have asserted that we can only think
by the aid of concepts, but we cannot do away
with an observed fact for the convenience of a theory.

We do not understand by " musical thought "
merely an act of intelligence, but also a work of
feeling, giving this latter word a meaning
different from the usual one. The difficulty is to
know how these two things go together. Certain
scholars do not consider their connexity proved by
experience : they make them appear at distinct
moments in a process of which they believe they
can reconstitute the history. This question is,
above all, psychological ; we shall only refer to it
here in so far as it bears on a definition of music
and gives us a new opportunity of confirming our
theory.

In his *Psychologie des Sentiments*, M. Th. Ribot,
wishing to show how a work of art can come forth
from emotion, puts forward the very shrewd idea
that side by side with intellectual memory there is
an emotional memory, that is to say, a real survival
or an attenuated prolongation of the emotion itself.

This survival is made up of partial sensations, weakened like an oft-repeated echo ; these are the residues of suffering or of pleasure—in a word, they are *abstract emotions*, analogous to abstract ideas. These emotions, reduced to the state of remembrances, may fuse themselves into one single state of consciousness, and finally, following the moving tendency which rules us, terminate in a musical work. What we call the creative imagination of a composer would only be the outward expansion of these states preserved within us by the emotional memory and carried further and further away from the circumstances in which they are produced. The concrete reality, tangible and visible, is thus transformed by the musician into an immaterial construction of sounds.

The plastic imagination furnishes us with a counter-proof of this ; it turns it round the other way : does a musical impression pass through the brain ? It excites it, but issues forth transformed into visual representations. Thus, Weber, after having contemplated a landscape near the Cascade of Geroldsau, writes a page of his *Der Freischütz*. Goethe, on the contrary, after listening to a piece of Bach's, said : " How grandiose and full of pomp this is ! It brings before me the vision of a procession of great personages in gala dress, descending the steps of a gigantic staircase." The first has the musical imagination, which purifies and spiritualizes the reality ; the second, the plastic imagination, which materializes abstractions.*

* Th. Ribot, *Essai sur l'imagination créatrice*, 3e. partie, chap. II. Alcan, 1900.

E

Such a clear-cut theory as this is very attractive. It revives with originality an old idea : that to create is to remember. By reducing the invention of the composer to an entirely internal work it satisfies the most exalted musical sense, which considers descriptive music as inferior, and finds its highest satisfaction in pure symphony. Yet it is disturbing from its extreme simplicity. Does any one really think that the emotional memory and the motor tendency which throws forth the residues unified by the consciousness suffice to produce a sonata, a motet, a stringed quartet, or even a melody of eight bars ? You enter into a garden, your foot presses a plate, and immediately a Neptune springs up, trident in hand. It would seem that impressions from outside, absorbed by a musician, end, by as prompt a mechanism, in a work of art ! However, I do not fancy that, in describing this process in such a general way, the eminent philosopher intended to propound a theory of music and to exclude other analyses.

Would a work like 'the Sonata of Beethoven dedicated to the Archduke Rodolph be formed out of the cold refuse of common emotions ? Rather is it an exaggeration, a conflagration which takes place in the composer's mind. What is necessary to him, if he is to write anything good, is the exaltation of sentiment, enthusiasm, and " Intoxication."

I fail to see how the passage from the commencement of the evolution to the final term, could happen everywhere automatically. The fusion of peculiar abstract emotions into a single state of consciousness is an impossible or barren synthesis from an artistic point of view, without the intervention of certain ideas of charm, of special technique, and of beauty. From the outset of the series of phenomena, the subject may be struck with impotence, unless he is endowed with a peculiar mind. To show that in music emotion is useful in everything, but sufficient for nothing, and that, if the mind is unable to grasp it at once and use it as the vehicle for a grand idea, emotion is rather an obstacle, we have a typical example, that of J. J. Rousseau.

Rousseau was *par excellence* the man of sentiment. Over his contemporaries and disciples he exercised, through sentiment, an influence which I need not recall. He loved music with extraordinary persistence. He insisted on composing; yet he was never able to become a true musician. He was a slave to his sensitiveness. It was impossible for him to escape it or to master it. His great mistake was to believe himself a musician because he had the emotion of music, just as he believed himself virtuous because he had the emotion of virtue. Berlioz was far more sensitive than Bach or Handel; he is not, however, their equal as a composer. It is not then sufficient to have emotion in order to compose; a special act of the mind is necessary to which sensitiveness alone cannot attain.

We have therefore to point out the part played by the mind in musical work. Several roads are open to this end.

Let us state exactly the antinomy we have to

resolve, and which it ought to be possible to
resolve.

1st. In a letter dated 27 March, 1828, addressed
to his friend Flechsig, Robert Schumann, who has
rightly been called the poet of music, expresses
himself thus : " Love and friendship pass their
life on this earth with veiled face and closed
lips. No human being can convey to another how
he loves him ; he simply feels that he loves him.
The inward man has no language ; he is dumb."
This declaration—which Schumann borrowed from
Jean-Paul Richter and repeats in another letter
(28 Jan., 1828)—recalls the words of Musset, who
indeed defines music as " the language of the
heart," but adds that it is a mysterious language—

> . . . ou la pensée,
> Cette vierge craintive et d'une ombre offensée,
> *Passe en gardant son voile.*

To sum up, *between a psychical state and any
formula, verbal or otherwise, there can be no possible
resemblance.* Such is the statement of Schumann.

2nd. And yet for the crowd, as for many composers whose testimony might be quoted, *music
and sentiment are two inseparable things.*

Here are two truths, one resting on as solid a
basis as the other. Can they be made to agree ?
A priori, we must answer in the affirmative. Our
researches into this agreement will carry us a little
more closely into the study of musical thought.

§ 5.   The Dynamics of the Passional Life and Musical Thought

Music cannot translate directly any given feeling, but it translates the intensity, the internal

and general dynamics of the psychical life with all its gradations ; and this mode of expression, joined to the images which complete it, is one of the secrets of its power.

Feeling always manifests itself in us by *quantitative* variations, which may be observed first of all in the " crescendo " or the " diminuendo " of all the functions of our organs. According to whether we are deeply or slightly moved, the heart beats faster or slower, the vessels contract or relax, and the secretions increase or diminish. All these phenomena may be easily measured. By the aid of ingenious appliances (the registering apparatus of Marey, François Franck, Potain, and Hallion-Comte) every one of the variations in the pulse, the heart, the respiration, and the troubles of the circulation can be exactly noted. If, from organic troubles, we pass to psychological observation, we find phenomena which it is no longer possible to measure, but are, in a certain sense, of the same nature. What we note is activity, accelerated, moderated, or in its normal state. Our vital and moral forces may be likened to a sort of internal capital in a state of perpetual renovation and, under the influence of feeling, subject to losses and to gains. An emotional state, whatever it may be (whether, as M. Th. Ribot says, a neuralgia, or the grief which Michael Angelo exhales in his *Sonnets*), may be summed up as an exaltation or a depression of the energy.

Now, it is first of all this—to take the simplest instance—that music can " render." It ignores the representations and the concepts bound up in the

emotional state ; it retains only its energy. It is, so
to say, the dynamometer of the sentimental life. It
appears indeed as if the great classical composers
had thus understood their art. At the beginning
of their finest symphonies they have written these
simple words : *adagio, allegro, andante, vivace,
presto.* Composers nowadays delight in multiplying the literary indications above a musical
score ; they sometimes pile up five or six in
the same bar, and daily add to their vocabulary
to apprise us of what they want to say. This
characteristic tendency of modern works is that
of an art which is ignorant of its limitations and
desires to come forth from itself at the risk of
losing itself or of compromising its originality.
There was nothing of this formerly. In the
manuscripts of Bach no other indication is found
save that of the "tempo." In this custom is the
best æsthetics.

Let us follow up the consequences of this fact.
Through neglecting the concepts and the external
circumstances inseparable from an emotional state,
music becomes what the Germans have called an
"art of inwardness," and what we may call simply
an *art of intimacy.* The *ego,* said Fichte, is pure
activity. Music, therefore, attains personality *in its
essence.* By binding itself to the reproduction of
the dynamics of passion taken from its deep source,
and nothing more (as far as direct imitation is
concerned), music acquires as much generality as
power ; for this energy of which it marks the intensity is not that unfolded by an individual in
his love or hatred for some other individual : it

is the vital force itself, taken at its source, freed from all concrete meanings, and grasped in its universality.

What is it that interests us when listening to the *Symphonie Fantastique* of Berlioz ? That which moves us is not Henrietta Smithson ; it is the intensity of Berlioz's passion ; it is, above all, the act of generalization by which the composer, rendering more vast and more magnificent the horizons of love, succeeds in universalizing a personal state, in absorbing it into the feeling of the general life. As Nietzsche remarks, the essential point in the act of artistic creation and in the effects produced on the hearer is the feeling of increased force and of plenitude. "Under the influence of this feeling we yield to circumstances, we force them to take a part of ourselves, we do violence to them, and this process is called idealization. It does not consist, as is generally believed, in a deduction, in the subtraction of everything small and accessory ; what, on the contrary, is decisive in it is a formidable projection forth of the principal features in such a way that the remaining features disappear. In this state one enriches everything from one's own fulness. What one sees, what one desires, one sees compact, powerful, overflowing with richness. Man then transforms things until they reflect his power, till they become reflections of his own perfection."

This brings us back to the admirable complexity of the musical art. The composer does not create with feeling alone, but "with his whole soul " ; that is to say, that to the increased passional force

is added an act of the mind, already observed in
what we are about to call the *images.* The emotion
and the thought mutually penetrate each other.
It is doubtful if in fact the first is not ordinarily
mingled with the second ; in any case, if it is
disjoined from it, the musical art would be impossible. Notice that between the dynamics to
which we have just referred and the rhythmic
sections, and the cadences of a period having
necessarily a limited extent, there is no analogy.
The thought is so intimately bound up with the
emotion that in this torrent of composition which
carries all before it, one may at times think it
predominates.

This is why Beethoven affirms that " Music is a
higher revelation than Science or Philosophy."
Carefully listening " to that which the Spirit inspired in me and told me to accomplish " (letter
to Schott, 17 Sept., 1824), he tells Goethe that
his greatest desire " is in no way to produce in
my hearers a more or less disquieting emotion, but
to touch their intelligence and be understood by
it " ; and he was only partly in error when, in a
letter—addressed, curiously enough, to a woman he
loved, Bettina d'Arnim—he says : " Emotion is only
good for women (all my excuses) ; for man, *music
must draw fire from his mind !* " He meant by
" emotion " those superficial troublings of the moral
being always associated with concepts. The force
he claimed to express was more general and came
from greater depths.

There is another means of solving the antinomy
mentioned above. We will demonstrate in the

following chapters that, in order to depict feeling, music takes a very ingenious bias by bringing in imagination, and that will put us in the right way to define later the part played by the intelligence.

CHAPTER III

MUSICAL IMAGES—EXAMPLES

WHEN we cannot represent directly a psychological phenomenon, a feeling, or an abstract idea, we employ a symbol, an image of which the exactness depends not on the real resemblance between the sign and the thing signified, but on the association of ideas which intervene and serve as a link between the two terms. This is the process continually used in ordinary language. We lend to ideas *a weight*. We talk of heavy or light ideas; or *a colour :* as when we speak of clear, sombre, bright, black ideas (to see things rose-coloured, to have the blues); or *dimension :* as in large, narrow, profound ideas; or *localization in space :* as in elevated, sublime, grovelling ideas; or *quality of resistance :* as in strong or solid ideas (a hard, a soft heart); or *geometric formulas :* as in a pointed wit, a square head, a circle or a sphere of ideas; or *flavour :* as in bitter, sweet, or insipid thoughts; or *temperature :* as in a warm, cold, or icy heart. . . . Such are the intermediaries with which instinct supplies us to express a phenomenon of the moral life; and we are about to make the best use of all this to explain our unexplainable music ! But let us follow the steps which will lead us to this end.

It is in the artistic language of poetry that these images multiply and develop. The usual rôle of a poet is not to invent feelings, but to translate into more figurative forms the ordinary emotional states. Victor Hugo knows the life of the soul no better than Racine ; it may, however, be said that he is a greater poet because he uses more images. Images are not everything in poetry—far from it ; but they are of the utmost importance. Take a piece of poetry or a page of sublime eloquence ; rob it of its metaphors, there will remain but a skeleton.

In music the expression is made up of sonorous sensations and not of concepts ; but is not the process often the same ? These sonorous sensations (a kind of realized images) have an imitative value only by the association of ideas that they awaken. Let us try to represent to ourselves Chopin improvising at the piano, under the influence of a powerful emotion, a nocturne or a ballad. He masters his sensibility ; the problem he has set himself (a problem which he solves without effort and by instinct because he has genius) is to create with sounds a plastic form capable of representing that which by its nature fights against all plastic form. He thus suppresses the antinomy of the moral and of the sensible world ; he projects the soul (*hervorruft*) into a system of forms ; he has performed a kind of miracle which astonishes us—but by processes of which we may say that they imitate nothing directly and that they can imitate everything indirectly. Considered from the point of view of expression, music would be a series of metaphors formed out of sensations and not concepts.

At times, the composer translates into musical metaphors feelings or objects known to both himself and his hearers (songs with words, symphonies with descriptions); at other times he translates feelings known to himself alone, and which he does not think it expedient to indicate to us exactly. Thus Haydn, it is said, when writing a symphony, not seldom wrote down a sort of synopsis for his own use. At other times, again, he translates feelings of which neither he nor his audience have any clear notion, because they are hardly conscious of them.

Let us deal with the first only. To constitute the metaphors, or the images which express them, the musician relies on associations of ideas which imply partial resemblances between two groups.

Gluck, in the pastoral of *Armide* (" plus j'observe ces lieux et plus je les admire . . ."), wishes to express the sharp struggle of Rinaldo, who, seized by the remembrance of his knightly duty, would tear himself away from the seductions which surround him. How does he effect this ? He employs —in defiance of all rules, I note in passing—three consecutive fifths, and the harsh impression produced associates itself in the hearer's mind with the idea of that which is painful in the struggle of the hero against himself.

(Gluck)*Armide*, II, 3.

Does Beethoven wish to express an intense, grievous or distracted passion ? He strikes a chord of the ninth, of which the dissonance is accentuated by a prolonged shake followed by a rapid run, disorderly in appearance, which puts in relief all the elements of the dissonant chord and gives the impression of a moan by reason of the happily placed intervals of semi-tones :

Presto de la *Sonate* op. 27 n? 2 (Beethoven)

To depict the majestic and harmonious course of the Rhine, Wagner uses an analogous effect differently worked out ; he uses two ninth chords, one atop of the other, or rather one chord of the ninth with a repetition of the lower fifth and a pedal—which awakens an idea of grandeur. But he writes these two chords in arpeggios so as not to leave a painful impression, and follows them up with a run which, instead of being inflected, irregular, and broken at every moment, as in the score of Beethoven given above, has the direct movement of a regular scale. The *Götterdämmerung* (Act III,

sc. 1) gives us the following image of the Rhine
with its powerful and harmonious flow—

Bach employs the same moaning and painful
chromatics as Beethoven to give an image of the
Agony of Jesus on the Cross. He naturally suppresses the passionate and free character of the
rhythm ; for he wants to represent human suffering
(he does so by means of an admirable altered chord
of the seventh)—but also the suffering of a man-God
dying with a thought of pardon, and with serenity.
Hence this melody, which *descends* by intervals of
semi-tones, slowly and with dissonances, ends with
a last tragic dissonance and resolves itself at once
as it were into an infinitely sweet and resigned
tenderness—

In all this we may say that there are images
accumulated upon each other.

When the author of the *Pastoral Symphony* wishes to express in an *Andante* the calm of nature, he employs successions of thirds, which by their symmetrical grouping and their rhythm realize the image of the poet—

Le bercement des flots sous la chanson des branches.

In the ball scene in *Don Juan*, Mozart wishes to depict the contrast formed by very different persons —lords and clowns—in proximity ; he puts one on the other, so that they may be heard simultaneously, a waltz associated in the mind of the hearer with ordinary people and their affairs, and a minuet associated with the idea of the aristocratic life.

To express terror, Berlioz proposed the following image : a diminished seventh chord (*Sol, Do* ♯, *Mi* ♮, *Si* ♭) played on four clarionets, of which two are bass. In music, the rhythm, time, movement, intensity of sounds, melodious design, harmony, consonance and dissonance, the timbres, everything— the rests, even silence itself—can form, or help to form, an image. It is by no means necessary for this image to be complete. It is enough that, on certain well-chosen points, the musician enables us to see a relation of resemblance between the language he is speaking and its subject, for our imagination, co-operating with his, to set obediently to work and construct a finished whole. This reconstruction is effected by association of ideas which play an intermediate part, and which, not being the same in the minds of all hearers, cause music not to be interpreted by every one in the same way. We cannot pass in review all those ideas with

which the composer deals ; his art consists in
creating and enforcing upon us the association of
ideas utterly unforeseen. Images are the creation
of the artistic mind, and do not result from simple
observation, as we should have to say if it were
true that there is "a natural language of feeling."   The imagination displays in them the
highest and the most delicate resources of the
invention, for the problem, solved at every moment
by the musician, consists in discovering images
capable of expressing what is, by its nature, inex-
pressible.

An image is never musical *on account of* its
(partial) resemblance to a given reality.   Herein
lies an important fact, which admonishes us that
we are only at the first stage of our study.   Not a
single one of the musical metaphors we have just
quoted is the imitation of a real fact. Every
one of them is the fragment of a thought which has
occasionally taken a symbolical form. We have to
show that a metaphor is only musical if it be organized, and to relate how this organization is effected.

Here what we have to analyse is the pure work
of the mind acting on passional perceptions : we
are entering the subject of true music.

CHAPTER IV

THE ORGANIZATION OF IMAGES

MUSICAL images, as we have said, tend to separate from all concepts and to organize themselves into independent systems. This organization is the whole of music; it is indispensable to examine it closely if we wish to ascertain wherein lies the originality of a composer's work. Unless we do so, we run the risk of only studying accessory phenomena, which are beside the real subject. It is certainly not the musical thought that we claim to grasp in the analyses which follow, any more than it can be grasped in a treatise on counter-point; but we can show its mechanism, its forms, and the whole series of facts without which the language of sounds would have nothing specific — and which, by suggesting the idea of a superior and reasoned work having no model in the reality, ought to maintain the idea of the musical art at a sufficient distance from that which is not itself.

When a reader, without previous knowledge of the subject, opens a book on advanced geometry he is confronted with complicated figures and formulas which appear to him somewhat cabalistic. Yet geometry had an empirical origin, and developed from the act of land measurement. Mathematics itself had a humble beginning. Certain experimental

data are first pondered over, then unexpected properties are discovered. We make abstracts and
progress, and hypotheses are framed without knowing whither they lead, until little by little there open
out unexplored tracks, which the mind follows
with delight, as if to the conquest of a new world.
Music has been formed in the same way.

I will take a very simple subject, the first five
notes of the diatonic scale—*Do, Re, Mi, Fa, Sol*—
which we will suppose to constitute (by movement,
intensity, evenness of emission, timbre, or any other
quality) a rudimentary image, and, endeavouring
to place myself in those frames of mind which have
marked, in succession, the principal epochs in the
history of this art, I will try to demonstrate how
this formula, subject to very varying treatment,
may culminate in a real musical work of a high
order. To commence with we will only deal with
the first three notes of our theme.

§ 1. A Melody, first Simple, then Ornate

1st. We may, in the first place, repeat our formula several times following, since repetition has
not the same drawbacks as in literature—

2nd. It may be reproduced in the octave—

This is the form of the echo, frequently employed

in orchestral music, and even in compositions for
one instrument alone.*   The first founders of instrumental music (Sweelinck, among others) often
used it.   There is even in organs a special " echo "
stop.

3rd. We may pass on this motif over all the
degrees of the scale, and, in the case of a polyphonic
composition, through all its parts.   If we reproduce
it as follows—

we have a march (and here we note a rather important fact, namely, that a reproduction strikes
the ear as sufficiently precise, even when all the intervals, semi-tones, whole tones, are not strictly
adhered to).   If we reproduce the motif in the
same part by changing the pitch, it becomes a
transposition; if we reproduce it in another part
either by transposition or by simple repetition, it
becomes an *imitation.*

4th. We may reverse the motif, and apply to it
the different treatments indicated above.

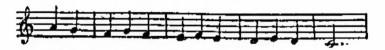

5th. We may increase or diminish the values,
either independently or together.

* Cf. Beethoven, *Sonatas,* op. 81 et op. 90.

6th. We may make the notes which come on a weak beat in this bar come on a strong beat.

7th. We may interrupt all the values of the motif by separating them by a rest of equal duration, so as to obtain a *staccato* instead of a *legato*.

8th. In the case of a melodious phrase of some length, we may reproduce only a part of it, which may itself serve as an introduction to a new idea.

9th. We may adorn or ornament the notes of the motif.

This will be like a person always the same and always recognizable, who appears in different clothes and altered gait. He may have a step now heavy, now light. Sometimes he will walk straight and with regular steps, and sometimes sideways, or backwards, or will perform the regular gymnastics of a dancer ; he will be clothed in a grand ceremonial robe or wear the slightest possible clothing. Lastly his countenance may be smiling and jovial, or thoughtful and melancholy. But he will always be the person we know.

§ 2. Grace Notes and Variations

We are now arriving at the subject of musical technique. As the idea just mentioned is of great importance, we will pause a moment to show its historical genesis and support it by a few facts.

Ornamentation, or *flourish,* must not be confused with *variations.* It has been possible to write a lengthy work on grace notes without mentioning the art of variations.* The *flourish* was not always written in old times; the variation, as a work of art and a personal work, could not fail to be written; but, historically, the one seems to be the origin of the other.

From the thirteenth century we come across flourishes, which were formerly termed *figuræ, flores, colores.* Pleasure was taken in decomposing rhythmic values and ornamenting them. The French writer Jean de Garlande (first half of the thirteenth century), whose tractate de Cousse-maker† published from the MS. of Saint-Dié, lays down the principle that every interval of a whole tone may be decomposed into two intervals of a semi-tone, and that, consequently, the chromatic altera-tion may be made on every degree of the scale. On this basis, he sketches out the theory of what, later on, came to be termed embroideries and pass-ing notes. Jerome of Moravia, who was in 1260 a Dominican monk in a convent in the Rue Saint-

---

* *Musical Ornamentation,* by Edw. Dannreuther. (Novello, London, 1892). The work commences at the end of the sixteenth century with Diruta.

† *Script,* I, p. 157 *sqq.*

Jacques, at Paris,* likewise concerned himself with grace notes. He defines the shake, which he calls *procellaris vibratio* (and was called, later on, *balancement* in French, *bebung* in German, and *tremolo* in Italian). The Englishman Tunstede, who was choirmaster to the Franciscans at Oxford in 1351, says that in polyphonic singing the tenor may venture on excursions to the note above or below, so long as he refrains from disturbing the main part, the *déchant*. Jean de Muris, born in Normandy, 1300, speaks, with regard to the famous short penultimas of the "flourishes," *floraturæ ;* the phrase " nulla nota brevis *floreatur*," with its barbarism, was even current at that epoch.

A proof that these ornamentations were in great esteem is that Robert de Handlo, in his *Regulæ,*† places the *flourishes* among several kinds of compositions, which he enumerates as follows : " Rondelli, Balladæ, Coreæ, Cantifractus, Estampitæ (dances), *Florituræ*." This word has so great an importance that it reappears, in a symbolic sense, among the titles—for instance, in the *Flores musicæ omnis cantus gregorioni*, one of the first collections printed (1488). In the eighteenth century, in Nos. 2 and 3 of the *Suites Anglaises*, published under the name of Bach (there is a doubt as to the authenticity of one of the pieces), are to be found two sarabands, each repeated twice, one quite simple, the other "with the ornaments,"so that the executant can make his choice. I will not here detail the writings on this subject by Scheidt (1624), Tosi

---

* Coussemaker, *Script*, I, p. 157 *sqq.*
† *Ibid.*, I.

(1723), Ph. E. Bach (1753), Marpurg (1755), Agricola (1757), Türk (1789). Between the grace notes of our harpsichordists, the manners and the coquetries of the eighteenth century, there is an evident connection.

The *Variation*, still more important, demands a distinct study. A point worth noticing is that we see it appear, among the predecessors of Bach, as a means of giving unity to the *Suite*, by varying a given theme instead of juxtaposing other themes. Walther calls l'Allemande " a proposition from which the other dances—the coranto, the saraband, and the jig—proceed, like parts from a whole."* The art of variation, though foreign to religious music, has played a great part in the sixteenth and seventeenth centuries, and has found its chief organ in the keyboard instruments. Sweelinck, Frescobaldi, Cornet have used it extensively. Samuel Scheidt, in his work published in 1624,† has composed variations on all kinds of themes. The history of music testifies, at each step, to the importance of this form. Bach, imitating the Italians in this, has written, in the fourth part of his *Claviarübung*, thirty variations on a saraband. On a theme from Chaconne in *Sol* ♮ major, Handel has composed sixty-two, which are one of the master pieces of the musical art. Following Haydn and Mozart, Beethoven has largely cultivated the same form ; he has composed fifteen variations (op. 35) ending up with a fugue ; twenty-four on the air *Vieni amore* of Righini ; thirty-three on the waltz

---

* Spitta, *J. S. Bach*, I, p. 262 *sqq.* ; p. 693 ; and II, p. 649.
† *Tabulatora nova, Cantiones, Variationes psalmorum.*

of Diabelli. I may also mention the piano sonatas op. 26 and 109. Some very fine works of Schubert and Schumann may be recalled. In a letter to Klingemann, Mendelssohn declares that he has composed some variations at the same time as a Passion, and that he was divinely amused by it. It is a play, it is true, but a play which three hundred years before occupied the minds of the greatest, and thanks to which the spirit of combination—that is to say, nearly the entire musical mind—has, little by little, rendered itself master of sonorous matter.

§ 3. CANON

Here are the .categories of new forms which present themselves to us.

An attentive examination and the luck of repeated experiments open up to us a path in which surprises of another order await us. Our melody *Do, Re, Mi, Fa, Sol* is capable of many other metamorphoses. It can *act as an accompaniment to itself*, and give us a composition in several parts—

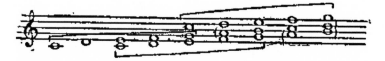

These bundles of notes are very heavy and appear to have little music about them! Here is, at the prelude of a piece by Sweelinck (beginning of the seventeenth century), a construction which, founded on the same principle, is more pleasing, clear, breezy and satisfying to the eye as well as to the ear—

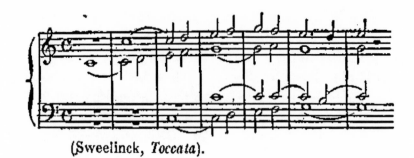

(Sweelinck, *Toccata*).

Imagine a person strolling by the side of some clear water and always followed by his own reflection as travelling companion; it will be something analogous to this complex and melodious movement.

We know that one of the parts may have a slower or a more rapid movement—

(Sweelinck) *Psalm.* III.

Here we have the hare and the tortoise, starting almost together and both arriving at the goal, but at different rates of speed, which allows the more nimble to return to the starting-point, to re-run certain laps and to play the truant a little.

This melody, which accompanies itself, thanks to its duplication, is called a *canon*, and if we take up the processes enumerated above relative to the transposition, the movement (direction of the design of the melody), bars, value of the notes, the rhythm, the number of the parts, we shall soon discover the possibility of a great number of new forms. These are canons in similar motion,

canons in contrary motion, canons with augmentation, with diminution, with syncopation,
with unison, canons at the second, the third, the
fourth, the fifth, the sixth, the seventh, the octave. . . . We can make some of these forms simultaneous, and obtain, for instance, a triple canon by
means of differences of duration in the notes of the
three parts, etc.

§ 4. SIMPLE COUNTER-POINT

Up to the present we have combined our motif
with itself ; we can doubtless combine it with
another, or with several other motifs,* and when

Such a fact shows that we are capable of simultaneous states
of consciousness.

seeking to make two different ideas progress together
according to combinations, of which experience will
show the charm as well as the stumbling-blocks,
many different paths open to us. This is what, in
the Middle Ages, was called descant or diaphony.†

The problem may be thus stated : We have
a given theme A; the question is to give it a
travelling companion B. How shall we set about it ?

* Thus in the *Meistersinger* of Richard Wagner (you will notice
the perfect chord at the beginning of the first theme).
† One of the best examples is to be found in MS. 383 of Saint-
Gall (written in the thirteenth and fourteenth centuries).

To *one* note of A we can always add one note,
or two or three, or even a larger number of
the motive B which we are seeking (ex. 1, 2, 3,
5). This latter form is what was called in the
Middle Ages the *broken* or *diminished* counter-
point, or, again, *duplicatio, triplicatio, conglobatio.*

We can also place the essential notes of the one
or other melody on the same long beats of the
measure, or else adopt syncopations (ex. 4)—

This little operation can be extended, while still
preserving the base *Do, Ré, Mi, Fa, Sol,* to three

parts to which we should apply the same mode of writing. (1) *One note against one note;* (2) *two notes to one;* (3) *four notes to one ;* (4) *a mixture of semibreves, minims, and crotchets ;* (5) *syncopation ;* (6) *syncopation mixed with semibreves and minims, or with semibreves and crotchets ;* finally, *quavers mixed with the other values.* The same operation may be performed with 4, with 5, 6, 7, or 8 voices (double chorus).

If, lastly, we imagine that the given subject may be placed in any one of the parts, and that the same holds good for the different processes employed in the structure of the melodies which happen to accompany the initial theme, we can see the already very considerable number of combinations possible.

§ 5. Double Counter-point

In the course of these researches we note that it is possible in certain cases to transpose two parts, to put above the one which was below, and conversely. This is what is called double, or reversible, counter-point. As in the fable the miller gets *on* his ass, having previously been *under* it. In music, where processes of this nature have a very great importance, it is a new way of saying " milk and water " after saying " water and milk," but it is much less easy and inoffensive than in the verbal language. First B accompanies A, and then A accompanies B.

This counter-point *double à l'octave*, used in conjunction with some of the resources that we are already acquainted with, allows constructions to be effected which have the greatest importance in the history of musical art, because they indicate the complete formation and the final emancipation of the musical mind.

This inversion may sometimes take place when dealing with two, three, or four parts ; one has then the double, triple, or quadruple counter-point—a delicate operation, requiring great care, for the inversion of the intervals may bring about many unforeseen effects. For instance, the intervals of 1, 2, 3, 4, 5, 6, 7, or 8 diatonic degrees, when reversed in the octave, become intervals of 8, 7, 6, 5, 4, 3, 2, or 1 degrees, and in their new order these parts have to produce as satisfactory a harmony as in their first.*

In these various realms, as will be easily seen, we are dealing more and more with relations and abstractions, leaving on one side any connection of musical formulas with the expression of a sentiment or of a picturesque idea. It is something like the game of chess, where, while keeping his eyes on the actual position of the pieces, the player has all the time *to think of the possibilities of the move*, bearing in mind the relative value of the pieces and not only their proper value or

---

* Beethoven gives a fine example of double counter-point in the octave, in the form of a canon in his Symphony in Si♭, *allegro vivace*, I. It is not possible to quote here examples of double counter-point at the 12th, 13th, 14th, and 15th. (See the *Traité de Contre-point et de fugue* of M. Th. Dubois, Paris, Au Ménestrel, 1901.)

form. There is also the well-known game of cat's cradle, which consists in stretching out a circular thread in the form of a saw on the fingers, held vertically with the two hands apart. The opponent then transfers it, with many ingenious combinations, on to his own fingers. Something akin to this is effected with melodious themes.

The selection and the synthesis of the above-mentioned processes lead us to the highest forms of composition : the motet, and then the fugue.

I give here the first bars of a motet by Vittoria (sixteenth century), *duo Seraphim clamabant**—

* I confine myself to transposing one note higher (to continue with our theme : *Do, Ré, Mi, Fa, Sol*) this prelude, which is quoted by M. Vincent d'Indy in his *Traité du Composition*, I. (published by Durand).

The given theme, rendered by the second soprano, is associated with another melodious design (B), formerly called *Comes*, or "Companion," which we have, so to speak, by withdrawing from it its personality, turned into the "accompaniment." In this case the "companion" is a counter-subject. Then we have a permutation; the theme A passes to the alto part No. 2 (and also to the superius No. 1), and B is laid upon it.

All this leads us directly up to the fugue.

To conclude, and to show whither the motive *Do, Ré, Mi, Fa, Sol* may get to, I will quote this exposition of one of Bach's fugues, in which the subject—our own theme—is first heard alone, and then repeated in the dominant (reply)—a combination which is reproduced immediately after in the converse order—

§ 6. The Methods of Counter-point in Pure Melody

The forms just mentioned raise in the mind a
construction in space with high, medium, and
low parts. No doubt the modern composer no
longer writes canons, motets, and fugues. But he
shows when writing a simple melodious period that
he has deeply assimilated these methods. We will
prove this by an example which will at the same time
enable us to point out new resources derived from
rhythm.

The elementary scheme of the melody is as
follows—

Having taken as a base a tonic (*Do*), there is
first a passage from the rest to the movement (*Sol*),
then a return of the movement to the rest (*Do*).

A formula of this kind is much too short to exhaust the feeling or the muscular power of the
singer and to please an assembly of men ; instinctively we are led either to link it with another
formula or to amplify it. It is easy to understand
that the first and the final part, having a function
regulated by a kind of law, it is neither before or
after, but rather *between* A and B, that new matter

should be introduced. The use of this last process
leads us to the following Gregorian melody*—

A is the first outburst of the phrase, the departure,
the abandonment of the tonic ; B is the conclusion,
the melody folding its pinions, returning to the
tonic and to the pause. Between the two are two
interludes, *a* and *a'*. The number of these can be
far greater. See how far Beethoven goes. Instead
of writing—

he writes—

* *Cantate domino canticum novum.* (*Paroissien romain, édition
des Bénédictins de Solesmes*, 1903, Preface.)

G

This admirable period, composed of thirteen or fourteen sections, calls forth two observations : (1) It may be considered as an image, the image of an energy which, after two preliminary efforts, returns to the task, with heroic obstinacy, and seems to attack the obstacle by a series of successive assaults after having wished to surmount it at one bound, arrives at last at the summit, plants there a flag of victory, and, after an unchallenged triumph, returns to rest again. (2) To a musician it is a work which requires no verbal interpretation ; it contains within itself a very complete and clear sense, the worth of which has no need of any commentary in order to be understood. If this be so, these four lines derive their specific interest from certain methods of composition : *inversion* of a subject, *transposition, repetition,* and *imitation.*

In a word, the methods of construction analysed above are not special to scholastic exercises. We meet with them again in the structure of a simple melody. They are therefore an essential part of the musical art.

§ 7. Rhythmical Organization and Timbre

We will continue our researches in this matter of the simple melody. We have a period. Let us designate it by the letter A ; and its repetitions by A′, A″, etc. We can now discover, in the order of pure sequence, combinations as interesting as in the order of simultaneity.

By combining (melodiously) a new idea with our period, we shall obtain the scheme A, b, A′, which, developed, will become A, b, A′, c, A″, d, . . . a series more or less extended, in which the important idea, enriched with episodes, is repeated in the form of a refrain. This form is that of the *Rondo*, which is found not only in the compositions bearing that name, but in most musical works, and has diverse forms : the rondo in two parts (rhythmical) : *A*, *b*, *A′* ; the rondo in three parts : *A*, *b*, *A′*, *c*, *A″* ; the rondo in four parts : *A*, *b*, *A′*, *c*, *A″*, *d*, *A‴*. By subjecting this scheme to certain modifications, we obtain a last form of the rondo : *A*, *b* (1st part), *c* (2nd part), *A′*, *b′* (3rd part) (example, in the finale of Beethoven's Pathetic Sonata).

These various forms lead to the Sonatina—then to the Sonata, which has more amplitude, and more suppleness and unity ; it forms the phrases by means of several subjects, the periods by means of several phrases, and the systems by means of several periods. The sonata no longer juxtaposes, it concatenates ; it gives life and movement to the subjects by transposition ; finally, it replaces repetition pure and simple by the ornate repetition or by one limited to a typical fragment. Henceforth, in this association of organized melodies, each component element derives its true value from the whole and not from itself.

Certainly there are many other constructions which, by researches and ingenuity, the musician has finally adopted. But let us indicate at once the last category of his resources : the timbres.

It is singular that the most immaterial of all the arts, that most exempt from all tangible reality and visual impressions, should have among its most moving and essential qualities, that of colour. Colour of what ? Of an object called forth by the mind ? Consequently, a colour created by pure imagination ? By no means. A colour unreal, and yet at the same time directly perceived ; a colour of musical ideas ; I would almost say, the colour of movement ! Timbres, we know, may be employed as images ; but that is only a secondary and casual function. Their organization is the grouping, by families or in " choruses," of wood, brass, and stringed instruments. It is, by a new progress and by a supreme creation of the musical mind, the inexhaustible series of combinations which can be effected with the elements of these groups.

§ 8. CONCLUSION OF THIS ANALYSIS

The forms which have just been briefly indicated were fixed (save as regards orchestration) in a period of some duration of which the points of maturity are the fifteenth and sixteenth centuries. In themselves they are somewhat dry. But within these learned outlines there soon appears an element of life which at first they did not enclose—

thought, and with thought all the brilliant freedoms which it allows. History permits us, at least, to grasp this new fact as the particular case of a general evolution in the arts of rhythm. A few analogies will throw light on this part of our exposition.

Let us see what took place in French poetry Before the seventeenth century, with some rare exceptions, there were, above all, writers who, in works at once pedantic and very useful, discovered extraordinarily complicated combinations of rhymes. They made, indeed, a sort of verbal counter-point and what they created was versification. After them come the Corneilles and the Molières, who certainly did not invent poetry, but who profited by the instrument handed down to them to express lofty ideas and human sentiments.

The same law appears in the history of Eloquence. Among the Greeks appeared first the rhetoricians, who discovered the period and taught the subtle symmetries of grammatical constructions; they also are makers of verbal counter-point. After them comes Demosthenes, who into this skeleton infuses movement, fire and life. Among the moderns, Balzac and Voiture precede Bossuet and prepare the way for him. But all this is subject to the reservation that neither poetry nor eloquence is of recent invention.

Let us now examine the situation of the artist-musician who has gone through all the formal work of which we have given the characteristics, or who gathers the fruits of this work done by his predecessors and is writing, let us say, about the middle of the eighteenth century.

In the first place, apart from music, a long heredity has formed him for the game of abstractions. Unknown to himself, he profits by the
special education which theologians and philosophers have conferred on the human mind from very
remote ages. If, in addition, he belongs to a race
which seems to have, as innate gifts, the taste for
abstruse speculations, the aptitude for searching
analysis, a leaning to reverie—if, finally, he have
that spark of talent which we cannot explain—
those forms of composition which his predecessors
have rendered supple and polished in so many ways
become familiar to him. He then exercises over
them an absolute mastery ; they are no longer an
ideal to be attained ; but they form the materials
of a language of which the use will henceforth be
quasi-instinctive. Finding them handy by reason
of their immateriality, his reason grasps them, re-
acts upon them, and puts into them something of
its own. The fugues of the *Clavecin bien tempéré*
and the six Brandenburg Concertos of J. S. Bach may
be cited as the finest specimens of the power of abstraction arrived at by a composer.

No doubt the modern musician will in future
rarely compose canons and fugues ; but in a simple
phrase of eight bars he will insert a thought which
will be due to a long practice of fugues and canons.

This thought will be an act of the intelligence ;
it will also be an irresistible impulse of the sentiment, a revelation of the whole mental man. Bach
is already, in the words of Spitta, "the master of
free fancy." With Beethoven and his successors it
is not only the most lofty reason, it is the whole

dynamics of human passion which comes to animate musical forms.

We have all of us experienced the following in many exercises : a series of movements, having for aim some direct purpose, is at first painful to us, and we only effect them awkwardly and slowly ; then, by use, the co-ordination of these movements becomes a simple sport ; it passes into the unconscious state and, instead of absorbing our attention, allows other concomitant exercises. Something analogous takes place in the technique of the art. Music is at first a work of mere form ; afterwards it becomes a work of reason *and* of feeling.

In his *Notes théâtrales* Schumann passes the following judgment on the *Euryanthe* of Weber : " It is the very blood of his heart and the noblest he has ; this opera has cost him a slice of his life." Schumann also shows us plainly the assimilation effected in thought, in feeling, and in the language of sounds when he writes to his fiancée : " I have noticed that my fancy never has more wings than on the days when my soul is strained with desire. . . . These last days, when I was expecting your letter, I have composed bookfuls. At this moment *I should like to burst into music.*"

The man who speaks like this—and this language might be that of every true composer—is a perfect artist, arrived at the final stage of the musical and psychical state. He transposes his feelings ; by an almost necessary consequence of their intensity and their identification with the idea of a special art which has permeated the whole of his mind he renders them objects, he dominates them, he *thinks* them in the language of sounds, and in that manner causes them to blossom into a lofty generalization.

Let us not forget that the secret of his " intoxication," as Nietzsche would say, is that such a strength of sentiment, of imagination, and of desire, by tearing him away from the world of concepts to replace him at first in the heart of nature, makes him dimly aware of the link between him and universal life. At the same time the special language that he wields appears to him a gage of perfect independence.

CHAPTER V

MUSIC AND MAGIC

WE have now established the following conclusions—

1st. Music cannot directly express a concrete, reciprocal, and conscious passion, maintained, so to speak, on the surface of the soul by exact concepts. It expresses a power much more general and deeper, only half conscious, perhaps identical with the sources of life and of which what we call passion—the passion of Othello for Desdemona, or that of Berlioz for Henrietta Smithson—is only a modality.

2nd. It employs a system of imagery which constitutes a wholly special language, unintelligible to the merely literary man, but perfectly clear to the musician.

3rd. The fusion of these two elements—the one springing from sentiment, the other from intelligence and technique—is effected by means of an act which we call the musical thought, which is at once the obscure *primum movens* and the brilliant result of " the organization of images." This thought is the most specific thing in the musical art.

As a solid foundation for this definition a demonstration may be produced whose object will seem paradoxical, but brings together facts well worthy of attention, and allows the verification, in a positive field, of ideas one would be tempted, at first sight, to abandon disdainfully to an æsthetics suspected of mysticism. I propose to prove that *at all* times music has been considered and cultivated as a work of original thought, distinct from the verbal thought. In order not to stray over the whole of history, I shall simply take two extremes which will allow me to include, in my conclusion, that which separates them.

1st. In the most musical country known to us, and one where poetry, romanticism, composition, and metaphysics are provinces with uncertain limits—that is to say, in Germany—philosophers and artists, though they do not use the phrase "musical thought," have given of music a definition which exceeds but includes our own.

2nd. The German conception of musical art, instead of being a peculiar view of the modern mind arrived at the highest pinnacles of abstraction, is in accord with the most remote origins of the history of music, *i.e.* with the opinion of primitive folk.

Nothing can less resemble each other than a Hegel or a Schopenhauer, in possession of a refined culture, and primitive man, who, in the anguish caused by ignorance, has recourse to magic and incantations. Yet they have exactly the same idea of the expressive power of song. All that is wanted to make this resemblance manifest is for the German æsthetes to found schools of sorcery conducted by musicians, and for primitive men to have made known, in beautiful books, the theory of their acts.

§ 1. German Opinions on Music

The systems which I am now going to summarize by characteristic quotations have sometimes been, even in Germany, accused of extravagance. They certainly deserve this reproach in the eyes of any one who, with regard to great problems, seeks a doctrine capable of submitting to the proof of immediate verification and of satisfying the rules of the experimental method. But it is in quite another spirit that they should be examined. In the affirmations of a Hegel or a Schopenhauer on the real nature of the musical art, I see an historical fact and not a matter for discussion—an object of science and not a science itself. The great metaphysicians should then be read rather as one listens to a quartet of Beethoven : it is not to the ordinary means of knowledge that they appeal. Truth to say, all Germans are not of the same mind ; but there is between them a striking family resemblance.

According to a remark of M. Bergson, the thinkers of a given country and of a given age, even when not of the same school, are more in agreement than thinkers of the same school, but of different countries and epochs.

In the country of Handel, of Bach, and of Beethoven the musician has been regarded as having an autonomous artistic life : he is "gifted with a special receptivity for the spiritual world, and is capable of producing ideas without external solicitation." There has been applied to him the definition which Novalis gave of philosophy : "It is the art of inventing, without any data whatever, an art of absolute invention." And, again, the saying of Fichte : " The ego is pure activity."

The cultivation of this state produces in the musician " faith in the authentic revelations of the mind : it is neither a *seeing*, nor a *hearing*, nor a *feeling ;* it is a compound of all three—it is more than the three united; it is an impression of immediate certainty, an intuition, a glimpse of the truest and inmost life." The manifest insufficiency of the corporeal and terrestrial form to express and organize the spirit which dwells within it, " such is the obscure thought which causes us to live, which becomes the foundation of all our thoughts." This it is which forces us to admit a world of Intelligibles, and an infinite series of expressions and of organizations for each mind of which the actual individuality is every time the expositor or the root (Novalis). Every perceptible event instantaneously enlarges itself so far as our intelligence is concerned into the image of an eternal truth so soon as it is reflected in the mirror of true music.

When it is not as a connoisseur of counter-point and of the various styles of the fugue, when, in consequence, he has to try and make out the real artistic substance of it, " the hearer ought to feel an impression similar to the one he would feel if assisting at the creation of the world by God " (Nietzsche).

Every activity which has the beautiful for its object is a liberation, so that music does not express the real feelings. On the contrary, it delivers us from their incoherence and oppression, and allows us to

" raise the tomb-stone of the life of the passions "
(Hegel).

The opera is only a sorry alliance of music with
a false poetry and rude sketches of the plastic art ;
it is an invention for the use of non-musical minds
which are unable to enjoy music without that
" thin broth," the erotic poetry of a libretto (Schopenhauer).

Real music is the symphony. Wagner himself,
who is considered an intensely descriptive composer,
writes to Mathilde Wesendonk : " Nothing catches
my eyes ; the objects, the scenes to which my eyes
are attracted, or might be attracted, might be the
greatest in the world, but do not amuse me and
are indifferent to me. My eyes now only serve me
to distinguish day from night, light from darkness.
It is really a death of the external world to me, and
of me to it. I only see internal images, which
try to realize themselves by sounds " (letter
dated Paris, 21 Dec., 1861) ; and, on another
occasion : " My poetical conceptions have always
been produced at such a distance from experience
that I must consider the whole moral formation of
my mind as caused by these conceptions. *The
Flying Dutchman, Tannhäuser, Lohengrin, The
Niebelungen, Wodan,* all existed in my head before
I saw them in experience. . . . There ought to be in
us an internal sense which becomes clear and active
when all the other senses, directed outward, sleep
or dream. It is precisely when I no longer see
or hear anything distinctly that this sense is the
most active and appears before me as the pro-
ducer of calm ; I can give it no other term. Is this

calm the same as the plastic calm ? I do not know ;
all I do know is that it acts from within to without,
and that through it I feel myself to be at the centre
of the world (letters date 19 Jan., 1859, and 1 Jan.,
1860).

Music should not be written to words, a commonplace and low task ; it is to music that words should,
if possible, be written.

A stranger, as it is, to the visible world, music
enables us to penetrate into the moral world. It is
a universe without matter, a paradise of intimacy ;
its forms are the forms of eternal things—that is to
say, of the Ideas. "Pythagoras, speaking of the harmony of the spheres, did not say that the movements of the heavenly bodies made an audible music,
but that it was itself a music ; which led Socrates to
say, very justly, that he alone was a true musician
who, from perceptible music, was able to raise him to
supra-sensible and intelligible music " (Schelling).
Musical sound is the soul of things. Musical rhythm
is a necessary, not a chance, succession which cannot
be said to be subject to time, but itself contains
time. The musical Beautiful is a "divine being
perceived in a form adapted to our human condition."

Music is made up of universals *anterior* to experience (*universalia ante rem*). When it is associated with an action, it reveals to us the hidden
meaning of it, a deep and original principle, while
neglecting its exterior and actual form. It reaches
up to the universal force, to the *Will* which main-
tains all things, and identifies itself with it.

The world is but a realized music (Schopenhauer).

When we listen to a symphony, we seem to see all the feelings reduced to their pure state and dancing for their personal pleasure an extraordinary ballet of joy and hallucination (*ibid.*).

From the fact that music is an imitation of the eternal laws of the world it follows that we have no poet so great as Handel, Haydn, Mozart, Beethoven, beside all whom Goethe himself is a blinded pagan. "In a kind of night these great composers behold the Ideas" (Ferd. Krause).

As the soul of the world is to us a mystery, a composer is forced to speak a language which is beyond him ; he resembles a somnambulist permeated with the magnetic fluid, informing us of matters of which, in his waking state, he has no notion. Finally, as *music exists in the heart of things and lives on their essence, it results that it has a hold on all objects whatever* (Schopenhauer).

Thus has music been characterized in the country of Beethoven, Bach, and Handel !

§ 2. PRIMITIVE FOLK AND MUSICAL MAGIC

Again I repeat that I do not discuss these ideas. I take them as an historical fact, and I note that they are in agreement with what occurs at the other end of civilization, quite in the "beginning" in the sense of the word as used by historians. The musical metaphysics of the Germans and primitive magic are one and the same thing.

Primitive folk largely cultivated magic, which took with them the place of science. If, in the oral rites of magic, they first gave the most important character to certain chanted formulas, it was by virtue of an unconscious reasoning which we can easily construct.

Primitive folk see on all sides moral forces and passions, and hostile or benevolent spirits. To them the slightest phenomenon represents a person or an emotional state. In the roll of the thunder, in the rising wave or the quivering tree, in sickness, in famine or abundance, even in the mineral, there is a *somebody*. Here we have the germ of that poetry which Homer, Virgil, Lamartine were in after times to set free. The old mythologies, in which the early beliefs of man embodied themselves, are a superabundant proof of this.

There must, therefore, be a close and direct relationship between the power of music and natural phenomena.

Since each of these phenomena is nothing else but a semblance behind which is concealed a sentiment (anger, hatred, sympathy, jealousy, cruelty, etc.), and, on the other hand, music has precisely the characteristic of translating all that is most general and most profound in this sentiment, does it not follow that music has the power not only to express nature, but to act on it ? The two privileges—expression and efficacious influence—go together. " Imitations effected by means of sounds," say the Greeks, " conduce to action " ; and Aristotle suggested this explanation : " Rhythms and melodious sequences are movements quite as much as are actions."

Musical magic is the anticipated, dimly seen, instinctive application of this doctrine : there is a living soul in nature, and music can directly grasp it.

Like the soul of nature, music is a breath, *anima*. From this identity results the idea of a power exercisable *by like on like*, which is one of the fundamental laws of magic rites.

At comparatively recent epochs we find these ideas clearly formulated, and we have authority for believing that they are but the echoes of very ancient beliefs.

In the *Li-Ki*, or *Memorial of Rites* of the Chinese, we read as follows : " Music is intimately connected with the essential relations of beings. Thus, to know sounds, but not airs, is peculiar to birds and brute beasts ; to know airs, but not music, is peculiar to the common herd ; to the wise alone it is reserved to understand music. That is why sounds are studied to know airs, airs in order to know music, and music to know how to *rule*."

M. Maspero, in the study of an expression relating to the importance of "the true voice" in certain funeral ceremonies of ancient Egypt, writes as follows : " The value of this expression is easily understood if one brings to mind the part that magic has played in the East and the importance of the voice in its operations. The human voice is the instrument *par excellence* of the priest and of the enchanter. It is the voice that seeks afar the Invisibles summoned, and it makes the necessary objects into reality. Every one of the sounds it emits has a peculiar power which escapes the notice of the common run of mortals, but which is known to and made use of by the adepts. One note irritates, appeases, or summons the spirits ; another acts on the bodies. By combining the two

H

are formed those melodies which the magicians in-
tone in the course of their evocations. But as every
one has its peculiar force, great care must be taken
not to change their order or substitute one for the
other. One would thus expose oneself to the greatest
misfortunes." * Very curious words! Not only have
we from such facts a kind of actual transposition
of all that has been said above, but from them we
might even draw a doctrine concerning musical
execution.

A further analogy, which enables us to bring the
extremes in closer contact, is this :

We have dwelt on the point that music was a
special and separate language with an original
meaning, but one inaccessible to verbal analyses.
After observing this in a Schumann or a Beethoven,
we discover it among the two sets of primitive
folk that we know—the non-civilized or savages
of the present day, and the primitive folk at the
dawn of history.

1st. In his study of the *Débuts de l'Art,* Grosse
notes the fact that in certain tribes the most celebrated songs are sung by people who do not understand the words. For the poet, the words of the
song may very well have an independent signification ; for others they only have a value when
joined to a melody. " Often, in fact, the sense
of a song is sacrificed, without hesitation, to its
form."

Many Australians, says Eyre, cannot tell you the
meaning of their own songs, and the explanations

* Maspéro, *Études de Mythologie et d'Archéologie Egyptiennes,*
T. I, p. 106.

they offer are, in general, very incomplete, for they
accord more value to the prosody than to the
literary ideas.

Another author writes : " In all their *corrobori*
songs they repeat or transpose the words so as to
vary or preserve the rhythm ; their songs thus become incomprehensible " (Barlow).

It is almost the same among the Mincopees ;
they endeavour, before all things, says Man, to keep
time ; in their songs, everything, even the sense,
is subordinate to rhythm. They take the greatest
liberties not only with the words, but with the
syntax. It happens, not infrequently, that the
author of a new song has to explain the meaning of
the words to his auditors.

Among the songs collected by Boas from the
Esquimaux there are five of which the text con
sists solely in a rhythmical repetition of an inter-
jection, devoid of sense. " This, therefore, forces
on us the conclusion that primitive logic, before
everything, offers a musical signification, and that
the poetical sense at times remains in the back-
ground " (Grosse). Thus Wagner tells us, in so
many words, that in *Siegfried* he wrote certain
melodies before he wrote the words.

This is in agreement with two other groups of
facts noted by us—

1st. Among the non-civilized of the present day
there exists a language, almost rudimentary, in
which the words do not attach themselves to concepts, but have a very various sense, general and
at the same time precise, so much so that behind
them there seems to appear the sentiment of the

unity which links together a number of things. Among the Hurons, the word *orenda* designates song, prayer, the formula of incantation, and the power attributed to it ; but, say MM. Hubert and Maus, dwelling on this point, " there is nothing in nature, and, more especially, no animated being, which has not its *orenda*. The gods, the spirits, men, beasts possess *orendas*. Natural phenomena are produced by the *orenda* of the spirits of these phenomena," etc. The words *mana* in the Melanesian languages, *deng* in French Indo-China, etc., etc., are used in a like manner.

2nd. The formulas of incantation made known to us by the magic papyri are not accompanied by music,* for the MSS. go back to a period when these formulas were simply recited instead of sung, and when, moreover, they were only preserved by oral tradition. But, when closely examined, by studying the combinations of sounds which they comprise, it becomes impossible not to attribute a musical character to them in the technical sense of the word.

Nearly all imply first the observance of a rhythm. One must not only invoke such and such spirit ; it must be named *three times*, for example.

Then I find in these successions of uncouth words musical processes : repetition of sounds ; imitation (or approximative repetition), inversion, or retroversion of a series of vowels ; development (repe-

---

* A French author, if I recollect rightly, M. Ruelle, once argued that the " boneless strings of vowels " to be found in the spells of the Magic Papyri of Greco-Roman and Christian Egypt were musical notes—a theory for which there is much to be said.—*Ed.*

tition, with variations of a given sonority) ; rhapsody, or linking together of different and undeveloped themes. We must not, no doubt, exaggerate the importance of these grimoires; still, I am not far from believing that there is in them a residue of primitive music, a dead song fixed by writing and a kind of " congealed music."

Cato the elder (*De re rustica*, 161) prescribes, to cure a broken limb, the singing of the following formula : "*huat, hanat huat, ista pista sista, domiabo damnaustra.*" Even had not Cato, to indicate this recipe, used the word *cantio*, showing that it was originally sung, I could not avoid seeing therein alliterations, combinations, and refrains having something musical in them. Those who have read in the German text the opera libretti of R. Wagner will not, I hope, be astonished at this observation.

§ 3. The Magic Chant

The belief in the efficacy of musical magic is one of the most important facts in the history of all civilizations, and there are perhaps none on which we have such ample information. The first weapon —offensive and defensive—of magic was the chant.

In these days we go to the Opera or to a concert to enjoy a pleasure without self-interest; above all, for amusement, for a momentary oblivion of practical life, its miseries or its cares. But our modern vocal music, with tendencies entirely æsthetic, suggests that before it there was quite another one with practical tendencies.

The first singers were not artists who appealed to the imagination of a chosen few, but experts whom the individual or the social group called in on all occasions of difficulty ; recourse was had to them as nowadays to the engineer, to the surgeon, to the doctor, or as in the days of the Renaissance one had recourse to the professional bravo. The chant was used to bring rain or sunshine, to overcome the antipathy of the woman one loved, to disarm a dreaded enemy, to bring forth abundance or famine, to cure the sick or to slay.

Jeanne d'Albret, before giving birth to the future Henry IV, sang, at the request of her father, a song of her native Béarn, which we still have, with the supposed object of preventing her from "having a squalling child."

In these days we content ourselves with saying that such a singer has much " charm " without attaching much importance to this word ; in former times the " charm " was a melody capable, according to a tenacious superstition, of changing the visible phenomena of nature : it was the *carmen* of the Latins, the ἀοιδή of the Greeks, the Zammaru formula of the Assyrian.

In the XIXth Book of the Odyssey (v. 457) Homer speaks of the sons of Autolycus staying, by the power of a magic song, the blood flowing from the wound of Ulysses ; and we know, by a great number of testimonies, that primitive healing was founded on the use of incantation.

Theocritus and Virgil have left us celebrated documents on the use of chants to inspire love.

The legislator had frequently to step in—as the

Church itself did in the Middle Ages—to forbid certain chants and to prevent the formidable abuses which they thought might occur with such weapons. The enumeration of the facts which might be quoted would fill a large volume, and belong to history. I must refrain from quoting them here, but will merely add that, in addition to the information gathered from philology, we have two other sources for the study of this subject—the sculptured monuments and popular legends.

Every one knows the legend of the great musician Orpheus, native of Thrace, a country which the ancients considered the classic land of magic. His life is merely a picture of the irresistible effects of harmony. At the sound of his lyre the animated rocks of the Symplegades, which threatened to break up the ship Argo, are stayed and become immovable ; the dragon of Colchis, the guardian of the Golden Fleece, becomes harmless ; Hell itself is moved and surrenders Eurydice. There is extant a representation of him, lyre in hand, seated on a lion couchant, having on his right a bird and a quadruped listening. A group in the Musée Guimet* shows us the Hindu Orpheus : it is Krishna-Govinda tending the flocks of Nanda, a sort of Apollo in the home of Admetus. While he plays the flute, the animals are grouped round him in comical attitudes of wonder and tenderness. The Finns have likewise their Orpheus : Waïnomoïnen.

As to the number of popular legends which testify to the magic power primitively ascribed to

---

* Musée Guimet, 1ère salle, galérie d'Jèna, Paris.

song, it is very great. An Englishman, Engel, has made a whole volume by collecting a small part of this very interesting folklore. I will quote but one example.

There were amongst the Hindus songs (Rags) over each of which a god representing a season presided : the wet, cold, mild, or hot season; the rainy season, the " rupture," or end of the rains. These Rags could only be sung in the season to which they corresponded, under the penalty of bringing about a sudden disturbance in the order of the seasons. There were also songs for the day and songs for the night.

A contemporary of the Emperor Akbar, having attempted to sing one of the latter in broad daylight, darkness immediately fell on the radius corresponding to the range of his voice.

Another Rag was called " the burner or the inflamer "; he who attempted to sing it, except under certain conditions, suffered death by fire. The Emperor Akbar, either from cruelty or scepticism, one day commanded the celebrated musician Naiq Gopaul to sing this Rag. Gopaul, after vainly seeking an excuse, bids farewell to his wife, then, profiting by a moment's liberty, plunges up to his neck in the river Jumna. Scarcely has he uttered two notes when the water commences to boil, and the sufferings of the poor singer become intolerable. He implores mercy, but the Emperor will be obeyed. Gopaul resumes his song, flames issue from his body, and, though in deep water, he is reduced to ashes. . . .

§ 4. The Identity of Primitive and Modern Ideas of Music

What a strange history is that of music ! Everywhere, in all ages, one sees in it something
mysterious and inexplicable which places it outside the other forms of human activity. At
the present time even, when we call to our aid all
the resources of our " sciences," we are unable to
explain clearly what it is that moves us when we
listen to a beautiful air of eight bars ; and the
modern mind, though freed from many supersti-
tions, is often obliged to speak the same language
as that of primitive folk.

Our operas, and the whole of our religious music,
may be considered as a survival of magic. When
Siegfried, while forging his sword, sings and enumerates the qualities of the blade, when Jeannette,
as she sews, says, " *Cours, mon aiguille, dans ta laine,*
etc.," they are performing acts reduced to meaningless symbols without efficacy, but imitated from
ancient magic. Lastly, we see how the two extremes
of history link themselves together.

What do we discover in the very beginning of
musical history ? Myths, ascribing to music divine
origins and incantations. Now, this is how the
greatest musician of yesterday expresses himself—

" The power of the composer," says Richard
Wagner, " is nought else than that of the magician.
It is really in a state of enchantment that we listen
to one of Beethoven's symphonies." * Is this the
brilliant epigram of a writer, such as we often find
in musical criticism ? No ; rather it is the phrase

* *Gesamm. Schriften und Dicht.*, IX, 86.

of an artist, a philosopher, and an historian all in one.

Wagner proceeds to develop his thought in the German style, with rather complicated but clear metaphysics, which are not without recalling the platonic myth of the cave-dweller.

" Till now we were gazing, in broad daylight," he adds, " on a painted and transparent image ; and here is Beethoven, in the silence of night, placing this image between the world of appearances and the *internal being of nature ; and it is from the essence of things that he draws that light which gives its transparency to the image.* Thus, by a kind of miracle, the image becomes a living one ; before us stands out a second world, of which the greatest masterpiece of a Raphael could not give us any idea " (*ibid.*).

This, stated more simply, signifies that the painter presents to us entirely superficial images ; the musician, even when we have closed our eyes " in the silence of night," puts us in direct relation with the true reality, with the internal soul, with the essence and the inner substance of things. And here we are in full magic ! The images of the painter are dead and cold ; those of the composer share in the universal and hidden life which upholds the world. Instinctively man believes that music expresses all that is deepest in living beings or in things ; he sees in music an imitative art.

" At an age when painting and sculpture did not yet exist poets were painters," says Langlois.*

* L. Langlois, *Rig-Veda ou Livre des Hymnes* (1848, T. I, Intr. vii).

We may add that the primitive poet was a singer ; this relation of *expression* and *imitation* he transforms into a relation of identity, and from the belief in this identity he at once conjures up the idea of a power all-powerful to sway natural phenomena, and sentiments and acts of living beings.

I do not say that all this is true. But these are the beliefs which were held by primitive man, and which the most civilized men have taken up again under other forms.

§ 5. Conclusions of the First Part

The conclusions to which this first part of our studies brings us may be summed up as follows—

1st. Music—a synthesis of sounds which must not be confused with purely sonorous phenomena—has a meaning untranslatable into verbal language ; it is formed by a thought without concepts, rhythmically constructed, of which we cannot anywhere find the equivalent.

2nd. It only translates emotions indirectly and by means of images organized in accordance with its proper technique.

3rd. The only thing it is able to imitate or reproduce directly in passion is its dynamics ; the power of expression which we attribute to it is founded on the following principle : Every movement represents to us the cause which produced it.

4th. Primitive folk and the non-civilized races of to-day, in their magical operations, and, after them, the greatest philosophers and composers in Germany, have attributed to music a supernatural power which seems due to two causes : first to the

absolutely special character, unique, and isolated
in the internal life, of musical thought; then to
the lofty generality of this emotional dynamics,
which is not that of a certain given emotion, but
that of life itself.

5th. It is likewise true to say that music is a
superior act of the intelligence and springs from the
depths of feeling. As a matter of fact, emotion
and thought are not clearly distinguishable.

We have thus ended the first part of our programme. We have defined music. We have now
to explain it, to say whence it came, and how it
came to be formed. As I said at the very beginning, it is, above all, the origins of the musical art
and the rules of its use that are here in question.

SECOND PART

MUSIC AND SOCIAL LIFE

CHAPTER I

APPARENT ANTINOMY—THE MELODIOUS ELEMENTS OF THE MUSICAL ART

IT frequently happens in the course of a conversation that two persons have at the same time the same idea, expressly or tacitly attached to identical terms : "I was just thinking of that"—"It is exactly what I was about to say." If such exclamations as these often occur between friends, it is because these persons belong to the same social group, which, by community of education, of manners, of speech, and of many habits, sometimes compels them to use the same manner of thinking and speaking.

Never, in music, does a phenomenon of this kind occur. Never is any melodious formula discovered simultaneously by two musicians.

It also happens sometimes that a somewhat extended group—a crowd—has the same thought and translates it by identical words. Needless to say in such cases it is in the social and not in the individual life that an explanation of this must be sought.

Nothing analogous to this is ever found in music.

We are constantly talking of the songs of the people, and we mean by that collective works; this is merely an illusion. A thousand or a hundred persons may, by combined action, build a pyramid or carry to a distance an enormous piece of rock, cut down a giant tree, hunt and capture a monstrous animal, or found a religion, a government, or a literature. But they are incapable of creating an air of four bars like *Au clair de la lune*, or *Marlborough s'en va-t'-en guerre*. For a work of this kind two persons are one too many.

The songs of the people are simply works which have become anonymous ; the people, in its collective form, is, above all, from the musical point of view, an agent of deformation. Nothing is easier than to give a practical proof of this. There exist to-day songs which, after having been applauded in the music-halls of Paris, have spread over France, Europe, and the universe. Every one knows them, but how many persons can say who wrote them ? In twenty years—unless they pass away—they will be " popular." In the second place, the tunes are no longer the same as before ; passing through so many lips and so many instruments, they have become modified and altered, sometimes by the suppression of notes, sometimes by additions.

The old songs are in the same case. Listen to a popular air in one of our provincial villages ; ten leagues away you will come across it again, but with variations.

As will be seen, this study of the relations between music and social life starts with important
reservations. It is, however, impossible a priori
that there should not be a connection between one
and the other ; especially if. we apply ourselves to
the study of the elements of the musical thought,
its modalities, and its evolution. In any case,
this is a difficult problem. Let us defer the examination of it. For the present, let us observe and
classify facts ; we will later on endeavour to recon-
cile them.

If the mass collectively does not create, it can
furnish all the materials necessary for musical
creation.

We need hardly recall that we understand by a
" sociological fact " one that supposes the existence of a society and exercises a restraint on individual activity. For example, the language and
the caligraphic signs I am using at the present
moment to express my thoughts are not the work
of one man, but of a group of men, and I cannot
help using them. There is in the collective mass
around me a principle of force, most often unperceived and concealed—as, perhaps, is the water to
the fish swimming in it—which, in manifold forms,
fashions and feeds my intelligence, and rules or
directs my will.

What does music owe to the social life ?

All music is the working up of the following
materials : (1) intervals ; (2) consonances and dissonances ; (3) scales and modes ; (4) time ; (5)
rhythm ; and (6) melody. This, then, is the programme we must rapidly run through.

§ 1. Perfect Consonances : the Octave and the Fifth

A classification which goes back to the first theories before the Christian era, and still figures at the present day in treatises on harmony, places in the rank of perfect consonances the *octave* and the double octave, the *fifth* and, by transfer to the higher octave, the *twelfth ;* in the rank of imperfect consonances, the *third* and the *sixth ;* and in the rank of mixed consonances, the *fourth.*

The notion of the interval of eight, or octave, may practically have been drawn from the fact which is at the basis of all society : the physiological difference between man and woman. When men and women sing the same tune there is always the interval of an eighth between their voices, although they appear to be in unison. Children also sing an octave higher than men. This is what the Greeks termed the " antiphony." This consonance has been dubbed " perfect " because it produces an apparent unison.

The sociological fact *par excellence* is language. Now, all theorists are agreed in acknowledging that the interval which appears most frequently in the inflections of ordinary speech is the interval of the fifth. It is that which the voice has covered at the end of an interrogative phrase (Helmholtz himself noted this fact on the staff of five lines) ; that is to say, of an expressive form which ought to be primordial since it translates a need. The Greeks have been the first artisans of our musical theory, and have made the fifth the pivot of music ; perhaps we may be allowed to recall that, like all Southerners, they were very demonstrative and fine speakers. The apparent meagreness of their primitive lyre, formed of a few intervals of the fifth assembled in the same octave, has been explained by saying that this system was no doubt appropriate to a chant founded on declamation.

Once declared perfect by the Greeks, these consonances were accepted as such by the Middle Ages, which, in musical as in many other matters, believed that it was the continuator of Grecian antiquity and had the superstition of its theorists.

In the ninth century Aurélien de Réomé thought to put himself above all criticism by writing : " Those who do not approve of my ideas, or imagine that they discover errors among them, should know that all the distinctions here mentioned, as well as the musical discipline as a whole, are from Greek sources." * The consequences of this fidelity to tradition were serious. For more than ten centuries the theory of music has been dominated, even tyrannized over, and stayed and impeded by the part attributed to these two intervals : the octave and the fifth. Even when one wished to write counter-point, one felt obliged to remain faithful to the old rule.

A theorist who died at the beginning of the tenth century (in 915), Réginon, quotes a passage from Martianus Capella, where it is said that " in the sacred grove of Apollo the trees repeat the melodies of the gods ; the highest and the lowest branches sing in octaves ; the middle branches are

* Quoted by Gevaërt, *La Mélopée antique*, p. 106.

I

at the degree which divides the octave into a fifth and a fourth."

The fifth certainly plays a capital part in music, as is indicated by the name of the *dominant* given to it by Rameau. It is the basis of the accord between the instruments and modulation. Upon it are founded the theories of the authentic and of plagal modes. " To first of all learn what the fifth and *double* " (that is to say, the octave) * are was the first duty of the contrapuntists from before the thirteenth century.

§ 2. MIXED CONSONANCE : THE FOURTH

It has been noticed that if an interrogative phrase ended on an ascending interval of the fifth, the reply usually terminated on a descending interval of the fourth.

It may also be said that the interval of the fifth, being given in the space of an octave, that of the fourth naturally occurs as the complement of the former. We must add that the excess of the fifth over the fourth gives the interval of tone which is the basis of the diatonic system.

One of the most characteristic facts in the history of musical theory is that the intervals of the octave, the fifth, and the fourth should have so long been used in part music to the exclusion of the third, which at the present day seems so natural to us. To the question of knowing how a given tune should be accompanied so as to produce harmony, every one in the Middle Ages answered

---

* Text copied from a series of notes in the popular language at the foot of the pages of a manuscript of the Bibl. Nat. (Fonds latin, 1539, p. 269).

by the Greek classification of consonances, employing solely those which were reputed " perfect." To find the true formula of the principle of harmony as we understand it to-day—that is to say, the real notion of the third and its rôle—we must hark back to the *Institutions* of the Venetian Zarlino, published in 1558. Practically, it is in the middle of the fourteenth century that we can fix the abandonment of the old routines (the parallel progressions of the fifths and the fourths), and that the third (at first considered as a doubtful consonance) received full justice and only tolerated "when space failed " or by way of "licence" (*abusivum organum*).

This change, as M. Gevaërt says in his *Traité d'Harmonie*, is like a great beacon shining after centuries of groping in the dark. What produced it ?

§ 3. THE ORIGINS OF THIRDS

According to a very fascinating hypothesis of M. Hugo Riemann (*Histoire de la Théorie musicale*), it is towards the Northern nations that we must now turn our attention.

A twelfth century writer, Gérald de Barri,† describing Wales, speaks of the musical qualities of the English at a date much earlier than the period at which he writes, and gives us some curious information. He first tells us that the English do not sing in unison, but in several parts, "so that there are as many different voices and sounds as there are singers." Then he adds these important

† Better known to English readers as Giraldus Cambrensis. —ED.

statements : " The English who dwell in this
country (the regions of North Britain beyond
the Humber) have not reached this special practice
by *art*—read for this, *science*—but by following
customs of very ancient date, which in time have
become a second nature." Polyphony is "instinctive
with them ; the very children, marvellous to relate,
practise it."

An English writer who taught at Oxford in the
thirteenth century, and whose writings are earlier
than 1275, informs us, on the other hand, that
in his time the use of the third in England was
considered ancient, and that his countrymen put
practice before theory. He himself declares that
the slight difference which calculation shows to
exist between certain intervals may be neglected.
Finally, Walter Odington is the first to mention
the perfect chord (with doubling of the tonic in
the octavë) : 64, 81 (for 80), 96, 128=4, 5, 6, 8
=*Do, Mi, Sol, Do.*

With these two pieces of information let us
compare the very beautiful and celebrated English
polyphonic composition of the thirteenth century :
Summer is icumen in. This delightful madrigal
can no longer be, as it has hitherto been, a source
of astonishment and an inexplicable and isolated
work ; it owes, in fact, its excellent harmony, notwithstanding a few consecutive fifths, precisely to
the use of thirds and sixths.

From this group of facts it would appear that
the rectified notion and use of the third, without
which the musical system would nowadays seem
incomprehensible to us, must have come from the

North to complete and finish the ancient tradition
which had too long been sterile. There would thus
seem to be two sources from which modern harmony has sprung : the one Southern and Greek,
the other Northern. Gérald de Barri, in fact,
declares that it is probably from the Danes and
Scandinavians that the musical qualities of the
English are derived. The first has given rise to a
current which may be called that of oratorical
music, borrowing its essential intervals from the
inflections of spoken language, and, in addition to
this, charged with the Pythagorean speculations ;
the second is the free development of a natural
and general instinct in nations who were strangers
to the scientific theory. The one has long imposed
on us the exclusive use of the octave, the fifth,
and the fourth ; to the other we owe the third.

From the union of these two currents in the
Institutions of Zarlino, in 1558, our musical system
has issued.

§ 4. General Remarks on the Intervals

From the classification of the intervals rules have
been drawn up fixing the somewhat narrow limits
in which the contrapuntist works, when engaged
in making several melodies go together. Before,
during, and after the Renaissance these rules
have been numerous and strict, and we must
give an explanation of them. They restrict the
musician to the exclusive use of consonances ; they
forbid him certain intervals, either altogether or
outside the first and last bar, or, again, when he
would use them more than thrice running ; they

proscribe "alterations," and with them all combinations which might imply a dissonance; and
they go so far as to fix the movement of the
melody, *i.e.*, the modulations.

The principle and aim of all these rules is the
pleasure to the ear.

Whose ear? That of the composer? Certainly
not, since he is not free, and, if he were, there
would be, on the same point of doctrine, as many
rules as there are musicians.

It is evidently a question here of the ordinary ear,
the ear of every one, the structure of which regulates the average impressions whence are derived
the general rules forced upon the individual.
Hence the composer finds himself in a situation
analogous to that of the writer, who is bound down
by a language which he did not create but is
obliged to respect under the penalty of being unintelligible. No doubt he can modify it, but only
to a partial extent, and never abruptly through an
act of purely individual fantasy. In music, as in
literature, there is no organic change excepting
where an innovation has obtained the approval and
sanction of the community.

The idea of "alteration," which plays so large a
part in musical grammar, is very conventional,
since, in reality, there are no "altered" sounds,
but merely periodical vibrations, differing one from
the other by their number per second. It is impossible in this to find any *raison d'être* other than
in the instinctive demands of the ordinary ear,
which, receiving the impression of an interval, at
times remembers or expects an interval smaller or

greater by a semi-tone. As we shall see later on, everything is done in music by attraction or inhibition.

§ 5. THE SCALE

The scale—a series of sounds comprised between one note and its octave—is but a systematization of the intervals above-mentioned ; that which is true of consonances, from the sociological point of view, is likewise so for the scale.

The musical scale, reduced to such a few notes when it might well contain a very large number, is an entirely subjective creation of musicians, and yet a fact which may be termed " natural," because it is the work of a collective instinct subjected to common physiological conditions. A sound constituted like the normal *La* (La_3), by 435 vibrations per second, has for its octave a sound which is constituted by twice as many vibrations in the same time, or 870 ; the following octaves are produced by 1740 vibrations, 3480, and so on. . . . There is, therefore, from a tonic to its octave hundreds, and even thousands, of possible sounds, regularly utilizable. Yet we only acknowledge seven, which, with the subdivision of certain degrees, give us in all twelve sounds. There are two explanations of this fact.

The first is that the ordinary ear is incapable of discerning too small intervals. We hear talk of very practised musicians who could easily distinguish and reproduce by their voice fourths and sixths of a tone, and even more. We only have to observe a great violinist tuning his instrument, or rectifying it in the course of a piece, to note that

his ear is sensitive to sounds of extreme delicacy.
But these are individual cases, and it is exactly for
that reason they have not given birth to the
rational and logical system which they might have
produced.

The system which has triumphed is certainly very
defective in the eyes of a scholar, and we should
condemn it did not so many masterpieces blind
us to its constitutional viciousness ; its triumph is
due to what pure theory calls routine, and what
the sociologist might call the tyrannic influence of
collectivity ; it is due to the state of the ordinary
ear which is not that of the virtuoso but of people
with limited powers, incapable of receiving very
minute impressions and imposing their way of
feeling upon the artists who, all said and done,
work for them.

The ancients, it is true, introduced into their
scales intervals much smaller than ours ; but from
an assertion contained in a treatise, we must not
always assume the existence of an actual usage.
Thus the most musical of the learned Greeks, Aristotle, declared that the quarter tone placed between
a *Mi* and a *Fa* (the enharmonic rise) could not be
determined and escaped the musical sense ; and he
acknowledged that two rises, differing in numerical
relation, were practically equal to the ear. We
know the trouble M. Bourgault-Ducoudray has had
in obtaining, in the East, the correct intonation of
intervals smaller than our semi-tone.   M. Gevaërt
has said rightly that this should give no cause for
astonishment, the ordinary ear only accepting what
has been termed " the universal diatonic."

The second explanation is that the organization of the scale has no other principle and no other aim than the following :—to form, with a sound arbitrarily selected (tonic) and some of the sounds included in its octave, such relations as may produce those consonances which we have already mentioned, and which the ordinary musical intelligence considers as the easiest to grasp because they are the most agreeable. This principle once applied to the space comprised between two limits like 435 and 870 vibrations, it was naturally extended to each division of the whole field of sounds available for the art, and thus grew up our musical system, which in great measure is only justifiable by reasons of a social order.

We shall fortify this point of view, which reduces the scale to the consonances, if we add that, in reality, there only exist in music intervals consonant or non-consonant, and that the scale is a theoretical fiction.

The scale has no more existence than has the " root " in the words of verbal language. It nowhere appears in the most ancient creations of popular genius. It is a system *deduced* from the analysis of a work ; and it is not a fact of observation which can be isolated in the examination of a given melody.

Historically speaking, the scale is primarily what we call to-day a product of the laboratory or of the study, the creation of a Pythagoras or of a Ptolemy ; according to these scholars it remains a bookish and pedagogic thing, and a handy means of exposition for purposes of tuition. Mozart, in the scene with the Commander in *Don Juan*, Beethoven, at the commencement of his first Piano Concerto, wrote, no doubt, for the instruments melodious sequences which may be called "scales"; but such works belong to a period when the theories of the schools made their influence on the genius of the masters to be felt.

Primitively one sings, and nothing more; now, there are no scales in the chant in unison or in part singing. At the present day the pupil who is "practising his scales," on the ivory notes or on strings, is devoting himself to an exercise useful for giving agility to his fingers, but he is without the pale of real music.

§ 6. The Major Mode

The same remarks might apply to the *modes*; that is to say, the various ways in which there can be established in a scale the succession of intervals of tones and semi-tones.

We must once for all take into account that the order in which musical theory presents the facts is precisely the converse of the historical and real order. At the present day, when we study music we begin by what is as it were the first compulsory chapter of the grammar; we learn first what a scale and a mode are, and afterwards we pass on to the melody. But the artists, known or unknown, who created music were ignorant of this scholastic process. They made melody at the outset, arriving at once at what is to us the crowning point of a sufficiently long study. In singing they had not the slightest idea as to what a mode was, any more than Homer, his contemporaries and predecessors, when making poetry knew of the twenty-four letters of the alphabet or the mechanism of the conjugation of the verb.

Later on appeared the theorists, the men of the laboratory and the study; they analysed the popular melodies, inquired into the basis of their construction, the rule of their " manner of being," and, to sum up their work of observation, they presented all the intervals used in these melodies in the form of a system which the Greeks termed a *harmony* and which we call a *mode*, an entirely subjective work, analogous to the formula given by the chemist after studying a gas.

In this manner the theorists have at times arrived at conclusions without the slightest relation to the reality. It is thus that, after having divided the Hindu scale into twenty-two *srutis*, some among them have counted more than a *thousand* modes in Hindu music !

This remark must never be lost sight of, and, strictly speaking, it should dispense us from developing it any further. However, in order not to look as if we wished to evade the difficulty, we will consider the modes as real things. At the same time, if they are an illusion on the part of the moderns, we ought to explain that illusion itself.

We have at the present day but two modes, designated by abstract words : the major and the minor.

The major mode, realized on the note *Do* taken as tonic, with two semi-tones, one between the third

and the fourth degree, and the other between the
seventh and eighth, has a preponderating importance in modern music. Formed of three perfect
harmonies (*Fa, La, Do—Do, Mi, Sol*—and *Sol, Si.
Ré*) and of two complementary ones (*Ré, Fa♯, La*—
and *Mi, Sol♯, Si♮*), it has been considered as the basis
of every musical system. The historian Ambrose
places it in the category of things known by instinct, " and which nature imparts to all living
beings " ; Rameau calls it " the first outburst of
nature." Certain musicians claim that there is but
one mode, the major, since the laws of modulation deduced from it are the same for the minor
mode.

In reality, the actual modal scale, *Do—Do*, came
late into music, and has only existed since the sixteenth century. It was, no doubt, known before
that epoch, but under another form. Instead of
being divided " harmonically," as at the present
day (a fifth, *Do—Sol*, then a fourth, *Sol—Do*), it was
divided arithmetically (a fourth, *Do—Fa*, then a
fifth, *Fa—Do*), as was the plagal mode of the
Lydian *Fa—Fa—*

Authentic Lydian mode—
(Finale) *FA-Sol-La-Si-DO-Ré-Mi-Fa.*
Plagal, or Hypo-Lydian mode—
(Finale) *Do-Ré-Mi-FA-Sol-La-Si-Do.*

The first person to give a proper position in
musical teaching to the scale—
DO-Ré-Mi-Fa-SOL-La-Si-Do—
was a learned humanist, a professor at Bâle and a
friend of Erasmus, whose latinized name, taken

from that of his native town, was Glareanus, the
author of a revolutionary work which appeared in
1547 (*Dodekachordon*, or *The Twelve Modes*).

As its title indicates, Glaréan's innovation consisted in increasing to twelve the number of modes,
which were primarily only eight ; among the four
which he added (two authentic, *La* and *Do*, with
the two plagals) is found our major mode of *Do*,
which has eventually absorbed part of the others.

I shall not enter here into the detail of the reasons
on which Glaréan relies to justify his reform.*
It is sufficient to state that, in order to rectify the
ideas of his predecessors, he draws his principal
argument from use ; he opposes the use to the
theory and desires simply that the latter, always
behind the times, should put itself in accord with
the former.

He states that this diatonic† mode of *Do* to *Do*
(with the division on *Sol*, and not on *Fa*) is very
widespread and greatly practised, though it has
not received any official rank among the others ;
he declares that he has found it in most of the
countries of Europe in great favour because it is
particularly favourable for dancing. "In the
ancient liturgical chants it is very rare to find a
cantilena in which it is used, but for the last four
centuries the singers of the Church have themselves
transposed many songs into this mode, having
been so much attracted, I imagine, by its sweetness

* I published them in the *Revue musicale*, 1906, p. 15 *et seq.*

† The word *diatonic* signifies that the strings giving all the
notes of the scale have their maximum of tension and cannot be
chromatically raised a semi-tone. It is what we now call a scale
"without accidentals."

and charm." Here was, therefore, a situation to
be regularized rather than a new fact to be added
to a theory. Thenceforth, instead of upsetting
another mode (like the Lydian, for instance, by
giving it a *Si♭*), so as to bring it into the Ionian
form (*Do—Do*), an independent existence for the
Ionian mode was recognized.

I would willingly sum up the theory of Glaréan
by comparing the mode of *Do—Do* to a person for
a long time known in the world under a disguise, which he threw off in 1547 to appear there-
after with uncovered face and to live in his own
home instead of with others (transposition).

As a matter of fact, this mode, which has been
called "masculine mode," or "perfect mode," and
has been proclaimed by Rameau the "master of
harmony," is of popular origin.

§ 7. THE MINOR MODE

It is the same with the minor mode, characterized
by the position of the semi-tone between the second
and third degree. Here, still more clearly, we have
to oppose the popular use to the thought of the
theorists and to show where the true principle of
musical life exists.

Since the seventeenth century the minor mode
has been somewhat roughly treated or held in dis-
favour by a certain number of theorists.

It was considered as "not being provided by
nature"; it was, they said, an artificial product. For,
to many thinkers (those of the eighteenth century
in particular), not to have sprung "from nature"
was to be branded as of irremediable inferiority.

The doubtful character and the "alteration" which seem to sully the origin of this mode, at the same time determines its expressive character; it is said of it that it translates the feeling, but, deprived of its normal frankness and strength, and somewhat astray, lessened, and veiled in cloud. The major mode, according to the theorists, gives an impression of light and serene power; it is a sovereign in full view, in whose person everything breathes health and whose countenance seems lighted up by an Eginetan smile; beside him, as if bathed in the penumbra of a prudent retreat, the minor scale appears delicate, pensive, not free from ill-health and with the *flebile nescio quid.*

". . . I do not say," writes Zarlino, " that a composer may not place one after the other two arithmetical divisions of the fifth (that is to say, two minor thirds); but he must not overdo this process unless he would give a very melancholy character to his composition." It is Zarlino who first uttered the aphorism, so oft-repeated after him : "*Si lontana un poco della perfettione dell'harmonia* " ("the minor scale slightly diverges from the perfection of harmony ").

In his *Traité des règles pour la Composition de la Musique* (3rd ed., 1705, p. 9) Masson declares "that the major mode, in general, is suitable for songs of joy, and the minor for serious and sad subjects."

This is the opinion of most French writers of the eighteenth century. "The major scale," says Rameau, "a direct shoot from nature, has a strength, a brilliancy, a virility, if I may use the

expression, which prevail over the minor and make
it the acknowledged master of the harmony. The
minor, on the contrary, depending less on nature
alone, receives from the art, of which it is partly
formed, a weakness which characterizes its origin
and its subordination."

The same note is sounded by the German school.
Hauptmann, who in a somewhat odd book has
traced the metaphysics of the two modes and
employs the terminology of Hegel, calls the minor
key a falsehood of the major (*ein gelaugneter Dur-
Accord*), and finds that it calls forth sadness like
" the drooping branches of the weeping willow " !
According to Helmholtz, who has special reasons for
thus seeing things (for the series of harmonics,
the basis of his doctrine, only gives the major
chord), it is far worse ! He does not hesitate to
say that the major mode serves to realize the
beauty of music, and that the minor is not only an
alteration of true music, but a means of expression
exceptional from the repulsion it excites.

" The major mode," says he, " is suitable for all
clear-cut sentiments, and also for sweetness, and
even for sadness, if impregnated with a tender and
enthusiastic impatience ; but it does not at all suit
sombre, uneasy, inexplicable sentiments, nor the
expression of strangeness, of horror, of mystery or
of mysticism, of savage harshness, nor of anything
which contrasts *with artistic beauty*. It is precisely
for all these that we need the minor key." In the
imagination of Schopenhauer, a Scherzo composed
in the minor mode brings up the idea " of a dancer
in tight boots which hurt him." Marx and M. Hugo

Riemann speak of the " bitterness " (*Herbigkeit*) of the minor mode.

Against ideas like these we may set up the following facts—

1st. We can call to mind by hundreds, nay by thousands, melodies which express happiness and are written in the Greek, Dorian, or Hypo-Dorian (tones of *Mi* and *La*), that is, in the minor mode. Such in plain-chant are the *Te Deum* of Easter Eve, the Prose of Easter Day, that of Whitsun and—what appears sufficiently significant—all the introits commencing with the words *Gaudeamus* or *Gaudete* (Rejoice !).

In the secular music of the Middle Ages, in the pastorals, the rondos, the musical games, it is always the minor which predominates.

In the sixteenth century the dances, the gaillards, the pavanes, the bransles, and the *tourdions* are all, with rare exceptions, in the minor mode.

Among the Italians of the latter half of the sixteenth or the very early years of the seventeenth century, who created the recitative and founded the opera—Cavalieri, Caccini, Jacopo Peri, and Monteverde—the minor predominates over the major ; it is also employed for the sentimental gallantry of the seventeenth century by their successors— Lulli, Cesti, Cavalli, Carissimi, and Stradella—at an epoch when the fusion of the ancient modes in two types was already an accomplished fact.

I open the collection of pieces, by Rameau, for the harpsichord (1706) :—allemandes, corantos, gigues, sarabands, gavottes, minuets—every one in the minor. In another collection of the same

K

composer (1724) pieces like the *Rappel des Oiseaux*, the *Poule*, and the celebrated *Tambourin* are in the minor mode. Bach and Handel have composed, like Rameau, whole *Suites* of dances in the same mode.

Secondly, the minor should have right of precedence over the major, for it is found everywhere in popular music.

It is inherent in oriental music. The firm of Breitkopf, of Leipzig, are at this moment publishing, in parts, a collection of pieces all which, as the title indicates, are in the minor. In the popular songs of Greece, of Thrace, of Macedonia, of Albania, of Crete, etc. (published by Pachticos, Athens, 1905), the minor constantly appears, as it does in the melodies of Lower Brittany, collected by M. Bourgault-Ducoudray (1885); and in the songs of the French Alps, noted by M. Tiersot, etc., etc. It leads one to ask oneself how Helmholtz could say that songs in the minor only existed in the proportion of " one in a hundred " !

There is, therefore, an utter disagreement, with regard to the minor, between what has been asserted by the theorists and the facts of the history of music, especially if popular works are taken into account. This says plainly enough that the minor mode is not a system set up by the authority of a scholar, but that it has its origin in the instinctive and the social life. This conclusion, founded on simple logic, becomes an observed truth when—confining oneself to the only field in which the problem can be set, that of the so-called learned music—we remember the way in which the minor mode was constituted.

§ 8. The Origin of our Two Present Modes

At the present day we only recognize two modes, and give them abstract names no longer recalling the idea of a living reality : they are the mode *plus* (major) and the mode *minus* (minor). But the process of abstraction and out-and-out simplification which has brought us to this poverty-stricken state and to this dry-as-dust mathematician's language should not make us forget either the richness or the significant nomenclature of the past. These two modes are the points in which end, by concentration, the eight modes which the Middle Ages practised and which they derived from the Greeks.

Now, among the Greeks the modes had ethnical designations which clearly recalled their origin : the Dorian from *Mi* to *Mi*, and its plagal, the Hypo-Dorian from *La* to *La ;* the Phrygian from *Ré* to *Ré*, and its plagal, the Hypo-Phrygian from *Sol* to *Sol ;* the Lydian from *Do* to *Do*, and its plagal, the Hypo-Lydian from *Fa* to *Fa ;* the Mixo-Lydian from *Si* to *Si*, and its plagal, the Hypomixo-Lydian from *Mi* to *Mi.**

As we see by these appellatives, the modes had been constituted by two social groups : the Greeks of the Peloponnesus and the peoples of Asia Minor. If we examine the ancient theory at the various epochs of its history, we should find other names as characteristic, such as " Ionian " mode, " Eolian " mode, etc.

---

* No doubt, the mechanism of these modes is not the same as in the Middle Ages, but the word " plagal " may be used here in a general sense.

To each of these modes there was attributed a particular " ethos " ; that is to say, a special emotional state ; and this musical ethos, as it is designated in the Greek writers, principally in Plato and Aristotle, agrees exactly for each mode with that of the nation whose name the mode bears. The modes with Asiatic names were considered as lascivious, suitable for banquets and dances. The nations inhabiting the west coast of Asia Minor, in the eyes of the whole of antiquity, passed for the types of effeminacy and brilliant seduction. The Dorian mode was regarded as virile, energetic, and proper for the perfect citizen. We know in what enthusiastic terms the ancient moralists exalted the warlike and civil virtues of the Dorians.

We have, therefore, two peremptory reasons for attributing to the modes a sociological origin : their names and their traditional ethos. Let us follow up their history.

In the Middle Ages, the Church collects and adapts to its own use, by making certain confusions which I need not dwell on here, the modal scales of the Greeks ; but it loses the feeling of their ethnical character and simply designates by numbers their order : *protus, deuterus, tritus, tetrardus ;* little by little the sense of their organic differences is also lost, and a phenomenon arises of which the history of the verbal language offers us an example.

We know that the inhabitants of our own country have in the end lost, in the use of names, the exact notion of the different forms of nominative, genitive, dative, accusative, and ablative, and that, in order to simplify matters, they pretty early reduced all the cases of Latin declensions to two : the objective case and the governing case.

A like evolution has taken place, though somewhat more tardily, in the musical modes, and this is due, as in Latin grammar, to the inevitable deformations of use, to ignorance, and to the spirit of simplification which follows the law of the least effort—in a word, to reasons of a social order. All the ancient modes which possessed a third from the tonic composed of a tone plus a semi-tone (Dorian, Hypo-Dorian, Phrygian, Hypo-Phrygian, Mixo-Lydian) have been identified with and collected into one single type which—from purely theoretical considerations substituted for the ethnical memories—has been baptized *minor* mode ; all those which possessed a tonic third formed of two whole tones have constituted the *major* mode.

It is not void of interest to add that, if this transformation was complete at the time of Carissimi (seventeenth century), it is impossible to affix to it any exact date.

CHAPTER II

THE RHYTHMICAL ELEMENTS OF THE MUSICAL LANGUAGE AND SOCIAL LIFE

IT is only by rhythm that the intervals, the scale, and the modes assume a really musical character. Before entering on this new subject, it is important to distinguish two things, most erroneously confused by a recent theorist (Karl Bücher), author of a very curious book, the substance of which we shall have to reproduce here, with two fundamental reservations. Time and rhythm, properly so called, could not be the object of one and the same explanation.

The bar is the division of a musical work into parts which all have *the same duration;* rhythm is constituted by a division of quite another kind, superposed on the preceding and giving to the parts of the composition durations *which are not necessarily equal.*

The bar is formed of a succession, always regular, and indefinitely repeated, of accented and unaccented beats ; rhythm obeys a totally different law. For it, there is neither accented nor unaccented beats ; it is constituted by the divisions and plan of the composition, by sections of phrases of greater or less length, by phrases and periods, and by groupings of gradually increasing duration.

The divisions of the rhythm may sometimes coincide, on certain points, with the bar, but this coincidence never occurs in a continuous and compulsory fashion. Thus a section of a phrase may commence on the first beat of a bar, but may end in the middle of the second bar, so much so that the next section of the phrase may commence before the third bar (this is termed an *anacrousis*).

The time, once given at the commencement of a composition, remains immovable throughout; it is a *mechanical* formula. The rhythm is an *æsthetic* creation. The study of rhythm in music merges into that of the composition.

§ 1. WORK AND MUSICAL TIME

The most diverse origins have been assigned to the bar, which we have just defined as a succession of accented and unaccented beats. Plato sees in it a reminiscence of the Absolute, the act of an artist obeying, like God, when creating the world, the law of numbers. Spencer considers it as one of the "First Principles" which underlie the constitution of things, and beyond which one cannot go back; others have seen in it an imitation of the movements of a pendulum, of the beat of the pulse, of the normal stride, etc. . . .

Karl Bücher, professor of political economy at the University of Leipzig, has recently studied the question of social work, and found himself, contrary to the original design of his work, forced to

draw from the observation of social facts a very
curious theory of the bar. The only criticisms one
can make on this are that he has confused time
and rhythm ; and then, that in discovering the
origins of the first of these he thought he had at
the same time discovered the origins of music
itself instead of supplying what is called in English a " contribution " to its study." *

Having made these reservations and removed all
confusion in cases even where the word rhythm
should be taken in its ordinary sense, which does
not conform to that of musical technique, we have
here the summary of an excellent theory founded
on carefully observed facts.

(a) Aristotle had already formulated a principle
which is that rhythm (for this, read *time*) is natural
to man ; to this principle must be added another,
to the effect that the savage has a much greater
tendency than the civilized man to movements
repeated with regularity, for two reasons. The first
is that he is naked, or nearly so, and freed from
everything which, in the former case, obstructs, and
even paralyses, at times, his activity. The second
reason is that the savage is not cultivated. Now,
it has been noticed that the physiological effects of
rhythm are in inverse ratio to the intellectual culture,
because the effects of music on a person who is not
intellectual meet with no resistance ; and hence
physiologists, pursuing in the laboratory researches
on the musical art, prefer to experiment on
illiterate people.

---

* We may add that, previous to Bücher, the theory we are
about to summarize, had already been sketched by Wal-
laschek (*Primitive Music*. London, 1893).

(b) It is a primary fact, that in a general way the savage has a particular inclination for time. We must, therefore, not be surprised that towards the end of the eighteenth century the traveller Meiners wrote as follows regarding African negroes—

" Marching, dancing, games, singing, work, everything with them is done in time. The most stupid negroes keep time far better than our soldiers, and far better than our musicians after a long course of careful training."

(c) But the exigencies of life—first the individual, and then the social life—favour and bring about more even than the climate an instinctive propensity to it. Let us first lay aside one prejudice. It has been said that the savage particularly likes laziness, and since the time of Tacitus it has often been repeated that "savagery and idleness are synonymous." This fact has even been adduced to explain brigandage, slavery, the sale of brides, and the custom of laying hard work and excessive burdens on women. This is a superficial and even a contradictory view; if there are among primitive folk some who live by plunder, this presupposes that there are others who like riches, and consequently somewhat put themselves out to acquire them. It is the same with slavery. It is said that it has acted a useful part in the education of humanity; but the slave who learns certain work must have had a master who initiated him into this work; if the master wishes to put the slave in a certain state of mind, he needs must himself have been in that state of mind. This is a sort of vicious circle.

In civilized society there may be—there are, in fact—idlers. In non-civilized communities every one, man and woman, is compelled to work more or less ; but the work is performed under special conditions. It is peculiar from two points of view : first, the absence of tools ; secondly, that of technique.

In order to build a hut or a canoe, to make hunting and fishing implements, to secure and prepare food, to fashion rude pottery and some semblance of clothing—without mentioning objects of adornment and elegance which make up his æsthetic ideals, for the savage is elegant in his way—primitive man is forced to compensate the want of suitable instruments by movements of the body, hands, arms, or legs.

Ignorant of technique, he makes up for it by patience and endurance. In certain tribes the work done by the women is so long and fatiguing that this is probably the explanation of polygamy. " In the district of Tanganika," says Stanley, " it takes more than three months to hollow out a tree in order to make a canoe." In Guinea some natives wear round the neck cylinders of white stone, the polishing and the fashioning of which (they are perforated with small holes) require, for want of metal tools, the work of two generations. Weaving also takes a very long time ; its progress has been compared with the growth of a plant.

All labour performed under such unfavourable conditions is made up of perpetual recommencements, endless mendings, and routine ; it demands, in short, *the repetition of identical movements.*

(*d*) Impelled by instinct, by habit, by the desire to avoid waste of time, by the care to escape useless efforts, and also by the wish to lighten as much as possible such an unthankful task, the workman, after a little training, executes uniform movements in uniform spaces of time. The idea of the object in view, which in the first instance guided his labour, and likewise the idea of the adaptation of certain measures to this object, fade from his mind by degrees. These ideas become useless, and little by little the man succeeds in replacing the energy of conscious will by an energy like that of an automaton.

(*e*) From that moment, the periodicity of movements is brought into the work. This periodicity has been noted over and over again. Already the elder Pliny, in his *Natural History* (Chaps. 18–54), had observed that wheat-sowing was an operation carried on in regular time; and (to take an example for brevity's sake from the other extreme of history) in a work which appeared in connection with the *Exposition universelle* of 1889, entitled *Les Colonies Françaises*, we read that the women of Madagascar, when preparing the soil for sowing rice, "resemble dancers performing a ballet," so striking is the rhythm of their movements.

Such are the first steps of our theory.

(*f*) What is now the unit which will serve to measure this incessant performance of work which has thus passed into the state of mechanical function.

It is determined by the very movement of the worker, by the nature of the muscular effort which he repeats time after time; and as this muscular effort is characterized by a tension followed by a repose, a group of values is created which has its equivalent in what versifiers term a foot, composed of a thesis and of an arsis, and by musicians a bar, composed of an accented and an unaccented beat.

The number and organization of these values differ according to the kind of work performed : the *iambic*, composed of one short and one long, the *trochee*, composed of a long and a short, are the rhythm of human feet treading the ground. The *spondee* is the rhythm of hands regularly clapped in time. The *dactyl* and the *anapaest* are beats (less ancient) of hammer-work, the smith always preceding or following the principal blow with two slight taps on the anvil. Blacksmiths have a significant term for this ; they call it "making the hammer sing." The various forms of the *ionic* time (6 beats) may be observed in the streets of our cities, where the instruments used to fix and level the paving-stones are always handled in regular time.

(*g*) There are other important facts which mark a further step in this theory.

This capital phenomenon of the creation of a bar occurs not only in individual and isolated labour, where the workman can make, in short, idle pauses at his pleasure without any serious inconvenience arising ; it becomes a necessity when the work is done in common, and particularly when it is a question of works where all the movements depend on one another. By beating time, the various activities contribute to the same end ;

without it they would hinder each other instead of helping.

Here are some men who are seated and rowing together in a pirogue. They are *compelled*, under penalty of grave and various accidents, to submit their movements to regular time. It is the same with the men shown on an Egyptian monument (now, I think, in the British Museum) who are moving over the ground an enormous block. In the same case are those who are sawing through a fallen tree, and those striking together on an anvil a mass of red-hot metal.

Other reasons compel the introduction of the beat into all labour performed in common and socialized. It has been rightly said that every individual has a tendency, either in working or in simply displaying his activity in some game or exercise, to adopt some special rhythm peculiar to himself. Thus, some persons become fatigued in walking fast, and others are tired by walking at a slow pace. Man, from this point of view, is like an animal. Every horseman, for instance, knows the pace that best suits his steed.

Beating time, in groups of workers, has as its aim and also as its principle the necessity of unifying individual paces.

The workers, when associated together, display an unequal energy excited by the zeal or rivalry which is established between them. In the Sixth Book of the *Odyssey*, Homer, speaking of the Pheacian women, who, together with Nausicaa, are washing their linen in the washhouses, says : "They beat their linen in little stone basins, and *try to outdo each other.*" All the more reason to regulate and discipline these various activities.

A third point to be noted is that the activity of a group when regulated and disciplined leads to better results. A German observer has compiled some rather curious statistics on this. Comparing the result of the work of workmen who sing with that of those who do not, it was shown that the former produced more than the latter. (Inquiry made by the Social Museum, Paris, *Les travailleurs du Bois à Dantzig,* 1905, p. 62.)

Finally, there are certain labours, somewhat exceptional it is true, in which uniform time has been employed very usefully, and almost as a matter of necessity. Among the very numerous documents which have come to my notice, there is one which appeared to me most odd, and yet one of the most serious. In a work entitled *L'Art musical au Sénégal dans l'Afrique Centrale,* the author, M. Verneuil, quotes a divers' song (do not smile!) when occupied in getting a vessel off a sandbank—a song which is consequently sung in the water—

" Imagine five hundred negroes swimming round a vessel lying on the sands and singing this air ; at the eighth bar they all plunge together, *mentally following the air while under water ;* at the twelfth bar they all push the vessel at once, and at the sixteenth come to the surface. Acting thus in concert, none of their efforts is lost."

(*h*) This time once created, by what means is it realized to the ear ? Here begins a new stage of the theory.

When the very movement of the worker produces
a regular sound by reason of the material used—
for example, the work of the smith hammering iron
on the anvil, or of the thresher striking the ground
with his flail—this regular sound helps to beat time.
In the other cases it is supplied by the most obvious
means : the human voice or that of an instrument.

On this point, documents and testimonies are
almost innumerable. The Malays row to the sound
of the tom-tom. In the Soudan and in China,
tasks are performed to the sound of the drum.
Here is a more classical proof : in the Louvre is
an archaic group from Thebes, in Beotia, representing four women, side by side in front of a
kneading-trough, and working the paste with their
hands ; on the left is another woman, seated, playing on the double flute. It is supposed that she is
there to regulate the movements of the others, or
possibly, to entertain them.*

It is also in regular time, marked by a flute,
that the Etruscans, according to a passage in
Athenæus quoted by M. Paul Girard, kneaded
bread, boxed, and even whipped their slaves. A
vase discovered in Greece and often reproduced
represents harvesters working to the sound of
music. Pausanias informs us that Epaminondas
built the town of Messenia to the sound of the
Beotian and Argive flutes.†

These are not legends. I recollect having in my
hands an official document, a " Report," in which

* Cf. Pottier, *Revue archéologique*, 3me Série, T. XXXIV, 1899.
M. Lindet (*ibid.*, p. 419) supposes that the flute-player " conducts
and *amuses* " the women at work.

† *Ibid.*, IV, xxvii, 7.

it was said that when the French Government was building a railway in Dahomey it had to make the negroes work to the sound of the flute.

§ 2. RHYTHM AND SOCIAL LIFE

In music, as we have said, rhythm, properly so called in the technical sense of the word, is merged into the plan of the composition. It is constituted by the following elements, which form, as it were, undulations increasing in size : the *foot*, identical with the bar or the element composing the bar (of 3, 4, 6, or 5 beats); the *section of a phrase*; the *phrase*; the *period* (which, conventionally, may be defined as a phrase composed of more than two sections); the *strophe* and systems of *strophes*.

Though the question is obscure on some points, it may be asserted that the characteristics of musical rhythm, like those of the bar, first presented themselves in the shape of real and socialized movements foreign to the art, and passing afterwards into song and finally into pure music, by virtue of higher and higher abstractions.

We have just explained the bar. The musical phrase, as we have seen, is constructed in the same way as a verbal phrase. Let us now deal with the higher elements of rhythm : the systems of strophes. I venture to say that, in order to give a sociological explanation of it, we have an embarrassing choice of alternatives. A method which appears to me scientific would be to admit *a priori* several explanations, and not confine ourselves to only one of them.

Every one must have noticed that in certain

children's games there is a series of collective acts executed by the entire group, and a series of individual acts in which, in turn, every player comes to the fore. As in all cases where there is an intense and prolonged activity (work, dancing, playing), these two acts tend to alternate. The rondo, when sung, is an example. The essential part of the song is the chorus in repetition, sung by the whole party ; between each chorus is sandwiched a varying episode, a solo, which each sings in turn unless there happens to be a sort of coryphæus appointed for all parts having an individual character.

Now, a melodious idea, repeated at intervals with episodes or "*divertissements*" placed before each repetition, constitutes, as already said, the scheme of a rondo, a general form of composition found in all kinds of works, and from which musicians, by successive transformations, have elaborated first the sonatina, and then the sonata with all their subsequent developments.

Another form of children's or popular games is the division into two camps, one of which repeats each evolution of the other by a sort of emulation or by an equitable division.

This division also reappears in certain circumstances of social life where women and children appear together with the men, but in distinct groups : a separation which probably had its origin in a religious idea. One has only, even at the present day, to enter a Catholic church in the country, or a Jewish synagogue, in order to feel that this belongs to reasons of delicacy of remote origin, women being excluded among primitive folk from most worships.

L

In the poetry sung during a religious ceremony this
division gives rise to the *antiphonal* or *anthem*, the
division into two choirs, and, in lyrical poetry, to the
antistrophic construction, where each system is accompanied by a repetition pure and simple: AA', BB',
CC', etc. Æschylus has gone so far as to include
sixteen strophes and antistrophes in the same series.

This extremely simple mode of establishing the
plan of a composition was adopted by Bach in his
French and English *Suites*, as also in those sonatas
for violin or violoncello which contain the *Suites*,
and by Handel in sixteen collections of pieces
belonging to the same category. It appears in
the *Scherzo* and in all modern dance music. The
antiphonal chant—with two choirs—of the Greeks
repeated the same melody in a higher octave ; it is
not without its use to point out that this custom is
almost universal and general in our music (see, for
example, the commencement of the *Adagio* in Beethoven's Pathetic Sonata).

Another fundamental construction in music is
represented by the following symbol : A,A,'B, that
is to say, a system (of phrases or periods), A ; the
identical repetition of this system, A' ; a third and
different part, B.

This rhythm is found almost everywhere, especially in the initial allegro of sonatas. It is the triad
—*strophe, antistrophe, epode*—of which the poet
Stesichorus, in the sixth year before the Christian
era, was supposed to be the inventor. Now, it may
be affirmed, almost with certainty, that it is of
religious origin.

A Latin grammarian of the Decline of the Roman

Empire, Attilius Fortunatianus, has handed down
to us some very precise information on the liturgy
of ancient Greece, which he no doubt extracted from
earlier works. "Formerly," he says, "the songs
composed in honour of the gods were in three parts.
There was first, turning to the right, a procession
round the altar (*strophe*) ; then the same, turning to
the left (*antistrophe*) ; finally, the song came to an
end before the altar in presence of the god (*epode*)."

From the liturgy this scheme passed into lyric
poetry, then into tragedy, which was at first connected with worship. It appears in the choruses
of the *Prometheus* of Æschylus, in those of *Electra*,
Œdipus at Colonus, the *Trachiniæ*, the *Philoctetes* of
Sophocles, the *Hippolytus* of Euripides, etc. . . .

If from Antiquity we pass to the Middle Ages,
an explanation of the same kind seems possible. Our
triad may be considered as an adaptation to poetry
of the rhythmical system of the Latin sequences.
The verses of these sequences, divided into two
sections, were sung by an officiating priest, then
followed by an Alleluia, at first taken up by the
whole people, and later by a chorus representing
the people ; this Alleluia, which was the germ of
a refrain, soon became a real chorus : thus we had
the type AA'B.

We must, therefore, not be surprised at this form
having been in such general use. It is again found,
in a more or less perfect state, in the poets of the
fourteenth, fifteenth, and even sixteenth centuries.
The theorists of the Middle Ages designated it by
the name of "tripartite *coué* rhythm" (that is to
say, with a tail, B).

Thus, as we find it in Latin, German, Spanish, and Italian collections, we may say that it is of popular origin. In Italy one of the forms of popular song is represented by the Tuscan *rispetti*, which have the scheme AB, A'B' plus an addition (*reprisa*), which is variable and gives the following aggregations: AB, A'B', CC; or: AB, A'B', CC, DD; or again : AB, A'B', AB, CC. This last type forms what has been termed the " octave of courtesy." All these forms can be traced back to the triad A,A',B.

I do not speak of the German singers, the Minnesänger, whose songs were composed of two equal strophes (*Stolle* and *Gegenstolle*), followed by an independent part (*Abgesang*).

The rhythmical type AA'B once discovered, it was subjected, like all others, to various combinations. Instead of remaining at the final, B has sometimes been placed between the two first systems, and the *epode* then becomes a *mesode*. B has also been placed at the beginning, becoming then a *pro-ode*, which in our vocal music, accompanied by instruments, is called in turn : *Symphony, Prelude, Toccata, Introduction,* and *Overture.*

To sum up, the following propositions seem established—

1st. The intervals of the octave, fifth, fourth, and third may be considered as sociological data ; before constituting the basis of musical theory they were suggested by the difference which distinguishes the voices of men from those of women and children, by the inflections of the verbal language and by an instinctive creation of the popular genius.

2nd. The scale, a simple orderly arrangement of these intervals, has only a theoretic existence ; the number of notes it contains is, moreover, determined by the tolerance of the ordinary ear, not that of the individual; on the same law depends the classification of consonances and dissonances, and also the rules of counter-point.

3rd. The major and the minor modes (of which we might say, as of the scales, that they have only an existence in theory) are the two terminals of a long evolution, similar to that which has, little by little, simplified Latin declensions ; they concentrate, in a double formula, ancient modes which all of them bore the names of peoples. These ancient modes (Dorian, Phrygian, Lydian, etc.) were only in themselves a conventional means, created by theory, of analysing the popular melodies of Continental and Asiatic Greece.

4th. Time is not a fact special to music ; it may be considered (though this is not the only legitimate view) as a law of work pursued in common forced upon man by the necessities of practical life.

5th. As regards rhythm, all musical composition is systematic, that is to say, is constructed on a regular plan, in which ideas are distributed into groups ; this plan seems to be the reproduction, freely interpreted, of real movements, gradually losing their special form, the type of which has been furnished by various forms of social activity : such as games, dancing, and liturgy.

We have now to study, from the sociological point of view, musical expression.

CHAPTER III

MUSIC AND LOVE

MUSIC, as we have said, is incapable (as, indeed, are all the arts of space subject to the law of symmetry, and all the arts of duration subject to the law of rhythm) of *imitating* an emotional state. The composer thinks, nevertheless, that he possesses the power of translating altruistic sentiments, and he conveys the illusion of having this power, thanks to " images," a kind of realized metaphors, of which the partial exactitude is indirectly obtained from associations of ideas. These associations, for the most part, are forced on the hearer by the ingenuity and dexterity of the musician ; but it is evident that the most skilful art can only produce intelligible results by giving them as base a fund of habits common to the imagination of the social group.

In reality, music, which knows no concepts, can only directly approach a real model by reproducing the dynamics of passional life ; this it is which renders its faculty of expression so general and, consequently, so powerful. By neglecting that assemblage of practical tendencies, of ideas, and of representations which form our conscious state, and, so to speak, the superstructure of our moral person, it penetrates to the deep and natural elements of interior life and reaches the hidden spring of *all* the passions.

This opinion on music we have seen erected into scholastic systems by the great German metaphysicians and put into practice (long before the birth of philosophy !) by the primitive magicians, who are everything in the origin of musical history. We shall see it associated by Darwin with the idea of the altruistic and social sentiment *par excellence* :—Love.

It is, at least, thus that I understand the theory sketched out by the celebrated naturalist in *The Descent of Man*.* Darwin has no more resemblance to a Hegel or a Schopenhauer than to a magician, and yet he upholds a theory which is in harmony with the doctrine of the metaphysicians as well as with the use of enchantments among the primitives. The love of which he studies the manifestations is something more than that spoken of in the libretto of an opera ; it is at the same time a universal as well as a social force. It resembles the Eros of Hesiod's Theogony, which, bearing in itself the germ of future societies, yet exists before humanity, for its only contemporaries are two other primordial elements : Space and Time.

Without going so far back, Darwin places the social rôle of love a long time before man, and among the living beings of whom man is the descendant. With the perfectly impartial mind, the unaffected good faith, and the prudence in assertion which make his work an admirable school of scientific probity, the English naturalist, who, at that period in his life, was very sensitive to artistic

* Second Edition, 1888, p. 571, *sqq.*

things, desires to solve the enigma :—Why has
music so great an emotional power ?   Why does it
so deeply move us ?   Whence comes the virtue of
this language to the charm of which we submit
without being able to account for it ?

To answer these questions Darwin relies on the
three following facts—

1st. Music has a somewhat limited power of expression (the word is here used in its commonplace
and current sense). It cannot translate fear, hatred,
terror, or fury ; on the other hand, it excels in
expressing *love and the joy of triumph*.

2nd. During the pairing season, animals give
utterance to sounds ; they even break into a rudimentary song.

3rd. Between animals and man there exists hereditary transmission.

These three facts are of a nature to enlighten
the æsthetic. If it be admitted that during the
time of pairing, when animals are carried away by
love and jealousy, by rivalry and triumph, the semi-
human ancestors of man used musical sounds and
rhythm, the deep and disturbing character of
musical expression becomes, up to a certain point,
comprehensible. In accordance with the principle
of hereditary associations, music would reawake in
us, in a vague and undetermined form, the strong
emotions of a very remote age.

Now, everything renders probable the hypothesis
according to which the manifestations of the voice
in our animal precursors were not a simple expenditure of energy, but a kind of language connected with altruistic sentiments, and a means of

allurement. We are authorized to believe that the use of this means produced, and still does produce, an agreeable effect. If, indeed, it be urged that the females are not capable of appreciating it, of being excited and allured by it, it must be admitted that the persevering efforts of the male and the complex organs he possesses to make himself heard are absolutely useless ; and this is impossible.

Darwin dwells much on the case of birds. The males, when endeavouring to attract the females, display all the resources enabling them to shine. They not only display the riches of their plumage, like the bird of paradise, which puts on what has been called its " bridal dress," but the instinct of reproduction makes artists of them, and they sing.

Nightingales engage in a veritable vocal contest to secure their mates. The capercailzie acts a curious pantomime interspersed with song. Perched on a low branch, he erects his long neck feathers, twists about, droops his wings, puffs himself out, stamps with his feet, turns up his eyes in a comical fashion, " then he emits clicks and clacks, slowly and separately ; then he continues quicker and quicker with one loud clack, followed by a series of sounds both piercing and musical ; . . . he ends on a prolonged note, and closes his eyes as if intoxicated with pleasure." *

The animal which has triumphed over its rivals becomes the founder of a finer progeny, since by his victory he has eliminated individuals less well endowed than himself ; and, as this progeny is

* Karl Groos, *Les Jeux des Animaux*, ch. iv.

subject to similar struggles and a like selection, it transforms itself by degrees. In time new species arise. What things may there not be in the song of a bird ! The whole future may be singing in his voice ; the delay in a species to touch "the divine shore of life" might be due to a nightingale breaking down in vocalization !

Man should be the continuator of the animal, in music as well as in everything else. The most charming melodies of our composers should be nought else than the prolonged blossoming, the conscious idealization, the survival culminating in a thing of art, of an initial fact connected with one of the strongest feelings of social life. And thus would be explained both the mysterious character and the disturbing effects of music. It is mysterious because it is now dislodged from its primitive function and applies to objects freely chosen by fantasy, a language which, in the beginning, was exclusively that of love ; it is deeply disturbing because it touches in us the vital instinct itself, the instinct of reproduction and of progress, and awakens, vaguely and unknown to ourselves, associations of ideas which a very prolonged heredity, many centuries old, have caused to pass into the world of unconsciousness.

What a pleasure it is to me to gather from Darwin's ideas that love and progress are one and the same thing. Two beings who seek one another do not solely desire reproduction and the perpetuation of life ; they desire its promotion towards the *better* and the *more beautiful*. Now, progress, if it really exist, if it be a law, must be attached to the very plane of creation, to a first principle regulating the evolution of beings. Thus musical expression would be brought to play a grandiose and magnificent part.

§ 1. A FEW OBSERVATIONS ON DARWIN'S THEORY

Facts are not wanting to commend to our attention this curious theory.

Certainly, if Darwin had claimed to give us a general and complete theory of music, we should have more than one objection to make to it. He would deserve the reproach of having simplified to excess an extraordinarily complex problem. We should tell him that the song of birds is not, properly speaking, musical ; the proof of this is that it is very difficult to take down in notation ; different birds singing at the same time do not impress us disagreeably, while simultaneous human voices not regulated by previous arrangement jar on us in the highest degree ; we should add also, moreover, that to recognize melody in the vocal manifestations of certain animals one must already be a musician, and even a refined musician.

We should also inquire, if we admit the hypothesis which attributes to song this precise part, how it is that hereditary transmission has changed its line in spite of circumstances, since nowadays vocal aptitudes manifest themselves especially in women, who thus substitute themselves for men in the art of pleasing.

But Darwin was too clear-sighted and too wise to forget the true nature of the matter with which he dealt or to desire to annex music to natural history, carelessly and in a paragraph of a special book. It is a simple contribution that he offers us. What he wishes to explain is the greatly disturbing effect of the language of sounds; and, on this account, his thoughts should be welcomed in a sociological study of the musical art, since the feelings of which, according to him, melody is the expression, presuppose the existence of a society.

The social point of view is not the artistic one, but it compels us to reckon with certain facts, even if some error be mingled with it.

We cannot refuse to birds the title of " singers," since it has been awarded them by all the ancient poets. They have even been regarded as masters. Athenæus says that the poet Alcman studied under them. Lucretius asserted that man imitated them before he knew how to speak. One of the popular songs in Languedoc commences thus—

Roussignolet du bois,
Roussignolet salvage,
Apprends-moi ton langage !

M. Zaborowski, the author of a little book on language, has had the curiosity to collect the names of a certain number of birds in the most diverse languages and dialects, both savage and civilized ; and this curious nomenclature shows that all these names contain imitative harmony and are veritable onomatopœias, implying the observation and imitation of animals by man.

The natives of Kamtschatka have a melody (*Aangitsch*) the origin and the name of which are both derived from a bird (*anas glacialis*), which appears in the country at fixed times in great flocks.

A flute, brought from Tonga Island (Island of
Amsterdam, in the Pacific Ocean) by Captain Four-
neaux, gives a succession of sounds which may be
considered as having been suggested by the song
of a bird—

Two sets of flutes now in the British Museum
produce, when blown into with force, the following
successions, which suggest the same notion—

To complete these short details I will add that
the organs of former times had a stop which was
called the Bird Stop (*Vogelgesang, Vogelschrei*);
that formerly the art of imitating the song of birds
formed part of the training of the *Jongleurs*†; and,
lastly, that composers often took a delight in this
kind of imitation.

* The melody in Siegfried by which Wagner depicts the song of
a bird has a similar cadence.

† *Livre des Métiers*, Etienne Boileau, published by Depping
(Paris), p. 287.

Clément Jannequin, the celebrated French (or Belgian) musician of the sixteenth century, wrote a well-known descriptive symphony, entitled *Le Caquet des oiseaux ;* Haydn, in the finale of his Quartet XX, imitates the clucking of the hen, in which he is followed by Mozart and Rossini ; Beethoven, in the Andante of his Pastoral Symphony, has not disdained to reproduce the cuckoo's note. Many others—and the list is long—have been bolder still. In his Sonata in *Ré* for the Harpsichord, Bach has not feared—in the middle of the fugue— to associate the cry of the cuckoo with the cackling of the hen. Pleyel has written a composition of the very highest order, taking as his motive the note of the partridge (which had already been done, according to Athenæus, by Alcman in his *Caccabides*).*

We must then register a first sociological fact, *i.e.* imitation, as dating from the very birth of music. Are we able to add that this imitation had for cause and as a basis the irresistible altruistic sentiment of Love ?   Yes, we shall answer, but with a slight modification of Darwin's theory, or rather by drawing from it everything implied in it, although it may not have been specially formulated by the great naturalist.

It raises at the very outset difficulties and objections which we must not disguise. Let us state these in detail—

1st. If song is an instrument of victory, and thereby subserves the progress of the species, there ought to

---

* In the collection Miscellanea Lipsiensia (Lips., 1718, III, p. 683), there is a dissertation by Geamœnus in which it is stated that the birds gave us the first lessons in song.   (*Natura homini per avium concentum præcinente*).

be a coincidence or parallelism between the progress of song and the hierarchy of living beings. Why is not the ape a greater musician than the nightingale? Among the mammals the noisy manifestations of the voice (they can hardly be termed anything else) are simple phenomena of inhalation and exhalation ; it is not sufficient that a certain gibbon should be able to utter an energetic note (Darwin) for it to be styled a musician. Brehms, in a work on animal life (*Tierleben*), complacently analyses the register of a certain ape's voice which, according to him, can give the complete chromatic scale, regularly and with correctness and facility ; we even recognize "retards" (*sic*) in it! It is a very suspicious or a very flimsy observation, but supposing we admit it at the risk of incurring ridicule, other difficulties remain to be solved.

2nd. If it be the language of Love transmitted by heredity and by evolution which has created music, primitive races ought to bear witness to the continuity of the progression by the character of their art. We ought to find among them a senti-mental music, all the more expressive and tender because it is the nearer to nature and more under the immediate dependency of heredity. Now, this is not the case.

According to the testimony of the Prince of Wied, quoted by Grosse, this is what the song of the Botocudos consists of : "The singing of the men resembles an inarticulate roar on two or three notes, sometimes high, sometimes deep ; they take a long breath, place their left arm on their head, some-times a finger in each ear, especially if they are

in public, and open wide mouths deformed by
the *bottock*." I do not think any one will be tempted
to see in this a specimen of the art of pleasing or
alluring !

As asserted by an excellent judge,* the savage
only recognizes in love the sexual act. " The Tinné
Indians of North America," writes Lubbock,† " have
not a word to express ' dear ' or ' beloved ' ; and the
language of the Algonquins (Red Skins) in the
neighbourhood of Lake Michigan have no word
signifying *to love* . . . . Though the songs of savages
ordinarily treat of the chase, war, and woman, it is
very rarely that they can be called love songs. . . .
Neither among the Osages (Indians of the central
regions of the United States) nor the Cherokees,
can we find a single musical or poetical expression
based on a tender passion between the two sexes.
. . . Though repeatedly asked for one, they have
never produced a love song." Not a single love
song has been discovered among the Australians,
the Mincopees, or the Botocudos. Rink, who has
studied the Esquimaux more deeply than any one
else, says that they are hardly acquainted with the
sentiment of love.‡

3rd. Take another point of view. If it is from
sexual instinct that music takes its origin, why is
one of its primary functions, in nearly all races, of
a religious order ? Whence come those war songs
which are the negation of love ?

How is it that the Australians (and many other

* Grosse, *ibid.*, p. 213.
† Lubbock, *Origin of Civilization* (Marriage).
‡ *Ibid.*, p. 68.   C. Grosse, *loc. cit.*, p. 185.

men) nearly all sing when they are by themselves ? *

Why, since the sexual instinct is universal, is it
that certain nations (like the Germans) are greater
musicians than other nations, who yet are of the
same kin, like the English ? The Germans may
be considered as the kings of music, since they have
produced a Bach, a Handel, a Beethoven, a Weber,
a Schumann. Is there any correlation between this
undisputed superiority and (by the hypothesis)
another innate superiority, among our neighbours,
in the art of pleasing and seduction ? Is there,
also, an exact correlation between the natural
gifts of seduction, which have always been attributed to the French, and their musical genius ?

It is, therefore, difficult to accept unreservedly
the theory of Darwin. The great naturalist
wishes to establish a continuous chain connecting
the music of civilized man with the manifestations
of the sexual instinct among the lower animals,
but there is, as we have just seen, many missing
links of this chain when we examine what happens
among the non-civilized. A slight modification,
merely consisting in pushing back the limits he
sets up, will suffice to modify the aspect of this
doctrine and to make it acceptable.

In reality, Darwin's theory does not greatly differ
from that of the German metaphysicians, who
attribute to music the privilege of expressing the
most fundamental part of our inmost being. What
else, in fact, is the root of our being but the love
of life, the desire to prolong and perpetuate it, by

* Grosse, *loc. cit.*, p. 226.

rendering it better and more brilliant ? This desire is the manifestation of a force which has other outlets open to it, but finds its most instinctive use in sexual love. It might then be said—and we are repeating the opinion set forth at the commencement of this work—that song and all the rudimentary attempts which preceded it express something very general, a sentiment identical with the vital force itself, in which the altruistic inclinations are no doubt contained, but are not everything.

In the account of his travels in Guinea, M. Claudius Madrelle speaks of the frenzy and sensuality with which the negroes cultivate music and dancing. " From the moment the sun sets the whole of Africa gives itself up to pleasure, and resounds with the beating of tom-toms." It is something akin to the distracting and deafening concert, with its weird rhythm, which on summer nights, after the overwhelming heat, all kinds of beasts keep up in the fields. This grandiose and rude concert has a reason and a meaning ; and it is by listening to it that we have some chance of understanding the soul of nature. With the first shades of night there seems to descend upon the beings here below an irresistible need to give more intensity to life, to perpetuate it in new and more beautiful forms. This is part of love, and therefore of something more general. Involuntarily we think we can seize in its flight the voice which the evolution of things assumes, the imperious cry of living beings who yearn and clamour for progress.

Our music is like that of the African negroes ; it is certainly better regulated, but it translates into sonorous formulas the same inherent sensuality. It systematizes, purifies, and refines those appeals of one sex to the other which, on June nights, envelope the country in a network of seduction and voluptuousness.   Love fills in it as great a place as in romantic literature, but it is only the translation of a deeper and more general force, which is the vital instinct itself.

Thus it is that all our great composers have been ardent votaries of love ; and, to a great extent, the emotion of their hearers is composed of the last echoes of their passion.

We have a very fine répertoire of music—plain-song—which has nothing to do with all this ; but we do not know to what the melodies, by the aid of which it is constituted, were primarily adapted, whether by simple transfer or by imitation, and, if we did, we should probably be surprised.   Without love, there would be no art ; and love is the chief manifestation of a universal force in which are included the whole of the social feelings.

CHAPTER IV

MUSIC AND LANGUAGE

LANGUAGE, which has sprung from the necessity of relations between like beings, is at the same time a sociological fact following upon the sentiment of which we have just been speaking. Its variations are now being studied from this point of view, at the Collège de France by Professor Meillet. We know already that the fundamental intervals on which the musical system rests may be noted in the inflections of articulate speech. Proceeding further on this line of observation, we may ask ourselves whether all the expressive characteristics of the verbal language are not to be found in music, where they are isolated and systematized, while developed and promoted to a higher degree of force.

Certainly, we do not deceive ourselves as to the value of these "expressive" characteristics. We are aware that they do not, in themselves, suffice to constitute music. We shall not imitate the physiologists, doctors, directors of lunatic asylums, and laboratory or hospital students, who, exaggerating the scope of certain excellent observations, only see as the origin of song some reflex muscular actions, so that, in order to explain an art, they commence by putting on one side the artistic sense.

The difference of the intervals which constitute the irregularity of the line of melody is but the externals of music ; to imagine that by it one gains a comprehension of the most simple popular song is much as if one claimed to know a person from the cut of his clothes. The theory we are about to summarize has been disdainfully rejected, in Germany, by musicians who " hope they have heard the last of it." It seems to us, however, very worthy of interest, when considered as a simple contribution ; its object is to explain certain modalities of musical thought, and nothing more.

Analysis shows us two parts in ordinary language. The one expresses the thought, or concatenation of concepts, and is constituted by words and their syntax. The other, which is a sort of accompaniment, expresses the emotional state joined to the thought.

The former is acquired, conventional, and partially intelligible ; the latter is instinctive, natural, and universally intelligible. The proof that they must not be confused is that it is possible for them to be in complete disagreement. There is a way of saying " yes " which, by the tones and inflections of the voice, may mean " no "; conversely a " no " may mean a " yes." It is on this duality that the art of the comedian is based. There is a pretty little monologue in which a young girl, making her début in society, is instructed by her mother to never answer but in these two words : " Oh ! Monsieur ! " But she makes up for it by giving to this formula all the shades of modesty, modest love, surprise, regret, fear, reproach, anger, sup-

plication, etc. . . . In a word, she is exceedingly
eloquent, and conveys all she feels without the
help of words.

It is probable, as M. Sully Prudhomme says in his
poem *La Parole*, that primitive man began by using,
in his way, this natural, instinctive, and universally intelligible language—

> La peine et les plaisirs s'exhalaient dans les cris,
> La terreur bégayait des prières farouches ;
> Le soupir échangeait les âmes sur les bouches ;
> Dans le rire éclatait l'étonnement joyeux,
> Et le discours trahi s'achevait dans les yeux.

These cries, these stammerings, these explosions,
and even these inhibitions result from the interior
force of the feeling which, in each particular case,
produces a special adjustment of the vocal organs,
and expresses itself outwardly by sounds which
differentiate a thousand shades of meaning. We can
imagine how much can be drawn from the gifts thus
furnished by the physiological nature of man, with
social life as a stimulant. Ancient orators like
Cicero and Quintilian assigned them an important
place in the theory of eloquence, and certain modern
writers have gone further still.

The opinion which considers music to have collected, accentuated, and idealized all the emotional
accompaniment of articulated and logical speech is
a theory of French origin, first formulated by
writers of the eighteenth century.

" We must," writes Diderot in the *Neveu de
Rameau*, " consider declamation as one line, and song
as another line which zigzags across the first. . . . It
is the animal cry which must dictate to us the line
most suitable." J. J. Rousseau many times main-

tained this idea, and drew from it the bold conclusion that the music of a nation has the same
characteristics as its language. I will only cite,
along with the first book of *Émile*, the whole of
the 48th letter from Saint-Preux to Julie in the
Nouvelle Héloïse. The same theory has been advanced, with all the pomp of eloquence, by Lacépède
in his *Poétique de la Musique* (1785) ; by Condillac
in his *Essai sur l'origine des Connaissances humaines ;*
by Villoteau in the *Recherches sur l'analogie de la
musique avec les arts qui ont pour objet l'imitation du
langage* (1785). Nor have the musicians been averse
from it : " Music," says Grétry, " does not copy
objects, but *the word* which describes them."

This saying agrees with the declaration of
M. Camille Saint-Saëns in *Harmonie et Mélodie*
(p. 259) : " When listening to fine verses well recited,
it has often happened to me to detect in them an
air which I could write down." The whole of the
early French opera was founded on declamation.
Let us not forget that plain-song has been characterized as the " blossoming of the tonic accent."
Now, instrumental music being only a transposition
and a development of vocal music, it would seem
that we have here an explanation of the whole art.
This was the idea of Herbert Spencer, who by
republishing the same theory has made us forget his
predecessors.

Here is a double series of phenomena which are,
so to speak, parallel in the articulate and the
musical language ; it cannot be said that they
imitate or reproduce emotion, but they accompany
it, they are one of its first effects, and, on that

account, pass as "imitative." They form an inseparable association of ideas.

1st. *Intensity of sounds.* In music, as in language, this is proportioned to the strength of the feelings.

2nd. *The pitch of the sounds.* In both it is determined by the same causes. Slight emotions leave the voice in the lower register ; strong emotions throw it into the higher.

3rd. *The absence, or the multiplicity and magnitude of the intervals* (a consequence of the preceding fact).

4th. *The ascending or descending direction of the melodious design* (as above).

5th. *The staccato, or the legato of sounds* (examples furnished by the expression of joy or of sorrow in all operas, *passim*).

6th. *Timbre.* There is in the most trivial conversation changes of timbre, called forth by the feelings associated with the different subjects treated and corresponding to modulations in music.

7th. *The rapidity or slowness of the movement.* There are conversations which, in proportion to the intensity of the feelings called into play, pass through all the movements of a symphony : *adagio, andante, allegretto, allegro, vivace,* and even . . . *furioso !*

The concordance of these facts in the two languages is easy to establish, and we shall not dwell on them. But there are two other parallel series, constituted by another use of the resources just enumerated. Spencer has not perceived them, and yet they would have completed his theory.

§ I. Descriptive Music and Natural Language

All the descriptive elements of musical language have their equivalent in the instinctive part of articulate language.

It has been said that music was applied to the translation of the inward life, that it had no grasp on material objects, and that, as it was deprived of any resources for depiction, it was obliged to reduce everything to vocalization—that is to say, to psychological expression—by transforming what was objective into the subjective.

We are, however, compelled to recognize, without attaching too much importance to these facts of a secondary order, that the musician can, if he chooses, speak a very picturesque language and reproduce certain characteristics of external things, such as their movements, their rhythm, their colour, and even their qualities in space. It is impossible to hear the works of Berlioz, Bizet, Saint-Saëns, Wagner, and of the Russian and so many other composers, and yet deny this.

Now, there are in articulate language all the elements of what is termed descriptive music. When they describe a fair, a hunting scene, a storm, a battle, a voyage marked with various incidents, the lower classes do not confine themselves to detailing the facts and to marking their concatenation; they adapt their language to the things they speak of, and give an approximate image of them. It is this which gives life to their descriptions, and it would require a great effort of will on the part of any narrator not to regulate all his

" vocal gestures " according to the nature of the objects of which he wishes to suggest the idea.

Here, again, there are intermediate forms to be noted before we come to music : these are the art of the mimic, of the reader, and of the comedian.

Gounod said, when comparing French with Italian : " Our language is less rich in *colour*. Be it so, but it is more varied and perfect in tints ; it has less red on its palette, I grant ; but it has violets, lilacs, pearl greys, and pale golds, which the Italian language will never know." This judgment doubtless may be disputed, but it is founded on a principle which is indisputable.

In his *Art de la Lecture*, M. Legouvé desires us to clothe words with all the colours of the prism and to paint them with the voice ; thus with regard to Lafontaine's lines on " the poor woodman, laden with branches," who, " with slow steps, regains his smoke-dried hut " : " Render me," he says, " these rugged contours of the branches with a rugged voice ; employ grey and smoky tones for this smoke-dried hut. Yet it wants a Decamps to do this, for it was Lafontaine who made Decamps."

In a letter quoted by Quicherat (and dated Venice, 25 Jan., 1838), Nourrit gives praise to an Italian singer, and, analysing the qualities of his natural voice, adds : " Unfortunately he has but two colours at his disposal : black and white." The celebrated Rubini has been greatly praised for the Rembrandtesque tints he employed so happily. An exact remembrance has been preserved of Devrient in *Freischütz ;* when she sang, *De quel doux*

éclat brillent les étoiles . . . , she phrased in a clear
and limpid voice, spreading, as it were, light over
the picture ; and when, exploring from her window
the depths of the horizon, she sang, *Des nuages
épais et lourds flottent là-bas sur la forêt,* she darkened
the tone at the idea of the storm gathering over the
head of her betrothed.

Let us also bear in mind that there are three
registers in the human voice : the chest (deep
sounds) ; the palate (medium sounds) ; the head
(shrill sounds). The position of the sounds in
space being determined by those of the parts of
the body, the deep sounds are termed *low* sounds,
because the chest occupies the lower position, and
the shrill sounds are termed *high* simply because the
head has the higher position. From the superposition of these registers, enabling us to speak of the
height of the sounds, it follows that the expressions *run up* or *run down* with the voice are used
to designate an adaptation of singing to external
movements and the directions of movements.

Without exhausting the analysis of these facts
and of their consequences, we may say that,
whether in the verbal language or the language of
sounds, the objective expression, although limited
to the reproduction of the most general characteristics of the objects, constitutes both a work of
instinct and one of art, and may comprise—

1st. *The reproduction of certain movements with
their direction* (upwards and downwards) ; *their
form* (movements of an arrow, of a serpent, etc.) ;
their rhythm, speed, and total duration.

2nd. *The indication of the size, great or small, of*

the objects in repose (by the varied volume of the voice).

3rd. *The imitation of light and darkness with their intermediate shades,* and an undetermined number of tints (thanks to the analogy between colour and timbre).

4th. *The indication of certain relations* (some of which are confined to music, that art of simultaneous expressions), such as the *superposition, parallelism, distance, nearness,* etc., of two objects situated in space (thanks to the facts stated as regards the registers of the voice, of which the extreme limits are extended by the orchestra, and thanks to the faculty of writing in several parts).

We do not find in language only the germ of all these resources of musical expression ; this approximation enables us to solve a question which has often been raised and which greatly puzzles amateurs : What is the degree of exactness to which expression in music may attain and what is its limit ?

We answer to this that, in principle, musical language has neither more nor less exactness than instructive language. Now, this latter is very general and, consequently, somewhat vague. A cry is certainly the translation of a very strong feeling, but it does not always indicate the true cause of it ; it may express fear, anger, despair, surprise, hatred, etc. . . . A moan may betray the condition of a wretch overcome by agony, or that of an ecstatic saint, or, again, that of an epicurean steeped in pleasure. Most of the physiological movements proceeding from the passions (change of colour, interference with the circulation, rise or fall in temperature, twitching of the lips, etc.) are in the same category, and may be produced by the most opposite emotional states.

It has been remarked that. the Saint Teresa of Bernin, in the Basilica of St. Peter, appears filled with a wholly voluptuous and sensual beatitude in the presence of the angel appearing to her. Théophile Gautier justly observes that in the *Femme au Serpent* of Clesinger the expression of grief resembles that of enjoyment attaining its paroxysm. Were we to go minutely into the matter, we should no doubt find that, beyond a certain degree of intensity, all passions merge in the same dynamics.

§ 2. Language and Rhythm

Among the many phenomena which Spencer might have pointed out in his analysis of language —in addition to the physiological effects of emotion—there are two of real importance.

1st. The first of these is the manifest tendency to keep to a certain time. In our Romance languages there are tonic and atonic syllables. If we study the sequence of the words which together form a sentence, we find, no doubt, that there is not equidistance of the tonic accents, but that to the principal accent there is habitually joined a secondary accent which introduces into the oratorical formula a commencement or rough draft of binary time. Thus in the 'word *département* the tonic accent is on the final; but the antepenultimate (*par*) is semi-tonic, so as to convey the sequence . / . /

In the language of primitive folk it is noticed

that the principle of repetition—the basis of rhythm
—has served to form a great number of words.
This fact deserved the notice of the English
philosopher (Spencer).

In his book on *The Origin of Civilization*, Lubbock
has devoted to this a special research, accompanied
by exact statistics. He takes the words beginning
with the letter A in the dialect of an African tribe,
and shows that, like children, savages greatly love
to repeat the same syllables. He then shows how
different are the modern languages of civilized
peoples. The first thousand words of the English
Dictionary of Richardson only contain three examples of repetition ; but this is what is found,
as regards the letter A alone, in one of the savage
dialects—

Ahi-ahi : evening.	*Anga-anga :* pleasure.
Ake-ake : eternal.	*Aru-aru :* to marry.
Aki-aki : bird.	*Ati-ati :* to hunt.
Aniwa-niwa : rainbow.	*Awa-awa :* valley.

Lubbock has drawn up some comparative tables
which are interesting. After having closely examined the vocabularies of the negroes of the Brumer
and Lousiada Islands, and that of the natives of New
Zealand, he arrives at the following conclusions :
In European languages there are *two* words in a
thousand where the principle of repetition is
applied ; in the " primitive " languages there are
from 38 to 170 per thousand, or, an average
of 104.

When it is admitted that song is but a development of the natural and instinctive language, it

may very reasonably be supposed that this instinct passed over into music and there produced the bar.

2nd. Verbal language is not only logical juxtaposition of words and continuity; it has its cæsuras, secondary, and primary stops, and divisions; now, we again meet these same things in the organization of song, and later in instrumental melody. This important fact should have found a place in Spéncer's theory. We have already pointed out this above and shall not again refer to it.

To recapitulate, it would be puerile to say, as Spencer has done, that music is only a simple development of certain parts of natural language. With ideas such as these we should have to give up all idea of understanding Palestrina and Beethoven. But it is very true that in music many expressive elements are found which already exist in the natural language. Did the one *precede* the other? It is probable; and in any case, from all the facts mentioned above, a "contribution" only to musical æstheticism can be drawn, and not the principle of a definition or of a complete bird's eye view.

Rapidly we have passed in review all the parts of the musical material: fundamental intervals, scales, modes, time, rhythm, and *expression*. Leaving this technical and general point of view, we will now examine music from the historical point of view, and endeavour to show that at each period of its evolution it has been a function in social life.

CHAPTER V

THE EVOLUTION OF MUSIC IN REGARD
TO SOCIAL CONDITIONS

WE shall group our observations in accordance with
the following plan, which is not however absolutely
rigid: (1) Primitive Folk; (2) the Greeks; (3) Plain-
song of the Middle Ages; (4) the Renaissance;
(5) the Bach-Handel Period and the eighteenth century; (6) Contemporary Music.

§ 1. PRIMITIVE FOLK

By the word "primitive" I mean the earliest
races of men which historical documents enable
us to conceive in the past, as well as the non-
civilized of the present day, who, though our contemporaries, seem to be still in the first stage of
social progress. Among both classes, as we have
seen, song appears as a very important part of the
oral rites of magic. Is this to be accounted a sociological fact? We shall be very brief on this first
point, for direct documentary evidence is either
lacking or very difficult to verify.

If we take, in relatively modern times, the
magician who, by the aid of incantations, claims
to stanch the blood of a wound, to cause rain
to fall on dried-up ground, to disarm an enemy,

to render a field barren, to evoke the shade of a
dead man, to inspire love in an indifferent or
hostile woman, etc., we doubtless shall have little
trouble in proving that all that he is and does implies the existence of a community.

The magician is only such by virtue of a qualifica-
tion given to him by society collectively and of the
attitude it assumes towards him. He can only take
his place by opposing it; he is a stranger, an individual made *singular* by certain physiological
blemishes; or else he is more cunning, or more
learned than the rest, a chief of a clan, or a priest-
king, one whom his peculiar authority allows to
communicate with the supernatural powers. If the
language he uses has any special virtue, it is for the
reason that, as regards rhythm, intensity, the intervals run through, the nature and combination of
sounds, it is distinct from the current language.
In addition, the formulas he chants leave him no
freedom of interpretation, as is the case with the
musical artist of modern times; rather is he a
captive to his own song; it is forced upon him
with an imperative character in its smallest detail;
if the incantations are efficacious, they act of
themselves, without needing, like our songs and
our operatic airs, a personality to make them of
use. This is because their virtue is founded on
tradition, and on the tacit acceptation by a group
of initiates or believers.*

As to the magician whom we place at the very
beginning of things, and who *creates* the tradition

* V. Hubert et Mauss, *Esquisse d'une théorie générale de la
Magie.* (Année sociologique, 1904. Alcan.)

N

(here lies the true problem) instead of being subject to it, a peremptory reason enables us to consider him as a function of a social life.

All the primitive incantations presuppose a belief
that everywhere in nature there are spirits ; it is
they who cause famine or abundance, sickness or
health. Now, these spirits are endowed with all the
feelings,—malevolence, sympathy, malice, greed,
etc.,—to be found among men. The belief in
spirits is, therefore, nothing but the transport into
the invisible world of that which has been observed
in an existing community. Without society incantation would have no basis and no existence. This
observation applies equally to the non-civilized
among our contemporaries.

Let us not linger over this prehistoric period, but
betake us to more solid ground.

It is customary to commence the history of
music with the Greeks, the founders of the theory
of the gamut and the modes, but this is evidently
incomplete and short-sighted. Too long have the
Greeks, intelligent and artistic as they were, pre-
vented us from seeing humanity as a whole. Before
their time there existed the whole of the East. If
we confine ourselves to those parts of the Old World
with which they had direct relations, such as Egypt
and Asia Minor, we discover documents which
suggest the idea of remarkable musical affinities
between the inhabitants of the valley of the Nile
and those on the banks of the Tigris and the
Euphrates, and which all attest the social part
played by music.

Among the Egyptians, the Assyrians, and the

Chaldeans, the inscribed monuments testify to an
art constantly connected with the magical beliefs
of the people and interwoven with their religious,
military, and civil life.

The texts of the Bible, as far as the number and
exact nature of the instruments are concerned, give
rise to doubtful questions on which the archæological researches of the nineteenth century, more
fortunate ·in other points, have thrown no light ;
but we are able to gather from them some interesting general ideas.

The flourishes of trumpets, mentioned as the
earliest of all instruments, gave rise (as in our
regiments of to-day) to a veritable conventional language, described in the Book of Numbers (Chap. X.).
The trumpet accompanies the Hebrews in all the
acts of their collective life : it summons the multitude to religious ceremonies ; it announces festivals,
the declaration and the end of a war, the accession
of a king to the throne ; it proclaims the Jubilee
Year, and gives warning of the anger of God.

There was a liturgical music, the object of a
somewhat complicated organization (1 Chronicles
xxv. 1), united with dancing and with instruments,
which were tabooed later on by Christianity ; but,
besides this, we can gather the existence of another
music more subtle, brilliant, and which seems to
have been voluptuous, reserved for the wealthy
classes : " a concert of musicians in a banquet of
wine is as a carbuncle set in gold " (Ecclesiasti-
cus XXIII.).   Job (XXI.) characterizes the ungodly
rich as they " who take the timbrel and the harp,
and rejoice at the sound of the organ." In Isaiah

(v. 12) divers instruments (the exact nature of which escapes us) are cited in conjunction with the most delicious wines as a symbol of effeminacy.

This duality of the religious and the worldly art passed to the Greeks, by whom it was enriched with a new idea :—the part music ought to take in the matter of education.

§ 2. MUSIC AMONG THE GREEKS

Among the Greeks, who were the successors of the Orientals, from whom they differ but slightly, and creative artists, who added their part of personal invention to what they imitated from abroad, music becomes the object of increasingly clear classifications, all having for foundation the ethos of the different social groups in which art took birth and received its characteristic stamp. The ethnical denominations of the modes do not only point out different successions of intervals ; they betray a political conception of musical art, and transport into the field of "harmonies"* the fundamental idea of what is national and what is not. Music is divided into different provinces, of which the boundaries coincide with those of the different States or races. The two principal types are furnished by Continental and Asiatic Greece. The first is the Dorian music, which Plato, in a celebrated passage, considers as reflecting the manly virtues of Sparta ; the second is the Phrygian or Lydian music, which was licentious, reserved for feasts, and endowed with enervating power.

It would be easy to prove, by the examination

* The modes were thus termed.

of later works written in the different modes, that
this distinction is, artistically speaking, untenable ;
yet it imposed itself on the whole of antiquity,
not from purely musical, but from political
reasons. This seems to me the only possible explanation of the astonishment it always provokes
amongst the moderns.

The employment of music in religious ceremonies
and in the education of youth is an entirely natural
sequence to the use of song in magic ; we must,
therefore, not be amazed that, in one of his comedies
(*The Clouds*, v. 967), Aristophanes distinguishes the
scholars of different generations by the choruses
they have learned at school. If, on the other hand,
a national and virile music and a music of pure
pleasure exist, it is the first-named which will
serve in all the circumstances where it is sought
to fashion the energy of the true citizen.

It follows from all this, that music can equally
serve to mark the unity of a people in the acts of
public life ; and, if this people be a democracy
founded on equality, the form adopted as the most
appropriate will be the choral chant. From this
cause, we have the considerable part assigned to
music in religious assemblies, in the primitive
tragedy of an Æschylus—a social work not yet
divided from a liturgy—and in the solemn Games.

This choral chant derived its beauty, not from
any artifices of composition, as the present-day
public demands, but from characteristics which it
is impossible to appreciate properly if taken apart
from their social circumstances ; the more simple
it was, the more it placed in a kind of serene light

the national idea associated with a religious one.
If it took the form of unison, it is by no means
on account of the æsthetic effect—a very fine one,
moreover, when the executants are numerous—
which unison can produce ; neither is it through
want of knowledge of harmony.

I am quite willing to believe, as so many documents allow us to conjecture (for example, the
position of the hands of the harpists, on the
inscribed monuments), that the Greeks, like the
Egyptians, were acquainted with composition in
several simultaneous parts ; but this art was probably not advanced enough to be associated in
their mind with the idea of a perfect unity in the
feelings and the ideas expressed by the execution ; in addition, it would have singularly complicated the task of the poet-musician, who before
the public representation had himself to teach their
parts to non-professional singers. We will add that
the writing of counter-point presupposes, for the
notation of real values and rests, a somewhat
advanced graphic system which at the beginning
was wanting.

In the study of Greek music from the sociological
point of view, there must naturally be taken into
account the myths which attributed a divine origin
to each instrument ; neither should we forget—
though we are only acquainted with them by name
—the popular songs. The Greeks sang while har-
vesting, while grinding the barley, when crushing
the corn with the hand-cylinder, when pressing the
bunches of grapes, when spinning and weaving—
all work founded on collective action and on the

spirit of co-operation. They had among them the airs of the shoemaker, the dyer, the water-carrier, the shepherd, etc. . . . . Through a slow evolution and changes in manners and customs, the original names of these kinds of couplets, associated with various collective operations, became unintelligible to the Alexandrians..

If we leave on one side the current of popular melodies (independent of *art*, properly so called), the two types of music, already mentioned in the Bible, reappear at the very beginning of the modern period : the one religious, the other profane and worldly, an object of suspicion to all who uphold the religion of the fatherland or of the altar. For a long time we see a predominance of the first ; then progress, slow invasion and arrival of the second, which little by little takes the leadership, and, by an evolution alike of the conditions of social life and the progress of the human mind, changes both the direction of the art and its technique. Thus can be summed up the history of music from the Middle Ages to our own times.

§ 3. Plain-song

For nearly ten centuries what was, later on, to be called " plain-song " was the only music deserving the name of art and of science. The musical language we now employ comes down from the Middle Ages by an evolution almost identical with that of the verbal language. How was this type of art formed which fills so large a place in history ? What links has it with ordinary life ? A well-known manuscript of Saint-Gall represents in an artless

sketch, a dove—the Holy Ghost—inserting its beak
into the ear of Pope St. Gregory while he is dic-
tating the " Neumes " to a scribe. We have only
to be acquainted with the various borrowings of all
kinds from pagan antiquity effected by Christianity
to comprehend that the true explanation, in music
as in other things, must have a less mystical
character.

In the Middle Ages the Church is the perfect or
nearly perfect type—we must not lose sight of the
theological differences—of a society, realizing what
political organizations pursue in vain or only attain
intermittently : viz. moral unity. The Church owes
this to the diffusion of the dogma which, by
implying obedience, removes the difficulty of the
problem, *i.e.* liberty ; but it also owes it to the chant,
which is inseparable from public worship. It is
easy to see that all the characteristics of plain-song
are of a sociological order.

The man who performs by himself an act of
worship does not sing ; he prays in silence. But
as soon as a gathering is formed song appears. It
is, therefore, legitimate to say, reversing the order
of the words : wherever we find chanting, there
exists a homogeneous community. " A very powerful bond of unity," says St. Ambrose, " is the chorus
formed by the assembly of the people."* In fact,
the chant is pre-eminently a collective work, and
on the other hand causes it to be a social bond, an
instrument of popularization, of deep penetration,
and of discipline.

* *In Psalm.*, 1 : *Magnum plane unitatis vinculum, in unum
chorum totius numerum plebis coire.*

Never has this function been more marked and more powerful than in the Middle Ages. At that period the word *cantus* did not only signify the melodies of the ritual, but song in general, as if the Church had not been *a* society, but *the* society. It was in this sense that Martin Gerbert still used this word *cantus* in 1774. Ignoring individual embellishments, the chant only exists by the community which collaborates * by means of it with the officiating priest; it is the "common voice"† of the religious society which chants, *una voce, una corde.*‡ "The chorus is a multitude united in one ceremony."§ It is no longer the case, as among the Romans, of special *sacra* for each family; through the chant the whole of lay society, interwoven with the religious, becomes a collective body which concentrates its feelings, its thoughts, and its words, into one act in common. The profane world is caught in the meshes of liturgical melodies, and thereby the natural or conventional characteristics which differentiate it are reduced to equality. Rich and poor, princes and subjects, clerics and laymen, young and old, men, women, and children are brought together, reconciled, and identified by music.‖ Such is the virtue of unification possessed by the *chorale.*¶

Like the liturgy itself, the chant is traditional. The Church chants "after the example of its predeces-

* *Succinit, respondet, ὑποψάλλει.*
† φωνή κοινή (Clément d' Alex.).
‡ Saint Augustine (*de Verbis apost.*, Serm. 10).
§ *Multitudo in Sacris collectus.* (*Ibid.*, ʟ. i, 3.)
‖ Saint Jean Chrysostom, *in Psalm.*, cxlv.
¶ *Ubicunque chorus est, ibi diversæ voces in unum canticum congeruntur.* (Saint Jérôme, *in Psalm.*, cxlix.)

sors,"* with the desire to revive the ancient spirit. Moreover, we are only acquainted with music founded on tradition, just as every one who speaks derives his language from some other person. The name of St. Gregory is by no means that of a composer, but simply an individual label given to the tradition when, at the end of the sixth century, it became fixed. St. Gregory confines himself to compiling, co-ordinating, and " centonizing." His musical work—supposing we have the right to use this term—is an act of administration which codifies elements descended from the Latins, the Greeks, and the Jews.†

Besides being traditional, the chant is also the object of faith (in the sense in which the observant historian may give to this word). It is too near to the sacred text not to borrow from it a ritual character. ‡ It is not used by reason of its beauty, as some pieces for the organ are now, but because it forms part of the things prescribed. In the churches there are as yet neither " audience " nor artists. The chant is one of the signs of the faith, for its prototype was believed to be " the choir of the angels celebrating the glory of God in Heaven."

---

* *Secundum exemplum prædecessorum nostrorum.* (Concile de Valence, III, ap. 855.)

† The Greek language was used in the Christian community until the third century, A.D.

‡ Unconsciously, modern archæologists have this train of thought when they endeavour to reproduce with so much precision from the manuscripts the exact version of the Gregorian chants. We must note, in passing, that no one dreams to do this work for the text of the Psalms, though it is known that the last Latin recension of them does not reproduce exactly the original Hebrew text.

In the Christian world it develops and propagates itself in accordance with the great sociological law of imitation, which is a kind of tradition radiating in space. St. Gregory, when regulating it, had only the Roman Church in view. By degrees the Roman chant became universal, but more or less influenced by the countries into which political circumstances and the expansive force of the religious idea caused it to penetrate. Hence its different forms (Ambrosian, Gregorian, Mozarabian, and Gallican chants), which have been compared to dialects having one single idiom for origin and assimilable to the Romance languages.*

From these first facts a few others might be logically deduced. Let us try to imagine the faithful who used to fill the churches in the early ages of Christendom, at a time when ignorance was so great; let us picture to ourselves, from the paintings of the primitive artists, the features of the contemporaries of Aurélien de Reomé (ninth century), for whom there existed no printed books, and who all might have said, with the mother of Villon—

> . . . Rien ne sais ; oncques lettres ne lus :
> Au moutier vais, dont suis paroissienne,
> Paradis peints où sont harpes et luths
> Et un Enfer où damnés sont boullus.

For believers† such as these the chant was an obvious system of mnemonics. For this purpose it

---

* A very fascinating hypothesis of Dom Mocquereau. (*Paléogr. mus.* T. I.)

† On the ignorance of the ninth century, *vide* the letter of Aurélian to the Arch-chanter Bernard (Martène, *Monumen.*, T. I., p. 121 *sqq.*).

is reduced to the greatest simplicity possible ; it is what was called later *planus cantus*, plain-song. Retaining its socio-religious function, it disregards systematically all preoccupation of *art*. Thus are explained the scruples of St. Augustine, who reproached himself with feeling too much pleasure in music. From those who practise it it demands at first no natural gift ; in virtue of the principle, "*corde, non voce cantandum*," it is within the reach of all, even of those of whom we should nowadays say that they have no voice.* Though capable, in certain cases, of translating the elementary sentiments, sadness and joy, it excludes *expression*, the impassioned cantilena,† and all the shades that this implies. It excludes the powerful intensity of sounds,‡ rapid movements, pathetic inequality of rhythm : in a word, everything now considered as musical and as constituting the *art* of the professional.

Sung in unison, average in everything, giving to its notes an equal length, it greatly resembles the verbal language of which it takes the appearance, the pauses, the inflections, and the cadences. In the origin it is hardly different from that " speech," *vicinior pronuntianti quam canenti*. In the most ancient liturgy, which is that of Milan, there are recitatives which end on an interval of a fourth or of a fifth, of which one could instinctively dis-

---

* The κακόφωνος may sing in the Church (Saint Augustine, *Confess* , ch. xxxiii. Cf. Nicct, *De Bono psal.*, ch. iii.

† *Constit. apostol.*, 1, V, ch. ix. Cf. Clément d' Alex., *Strom.*

‡ *Rule* of St. Benedict, ch. xx, lii.

cover the musical design by simply reading the words.*

The general principle of the organization of plain-song is, in the most important of the sociological facts (language), a paramount phenomenon, viz. the tonic accent. The chant is its development and full flower, from which it draws its system of notation.†

With the melodies that it thus liberates it forms a répertoire which, in spite of the size of liturgical books, is very limited. This is confined to a few characteristic tones, so few at first that oral tradition could preserve them ; but later, when the liturgy developed, it was thought to fix them by very general graphic signs. Even at this recent period itself, when new services demanded new airs, old melodies already in use were employed, an adaptation contrary to our ideas of art, but in conformity with the habits of the collective activity, which proceeds by repetition and imitation.

In practical execution, the principal forms adopted are traditional or of universal popular origin. These are the antiphonic chant (division into two choirs) and the responsorial (one choir responding to a soloist).

The modes used are borrowed from the Greeks,

---

* For example, the ordinary lessons of Matins (Jube Domine *benedicere*, Tu autem Domine nostri *miserere*), the Lessons from Scripture on Sundays and Feast-days, the Passion of the Martyrs, the Epistle, the Gospel, etc.

† The acute accent, according to decisive proofs found at Mont-Cassin by Coussemaker, at first drawn from below upwards by the transcribers, and then from above downwards with a heavy stroke, gave rise to the virgule of the neumes, and later to the modern crotchet.

as indicated by their names : *protus, deuterus,
tritus, tetrarchus ;* and the Greeks themselves received from the Orientals of Asia Minor some of
these modes, which were shortly afterwards to
reappear, with their ethnical designations, in Occi-
dental music.

The *clausulæ* of the Gregorian melodies and the
principal features of their structure are not determined by artistic reasons, but by the nature of the
liturgical text (Catalogue of Réginon).

Finally, plain-song is impersonal and anonymous.
It has remained so, even when in the course of ages
individual talent has enriched it. The melodies
never, as in the present day, bear a composer's name.
They are considered as the work of the community,
and consequently as its property. (We should note
that this is the case neither for sermons, nor for
the text of the hymns, nor for the liturgy properly
so called.)

Neither are the names of the most talented singers
—there must, naturally, have been some ordinary
and some excellent ones—brought into prominence,
or even simply recorded by historiographers, notwithstanding the special schools in which they were
subjected to a hierarchical discipline. Here again,
it is the voice of the community which is on their
lips ; every individual musical element is absorbed
and disappears. The assembly alone seems to have
an existence.

Even didactic works, whether signed or not, do
not escape this law. In the period before counter-
point—which marks a revolution and a new era—
they are impersonal. Generally, the monk who

writes a treatise on music in no way seeks to set forth and uphold original views ; having to supply the library of his monastery with a book it does not possess, he is somewhat in the position of one of our pedagogues who has to teach the metric system or some other " matter " ; he is, above all, anxious to set forth with precision a sort of anonymous knowledge and to conform to tradition. Far from avoiding what has been said before, he is bound to seek it out. Hence these treatises, differing as they do from modern " plagiarisms," though at every moment they bring them to mind ; hence this untiring diligence, fastidious to our minds, in reproducing uniformly legends which hark back to Pythagoras, to the Bible, and are embodied in the " doctrine."

Such are the characteristics of the religious chant of the Middle Ages. It has issued from a certain very pure type of social life and of its historical antecedents ; and at the same time it is charged with maintaining the unity of it. Between this music and the collective life there is constant action and reaction.

§ 4. COUNTER-POINT AND ITS FUNDAMENTAL RULES

Restricted to unison and tied down to traditional forms, plain-song was incapable of making progress ; when new services were introduced into the liturgy, it could only repeat itself or adapt to new Latin words unappropriated melodies. From about the eleventh century there appears and develops by its side a type of chant which is the really original and fruitful creation of the Middle Ages :

i.e. counter-point. It made its appearance awkwardly and painfully, but to it belongs the future. It was destined to invade the old religious music, and to lead up to Palestrina, Bach, and Beethoven. . . .

The division of the primitive cantilena into several simultaneous parts, differentiated by the compass of the voice, was obvious to any musician desirous of novelty by the natural classification of the voices, such as voices of children and women (soprano, alto), and those of men (tenor, bass); it was equally suggested by the wholly natural desire to adapt music to the differentiations of the collective life and to present an image, in the choral chant, of the social groups. It is not without interest to remark that polyphony especially developed itself in countries where, as in Flanders, there existed a spirit of municipal freedom and corporate existence, and in those which, like Venice, carried to extremes the luxury and the pomp of aristocratic assemblies.

A community, according to the definition of Tarde, is constituted by persons who imitate one another and yet are individually distinct. In this new music, in which the problem consisted in reconciling multiplicity with unity, *imitation* became the general law of composition.

The first important style in which musicians practised is Canon, in which the same melody repeats itself in one part after another, like an undulation, the field of which grows larger and larger. For a long time the progress of Canon was confused with that of the musical art itself. Then music gains more independence ; it organizes its motets and its

madrigals in accordance with the triple principle
which is at the base of all social life : imitation,
opposition, and adaptation.

Pure instrumental composition is unknown to it
for a very long time ; it remains under the direct
influence of the verbal language, and only commences
to break away from it later, in an age of transition
which may be assigned to the time of the Renaissance.
We have only to peruse the titles of the works published in the second half of the sixteenth century—
Collections of Dances, Gardens of Music, Treasures,
Orchards of Melodies, etc.—to see that they are
" written as much for the voice as for all musical
instruments," and that they serve " per cantare e
sonare d'*ogni Sorte*." The idea of writing a piece
for a special instrument is as yet not existent, or
hardly so.

One is startled at the multitude of social facts
and at the complexity of the events of political
history which we should have here to analyse if
we desired to explain in complete fashion how
polyphony, after having developed in the sixteenth
and seventeenth centuries, succeeded in constituting various kinds of compositions, which appear to
us at the present time as free from all links with
the surrounding realities, and in a kind of splendid
isolation. To avoid losing ourselves in a subject
which is in touch with everything, and of which it
is impossible to say everything concerning it, let us
take one of the works which developed into the
grand orchestral symphony, and let us try to reconstitute its genesis.

o

I open a collection of the works of J. S. Bach. The first piece is a Sonata in *La* minor, for the piano. It is composed of four movements : an *adagio*, of free form (non-periodic) ; an *allegro*, a fugue for three voices ; an *adagio*, of the same form and the same extent as the first; an *allegro moderato* (allemande), followed by an *allegro* (coranto), an *andantino* (saraband), and an *allegro* (gigue). An examination of this very complex work prompts the following observations—

1st. The abstract form "Sonata in *La* minor" is, first, the terminal point of an evolution which started from the concrete form, that is to say, from music associated with language, to arrive at the abstract form (music without words). The first symphonic pieces, published in 1597 by Giov. Gabrieli, were for the "voice *or* for instruments." Down to 1651, the terms *Sonata* and *Canzone* are indifferently used ; it is subsequently to Neri, the organist of Saint Mark's, at Venice in the middle of the seventeenth century, that the word *Canzone* was definitely replaced by the word *Sonata*.

Dances, which come to play so large a part in the genesis of the classical Symphony, and which figure to the number of four in Bach's work, were also primitively written on airs for the voice with words. The Italian composer, Gastoldi, published at Venice in 1591 some *Balleti a cinque* (five voices) *con li suoi versi* (with their verses) *per cantare, suonare et ballare ;* the English composer, Thomas Morley, had written *Ballets for Six Voices* (London,

1595); the German Valentin Haussman a collection of thirty-seven Pavanes (Nuremberg, 1604),
the first ten of which are accompanied by erotic
words, etc.

Therefore, from the chanted language to the pure
instrumental music there must have been steps
which we cannot discover. Some of these are
supplied by the Italian composers; we know that
Bach had, on certain points, been their pupil. We
shall later see further proofs of this.

2nd. This Sonata in *La* minor appears at once,
from the simple headings alone, as the juxtaposition of two works of different kinds, each
comprising an *adagio* and an *allegro*. The first is
rightly the Church Sonata, *Sonata da Chiesa*, which
generally commenced with a grave and majestic
movement, "after which was taken some gay and
animated fugue"; the second is the *Sonata da
Camera* (chamber), "formed of a succession of
little pieces, suitable for dances" (Brossard, *Dict.
de Musique*, 1703). By analogy, and to give symmetry and a regular rhythm to the composition,
this second part here begins, like the first, with an
adagio.

Bach, therefore, has united a profane subject
with a religious one; that he was able to do this
shows that this conjunction had been made
before his time by the evolution of manners. In
Italy the churches were concert halls as well as
museums. At St. Mark's, Venice, during the seventeenth century there was a real orchestra, composed
of violins, *Viols da gamba*, theorbos, cornets, hautbois, and trombones. At Salzburg, as late as 1783,

between the Epistle and the Gospel a Sonata was played (Mozart composed seventeen for this purpose). We have already left plain-song far behind us. The Church has undergone evolution as well as the community.

3rd. Following these general observations, let us examine the style itself of our Sonata. At first sight it seems more adapted to the violin than to the piano. This is in no way the result of individual whim or habit ; notwithstanding the example of his father, notwithstanding his competence in technique and the functions he held at Weimar for nine years in the chapel of the Grand Duke, Bach was by no means a violin virtuoso : he here submitted to the influence of an external and very general state of mind, to explain which we shall again have to bring in the practices of the Church.

The instrumental works composed in the sixteenth century in North Italy by the organists and virtuosi of Venice, by the members of the *Academies*, or by the Roman School, all offer the following peculiarity : the violin predominates (no doubt because of being the instrument most fitted to imitate the human voice and to *sing*). In adopting it, the Church had done what was hardly possible to an academy, a school, or to lordly artists : it had popularized it. Bach yielded to this kind of fashion by letting the style of the violin slide into the piano.

4th. The *adagio*, written in this spirit, is, in reality, a prelude. This does not imply to our mind either the *exordium* of the orator, or the *intrata*, or the *overture*, or the recitative preceding the " air," or the liturgical *introit*, or any of the forms which announce or prepare something important or rhythmical, but simply an organ prelude, destined to tune the voices of the faithful who are about to execute a chorale. This organ prelude at first became a simple prelude not followed by singing, and then, by a final transformation, an *adagio*. It is a transformation resembling that which, later on, in the symphony, is to replace the minuet by the scherzo. This reminiscence of the functions of the organ will become habitual (in the form of an introductory *adagio*) in the symphonies of Haydn, less frequent in Mozart's, and rarer and rarer still in their successors—and the sociological reasons of this are easy to understand. Like the public mind, the musical mind gradually liberates itself from the Church.

5th. The fugue which follows is, in fact, a chorale without words. It is customary to distinguish the instrumental fugue, in which Bach excelled, from the vocal fugue, of which Handel was past-master ; in reality there is but one kind of fugue : *i.e.* the vocal, written for a *group of categories* of singers, since it is formed of " voices " which execute simultaneously different melodies moving within a normal register. Bach followed the models which were handed down to him by the Netherlanders, the Flemish, the Germans of the seventeenth century, and the Italians ; he is not the creator of the fugue ; he obtained it from the masters of the North and of the South.

6th. The second part of the work, the " Chamber " Sonata, welded to the first, begins with an *adagio*, to which is added a *Suite* formed from dances : *i.e.* the allemande, coranto, saraband, and gigue. The co-ordination of these dances into a whole possessing tonic and thematic unity, is the result of a further evolution in certain facts of the profane life, of which these are the successive phases—

First of all a dance, with a song used as accompaniment.

This song has an instrument added to it.

The song disappears, and the instrument is used alone.

The idea occurs to give the song dissociated from the words and become instrumental elsewhere than assemblies for dancing.

Travelling musicians carry the dance tunes from town to town and country to country ; and international relations favour and extend these exchanges.

In presenting dance tunes, they were arranged in such an order that a pleasing contrast arises between slow and quick rhythms, from the succession of ternary and binary measures.

It was during the Thirty Years' War (1618–1648), when the common use of arms had brought about a similarity of manners and customs among Italians, Spaniards, French, Swedes, Danes, Poles, that choregraphic cosmopolitanism was instituted ; and, in all probability, it was a musician of the school of the Dutchman Sweelinck (*obiit* 1621) who created the *Suite for the piano*. Bach was born in 1685.

Finally came the idea of uniting these dances into an artistic whole, called a *Suite*, which passes into the Sonata, reaches there its last degree of unfitness, and soon dies out, though not without bequeathing to symphonical music rhythms and outlines of time, which are still noticeable at the present day.

Religion, profane life, chant, organ music, violin music, dances brought from Italy (the coranto), from Spain (the saraband), from Germany, and types of composition borrowed from the North and South and themselves constituted under the influence of multiple social facts—such are the elements which a rough analysis, limited to the notice of the most apparent facts, discovers in one Sonata of Bach.

It will be seen that the composer is far from inventing everything himself, and also how incorrect is the judgment, repeated a hundred times, that Bach is "a pure German," *echt deutsch*, as our neighbours say. One of the most manifest errors committed by both nations (an error instinctively fortified by the complicity of Chauvinist criticism in each country and by that of a criticism ill-informed outside each country) is to imagine that it is their mission to create a really national work and to protect jealously against all alloy the pure substance of their genius. As a matter of fact, there exist between nations the same necessary links as between the individuals of the same country : each receives, modifies, and transmits a civilization in progress which he did not create, and can only mark, on its passage, with a new imprint.

It goes without saying that, if we had examined an oratorio, a cantata, or an opera, the search for a sociological conclusion would have been still more

easy! For it to have been complete we should
have had to enter into the matter of style. I shall
not perform here this meticulous task; I shall confine
myself to a single observation, to show that it would
be possible and legitimate to connect with the state
of the collective life, at a given moment of history,
certain characteristics of musical phraseology.

§ 6. Music under the Ancient Regime and during the French Revolution

Here are two facts which appear to me significant—
1st. Our French music, under the ancient regime,
is full of "ornament." Every moment the line of
melody is inflected by grace notes : the slur, the
mordant, the gruppetto, the trill, and what has been
termed in French "broderie," and in German
manieren (cruel word!)—all these are lavishly employed.

This practice, carried out even in pieces for the
organ, no doubt comes from the clavecin, which
has been the basis of our musical education, and
in which the notes, being rather short, need to be
sustained or amplified by accessories; but may we
not also find its explanation in the condition of social
manners? These "graces" are the curl-papers,
the ribbons, and the patches of an essentially
worldly music, of which Saint-Aubin has given us
an exact idea in his celebrated engraving, "The
Concert," where the wit and the coquetry of the
salons find their equivalent. One of the Couperins
wrote that, when playing, the performer on the
clavecin should look at the audience with a smile
on his lips; this advice would have come home to

us even had it not been formulated. Very far removed from the period when the art was popular, the musician is then a functionary of an aristocratic élite ; he only lives by it and for it ; the desire to please by sweet effects is the great law of his art, which appears to us all curtseys and festoons.

2nd. Let us now run through the very considerable répertoire* of the music appearing after 1793. The style is quite different. No more "graces" and "manners." During the revolutionary period, the musical art is characterized by the abandonment of instrumental prettinesses, by an artless and declamatory enthusiasm which manifests itself by the freedom of the rhythms, the simplicity of the line of melody, the use of vocal masses, the ignorance or disdain of harmonic subtleties. How is it possible to deny the concordance of these facts with the change in manners ?

If we wish to convince ourselves that the evolution of music is determined by the evolution of society, nothing is, finally, more instructive than the spectacle of our contemporary art.

§ 7. The Present State of Music

We might commence by stating, after grouping secondary facts round the epochs, that music also has had its three ages. It has known a theological age, with plain-song ; a metaphysical age, with the great symphonists Bach, Haydn, Mozart, Beethoven ; and the present with composers so preoccupied with realism, we might term the positive age. One of the laws of civilization is that the lay

* Published by M. Constant Pierre (publications de la Ville de Paris).

spirit, governed at first by the religious spirit, gradually detaches itself from it, differentiates itself, and organizes itself apart from it. This law is the same for the arts of rhythm. Music separated itself from the Church after having been its thing ; it liberated itself, in appearance to enjoy worldly freedom, but in reality to secure the expression of its natural feelings outside dogmas.

What a Beethoven represents, historically, in his symphonic works is the definitive emancipation of an art which began to free itself from its early tutelage at the epoch of the Reformation and the Renaissance, and henceforth only recognizes humanity, nature, and natural religion.

What our contemporary composers represent is that absolute liberty, no longer exercised only *in abstracto*, as in the classic symphonies, but restored to its concrete, naturalistic, and sociological applications with an independence which is entirely free from restraint.

It is a state which has its grandeur and its perils, and numerous facts give evidence of its connection with the evolution of politics. To-day, the division of music into distinct kinds, hierarchized according to their nobility, a division which resembled, in former times, that of society with its graduated stages, becomes more and more effaced. This confusion of genera, a result of the confusion of classes and of the throwing-over of all conventionality, is, above all, visible in the theatre ; grand opera and *opéra-comique* continually encroach on one another, and have become almost indistinguishable. This transformation is equally visible in the Symphony. In what category can we place a work like the *Prélude à l'après-midi d'un Faune* of M. Debussy? All the old forms are broken up or are no longer useful.

What characterizes our organization at the present day is a state of deep and complete renovation, in which the democratic and individualistic pressure overthrows or causes to totter the old conventionalities of all kinds. The same fact is happening in music. It may be summed up in the one word: anarchy.

In politics "anarchy" signifies the *absence of a ruler;* in the matter of art it means the absence of all law of any kind forced on a composer.

There no longer exists a preponderant school, with a quasi-official chief to group around him the majority of talent; the systems of æstheticism are as numerous and as diverse as are the political parties. Among our musicians there are revolulutionaries, independents, conservatives, liberals, classic irreconcilables, reconciled neo-classicists, socialists, who vow to write only by the people and for the people, and for whom the hill of Montmartre supersedes the Olympus of old.

No longer is there a general and common direction. Absolute liberty in the choice of subjects — formerly taken from mythology — and in the manner of their treatment. The rhymed operatic libretto is followed by the prose book; the behelmeted and gaudily dressed hero is replaced by the workman in fustian, as depicted in the novels of Zola; the regular melody by a sort of inorganic recitative; the preponderance of melody over accompaniment by a mixed and undivided regime which levels everything ; to the judicious use of the orchestra and to the voices of the artists, succeeds an unbridled flow of instrumental force in which one seems to hear growling the formidable voices of the crowd.

Even the grammar of music, with its long tyranny of rules, has no longer any absolute authority. Between the language of Rameau and of Gluck and that of certain musicians of to-day there is as great a distance as between the style of Boileau and that of Stéphane Mallarmé or any other "decadent." The pure consonances which formerly gave to music a mundane decency of good taste are now almost the exception : everything dissonant, unusual, aggressive is regarded as expressive *par excellence*. Regularity of rhythm is carefully avoided. It is thought that work to be beautiful does not need to be clear.

What favours this state of dissolution—and, at the same time, of fruitful regeneration—is that those learned in acoustics, who might impose certain bases on musical syntax, are not in accord. They also have been rent asunder by the critical spirit. The leadership of Helmholtz was a fugitive one ; and musical physiology has been, in one sense, the liberation of music, because, while it says nothing which has an evidential character like the problems of geometry, it has lost the right of giving directions to the artists.

Lastly, there is a final standpoint which sociology might choose in order to explain music. Every composition needs, in order to exist, certain instruments for its execution, and, conversely, the number of instruments available for use exercise an undoubted influence on the nature of the composition. Now, the manufacture of a musical instrument is a very delicate and complicated work which presumes a certain degree of science of industry and of international relations. I shall not enumerate the inventions due to the instrument-makers in the course of the nineteenth century, which have enabled musicians to obtain effects unsuspected two hundred years ago. Concerning the Sonata referred to above, I will only recall some of the parts which enter into the construction of a violin, taking the case (the least favourable in appearance to the sociological theory) where the violin is not manufactured by machinery, but by the hand of one workman alone.

The violin-maker levies contributions from a great number of countries and trades. He requires Swiss or Bohemian maple for the stock, the thin sides, the finger-board, the head, and the bridge of the violin ; Swiss fir for the sounding-board, the bar, and the angle-joints ; ebony for the fret, the tail-piece, the knob, and various parts of the bow ; ebony for the pegs ; iron-wood, ivory, and mother-of-pearl for the stick ; Cologne glue for joining the various parts ; silk, silver, brass, or bronze wire to go round the string of the *Sol*. The first string must bear a tension of seven and a half kilogrammes ; the *La* of 8 kilos. ; the *Ré* of $7\frac{1}{2}$ kilos. ; the *Sol*, $7\frac{1}{4}$ kilos. ; and these measurements require the attention of several specialists.

With the varnishes, the large and small brushes, the wheel to spin the strings, the sulphur vapour to bleach them, the violin-maker requires a set of tools almost as numerous as a joiner—about thirty, in fact, each of which is the finished product of collective labour. And it will be readily guessed that the choice of these materials and the rules for their use are the result of a long period of practice, of experiments and of comparisons, in which each one imitates and corrects his neighbour, profiting by his errors as well as his discoveries.

§ 8. Conclusions of the Second Part

To sum up : the forms of composition, as well as the expressive parts of music and the elements of its grammar, are tributaries of social life ; they owe to it their *habitus* and their intelligibility. From language, music borrows its inflections, its cadences, cæsuras, movement, timbres, imitative harmony, its affinity for the "images," which take the place of things it would be impossible to reproduce ; from liturgies, games, and dancing it borrows its chief rhythmical constructions. Lastly, from one end of its history to the other, it has an evolution parallel to that of society by reflecting all the changes of public life, the progress of the lay mind, of science, and of industrial labour.

Have we in this an explanation of the whole phenomenon to be studied ?

I dare not affirm it. There are theorists who may perhaps be satisfied by the analyses we have made. I cannot repeat how puerile, pitiful, and anti-scientific would be a method which consists in explaining an art by ignoring the paramount artistic fact which is essential to it and constitutes it. It is already a great deal, no doubt, to be able to give an account of all the modalities of compositions in unison and in parts; but there remains to be explained the special act of synthesis which animates all these forms—in a word, the thought. To ignore this last fact is to place ourselves without the pale of music, and to condemn ourselves to dissertations on side-issues, which the musician has the right to consider as trifling matters when it is proposed to give them any greater value than that of a modest and limited contribution.

It is not sufficient to urge that musical thought, under the pretext that one of its characteristics is the absence of concepts, is like the terminal point of a series of ever and ever more sublime abstractions. The mathematician and the algebraist likewise think without concepts; all that we can affirm—leaving on one side the problem of its origins, which escapes us—is that during that period in which the history of civilization can be directly studied by the aid of positive documents, we see the mind of the composer becoming formed in the same way as that of the writer who uses the verbal language. He assimilates information; he forms part of a school, even if unconnected with Conservatoires; he reads or hears much music; he stores in his memory a number of formulas which are unconsciously in his mind, and cause him, unknown to himself, to imitate or counter-imitate. He is always the follower of some other composer, even if he adopt habits of style opposite to the views of the latter. All modern symphonists, French or foreign, owe a part of what they are to Beethoven. Now, Beethoven proceeds from Mozart ; Mozart from Haydn ; all from Bach and Handel, who are the culminating point of the Renaissance. This last is the development of the music of the Middle Ages, which, in its turn, is governed by plain-song ; and plain-song is the meeting-point of several melodic arts, still imperfectly known : to wit, Latin, Greek, and Jewish art.

Everything is related and linked together. But this series has a beginning, and taking history backwards simply pushes the problem further back.

Our sole resource is to admit that this delicate act, by which a syntax of sounds develops into a very expressive language, is not the privilege of any special artist refined by centuries of civilization, but has its affinity in humanity itself, of all ages and of all latitudes. Everywhere mankind is sentimental, imaginative, and superstitious ; it is therefore a musician, at bottom, by virtue of an obscure instinct which by degrees becomes precise and realized. An assembly of people is never insensible to fine music ; no doubt there are persons who, when listening to a symphony, are cold, do not understand, and are unmoved. But they may be classed as " abnormal." We must remember that there are many hunchbacks, many halt, many persons born blind, etc. But it is not from them we take our definition of mankind.

THIRD PART

MUSICAL THOUGHT AND PHYSIOLOGY

GENERALITIES

BEFORE he undergoes emotion, thinks, and forms part of an active social group, man is constituted from the working of certain organs ; and the study of his physical nature generally serves as the basis or as the introduction to the study of his intellectual nature.

In discussing physiology only at this part of the book we are following an unusual order, and one which may seem paradoxical. We have been forced to do so by our anxiety to begin the inquiry by the observation of a specific fact, capable of serving as basis to a certainty, and by the design of not entering till later upon the field of hypotheses. This specific fact is musical thought, without which there can be no music ; the field of hypotheses is what the vulgar call " science."

After having studied the modalities of musical thought, we will now study its conditions. The first is the structure of the ear ; but here begins a fresh realm, that of the very complicated and obscure phenomena on the border-line between the subjective and the objective life, regarding which the most ingenious observers, notwithstanding their endeavours to remain faithful to the scientific spirit, can very often only make hypotheses which escape all experimental check. They are not, it is true, reduced in every case to a confession of ignorance. Thinking over what is known, and also what is not yet known, it may be said that physiological acoustics form a world of marvels.

First, it is certain that sound impressions produce in us involuntary reactions which are purely mechanical. Careful experiments, the results of which have been noted with mathematical precision, enable us to accept this as an established fact. Music causes reactions on the respiratory system, on the circulation, the nerves, and the periphery. No doubt, if in examining these phenomena the effect produced by the audition of a major or minor scale, of a single consonant or dissonant chord, of a single high or low note, had alone been considered, no conclusions could have been drawn without an incorrect use of the word "music"; but experiments have been carried out with real compositions—a funeral march of Chopin, an elegy by Massenet, a melody of Wagner, Gounod, etc.—and the results obtained have the same weight as any other well-observed fact.

But here begins a veritable usurpation on the part of physiology. It has been attempted to use the reactions observed to explain musical emotion by applying to music the ideas of James. According to this last, we must not say : this man turns pale, trembles, breathes heavily, has a haggard look, etc., *because he is frightened ;* we must say : he has a feeling of fear *because, under the influence*

of an image, he has turned pale, trembled, etc. We
must not say : that young girl blushed through a
feeling of timidity ; but : she felt timid *because
she blushed.* In a word, the psychical phenomenon
is only the reverberation within the consciousness
of the physiological phenomenon. It is the latter
which should determine everything.

This manner of understanding the order of things
is very paradoxical—which by no means signifies
that it is false—but it seems very difficult to apply
it to music.

It is certain that if we first admit that music,
not operating on concepts, is a matter of pure
sensation (which is very nearly what Helmholtz
says), the explanation of the musical phenomenon
is relatively easy. But this principle is a postulate.
When we experiment on other things than the
rattling of shovels as heard by dogs, sick people, or
idiots, the psychical phenomenon and the physiological phenomenon form such a complex, and
so suddenly, that it is impossible to say which is
earlier than the other : the purely scientific method,
anxious for affirmations easy of control, does not
permit of such dogmatism.

Objections of a less general nature may be made
to the uncompromising thesis of the physiologists.
Thus many persons are affected in their respiratory, circulatory, and nervous system on hearing a
beautiful poem recited by a reader unable to use
the art of the comedian and the seductions of the
voice on the ear. In such a case, is it not the
sense of the words, and not their acoustic organization alone, which produces the effect?

There is a shuddering of the periphery which is
supposed to be a sign of the impression of the
" sublime." I note that it is felt not infrequently
at the theatre or concert, all in connection with
matters insignificant enough in themselves, which,
however, the mind of the hearer, by virtue of its
own activity, interprets after its own manner by
putting into the formulas employed a sense different
from that intended by the author.

Finally, there are observations manifestly incorrect or of exceptional order, which certain physiologists have thought proper to take as the bases of
a doctrine by reason of illegitimate generalizations.
For instance, in a *Bulletin de l'Académie de Médecine*
(1895), we read that the minor mode has a " character of weakness, of indecision, and of sadness,"
and possesses " a special aptitude for the expression of the *depressed* states of humanity." These
assertions of M. Ferrand enable us to mark how
deceptive is the " scientific " label. It is possible
that in certain cases and with certain subjects the
minor mode may have produced these restrictive
effects of sadness and depression ; but what gives
us the right to generalize ? We have shown in
former pages that there are thousands of popular songs which express joy and yet are in the
minor. Personally, I am inclined to assert that
this minor mode expresses virile energy, with
a serious character and a tendency to action which
is exactly the opposite of sadness and the " depressed state " ; moreover, this was the opinion of
all antiquity, which saw in the Dorian mode—one
of the types of our minor mode—a reflection of the

genius of Sparta! What then is the worth, from a
" scientific " point of view, of a doctrine which
stumbles against such objections as these ?

Too often do physiologists argue on abnormal
cases, ignore contradictory facts, and yet draw
inductions which comprise everything. In the name
of scientific thought, they should be taught more
prudence.

Here is another material error among many
(I mean by this a certain number of legends which
have been accepted as real truths and as a base
of doctrine). In most of the works devoted to a
physiological theory of the musical art we find
mentioned this fact—by way of argument—that in
all times there has existed a therapeutics based on
singing or on instrumental melody. It seems to
me difficult to interpret the facts of history more
against their plain sense. It is perfectly true—we
know it by many testimonies—that music has been
used for the attempted cure of certain diseases ; but
if we go back to the origin of this usage we come
upon the belief that a sick person is one in
whom dwells an evil spirit, and that music may cure
the patient because it acts *upon spirits*. Such a
superstition as this has for basis a fact, the moral
power of song, which is the exact opposite to the
physiological thesis : if it can be put to profit by
any system, in the matter of music, it is by the
intellectualistic, and still better by the metaphysical
—even the transcendental—system.

Let us, then, admit that music produces reactions
of the organism, but let us acknowledge that in
certain cases it will be impossible for us to assert,

when formulating a law, whether these reactions are earlier than, concomitant with, or subsequent to the purely psychical effects of expression. If we hear an experiment quoted, we shall first assure ourselves that it had for object a real musical phenomenon ; we shall insist that all the conditions of the phenomenon shall be realized ; and we shall inquire on what the generalization is based.

Lastly, in taking up this new part of our programme, we must be prepared to receive another contribution, and not a tyrannical cut-and-dried doctrine.

CHAPTER I

LET us indicate the stages of the journey accomplished by sounds before arriving at the special
sense which makes of them a synthesis and
transforms them into music : (1) An elastic body,
outside ourselves, is set in vibration ; (2) this
perturbation communicates itself to the air and
propels itself in it ; it arrives at that receiving and transmitting organ, the ear ; (3) it
penetrates into a part of the ear, *i.e.* the laby-
rinth, where it affects the extremities of the
network of a special nerve ; (4) the sound
is transmitted to a centre localized in the
brain ; (5) thence, it is conveyed to the consciousness.

The two first stages of this journey have been
completely explored ; we can *see* and *describe* in
writing all the movements which take place
there. It is in No. 3 that the difficulties
begin.

The general construction of the ear is known to
us, but all its anatomical elements do not appear
to have been exhausted by analysis. Especially it is
not known what is the part played by each portion
in the triple function of receiving, transporting,

and communicating the waves of sound to the
sensitive parts.

I never read, in the most recent works, a descrip-
tion of the ear without thinking of geographical
treatises, where certain distant countries in the
neighbourhood of the poles bear the names of the
fortunate explorers who first discovered them.
Discoveries have been made, and no doubt more
will follow, in the auricular tissues, discoveries to
which the names of scholars will remain ap-
pended ; but we are still very far from being able
to define in a complete and satisfactory manner
the mechanism of hearing.

We are confronted by two theories : the one of
partial, the other of total, variable, and flexible
accommodation.

1st. The first has been adopted by Helmholtz.*
When new elements in the field of the infinitesimal
are just discovered, it is difficult to resist the
temptation of assigning to them a decisive part in
the solution of the problem in hand. According to
Helmholtz, the ear has a special organ for the re-
ception of each sound, one of these elastic pillars,
termed *pillars of Corti*, forming an arch over the
basilar membrane and stretching over the tops of
the others.   An idea of their size will be gathered
from the fact that over three thousand of them have
been counted.   They might be assimilated, when
they receive the impact of the sound waves, to the
keys of a piano yielding under the pressure of the
player.   It has even been said that each of these
pillars, when vibrating under the influence of a

* *Die Lehre von der Tonemfindungen*, edition 1877, p. 227.

given sound, can divide itself and give partial impressions in accordance with the laws of multiple resonance.*

Though this theory (stripped of the improbable hypothesis just mentioned) is not yet a definitely accepted doctrine and is somewhat repugnant to me, I am bound to say that it has found a serious champion in the Abbé Rousselot, who has continued and perfected in many points the work of Helmholtz. Here is a very brief account of the researches which the Abbé Rousselot has effected in his Laboratory of Experimental Phonetics at the Collège de France.

The sound of each of the vowels *ou, a, e, i, o, u,* is not simple, but formed of a group of compound sounds of a fixed intensity, among which one or two are characteristic. To ascertain positively this most important phenomenon, the Abbé Rousselot has constructed a very ingenious resonator, greatly superior to that of Helmholtz, for, instead of only serving for one simple given sound, it allows the whole series contained in a given compound to be observed. It is in form a cylinder with a movable bottom ; and, while a vowel is being emitted in front of one of its extremities, the bottom of the instrument is drawn forward by a steady movement towards the source of the emission. The length of the column of air is thus modified, and this causes the resonator to vibrate successively, by sympathy with *all* the simple sounds it meets on the road, and these are made recognizable to the ear by isolating them one after the other. It suffices, at

* Mach, *Beiträge zur Analyse der Empfindungen*, Jena, 1866, p. 113.

any given moment, to note the dimension given to the cylinder in order to obtain the wave length and, consequently, the number of vibrations, thus allowing the sound perceived to be identified.

This experiment, the basis of all the explanations which follow, once duly established, the following facts are observed. Certain defective ears, instead of perceiving the compound sound, as is usual, have quite a different impression ; *u* is uttered, and they hear *o* for *e*, *i*, etc. The explanation would seem to be that in the series of receptive organs these ears have gaps or islands of deafness which, in certain cases, do not allow them to grasp the characteristic components of the vowel emitted. They have, at the same time, some remains of the auditory apparatus which, acting separately, cause them to hear with predominant intensity *one* harmonic which ought to be, as it were, merged. in a synthesis ; and, according to whether this harmonic is more or less distant from its normal characteristic, the tone of the vowel heard becomes modified. The result may be different, but of a like nature, if the ear perceives *two* harmonics bordering upon the characteristic one.

From all this, consequences may be drawn which it is easy to foresee. If, by the aid of the improved resonator (called the Universal Resonator), we commence to determine objectively, the composition of all the vowels, and if, on the other hand, we observe in a single case the way in which a defective ear perceives a vowel, it is easy to deduce how the same ear will behave towards all the other vowels. In the second place, we are brought to believe that *everything happens, in the mechanism of hearing, as if there were a special organ for the perception of each simple sound.*

This is a fascinating idea, but has it any character of certainty ? First, how can we admit that fibres one-twentieth of a millimetre long can sympathize with sounds of considerable wave-length ?

Granting that there are 200 fibres for the perception of noises, this would leave 2800 for the musical sounds ; and as these musical sounds do not comprise more than 7 octaves, it makes 400 fibres for each, or a little more than 33 sounds in an interval of a full tone. In other terms, between *Do* ♮ and *Ré* ♮ we ought to be able to perceive, in the easiest way, 33 different sounds (since we have, according to the hypothesis, a special organ for each) !

The objection has also been made that birds, which have such delicate hearing and a relatively well-developed musical sense, do not possess these pillars. This objection appeared decisive. Thus one had to fall back on the fibres called those of *Hensen,* to the number of 60,000, each one tuned to a given sound.

2nd. The second principal hypothesis (there are some secondary ones) is that of total accommodation. The ear would thus be a very flexible instrument, whose elements would have no specialized function ; but which would become modified, in response to solicitations from without, by adapting itself in its entirety to the various sounds perceived.

This opinion raises fewer difficulties than the other ; it is the one we should willingly accept, but

on one condition, to wit: that it be granted that
the ear does not, solely and necessarily, accommodate itself according to the sensations arriving
from without by a kind of pure mechanism, but
according to the images already localized by habit
in the cellular centres of the cerebral cortex and
according to an idea which imposes its form on
the sensation: in a word, by the musical sense
itself.

Let us take an example. Here is a formula of
Wagner (*Rheingold*)—

which, played on the piano, makes me perceive the
group *Sol*—*Mi* as an interval of the sixth belonging
to the third inversion of the perfect chord *Do, Mi,
Sol.* Here is another formula from the same
score—the wail of the Rhine maidens who have
lost their gold—

Here I perceive the same group (emitted by *the
same keys* of the piano) as belonging to the chord
of diminished seventh, having as fundamental the
dominant of *Do.* This distinction is not a subtlety
of analysis: every listener will grasp this change,
which produces the very beautiful effect of a
mournful and strange wail, which is steeped in
poetry.

Between *Sol*—*Mi*♮ and *Sol*—*Fa*♭ there is a fairly

notable difference. $Sol-Mi \natural$ $\frac{1}{7}\frac{2}{5}\frac{5}{}$; $Sol-Fa \flat$ $\frac{1}{7}\frac{2}{5}\frac{8}{}$, or say, an interval between the two, expressed by the relation $\frac{1}{1}\frac{2}{2}\frac{8}{5}$. Why, with an instrument with fixed notes like the piano, have I the very clear impression of this non-identity? Why is $Sol-Mi \natural$ perceived as a consonance, and $Sol-Fa \flat$ as a dissonance, although on my keyboard the vibrations producing these two groups are exactly the same? Is it not, in one formula as in the other, in consequence of that which precedes and follows the two intervals? Their antecedents and their subsequents are not the same; which accounts for my hearing them differently.

The acoustic impression therefore resolves itself here into the perception of a relation. Now, a relation is never given by a sensation; no fibre, however delicately organized we may imagine it, can do that; the intervention of an act of the intelligence is necessary. The ear, therefore, would appear to accommodate itself according to other laws than those of physiology.

Any enharmonic modulation should offer a similar example. There exists in this case an instantaneous transformation of a sound-phenomenon into a musical phenomenon, which constitutes precisely the originality of the physiological facts. The ear does not make the hearing as a mould gives its form to the fluid matter poured into it; to its passive receptivity there is added a rapid act which appreciates, undoes, reforms, and makes perfect the work of the auditory sense.

There is no more disagreeable dissonance, taken by itself, than that of $Mi \natural$ ($\frac{5}{4}$) against $Mi \sharp$ ($\frac{1}{9}\frac{2}{6}\frac{5}{}$),

yet Schumann produces with it a charming effect
in his song *Mondnacht !* The dissonance of major
second and minor second comes in no less than ten
times in an exquisite pianoforte piece by the same
Schumann : *Einsame Blumen* (" Lonely Flowers ").
Anywhere else they would be intolerable ; in this
case, again, it is the progression of the parts, the
antecedents, and the subsequences of the counter-
point—in a word, the *sense*—which imposes on the
ear a very pleasant impression.

We can quote a phenomenon of the same nature
in very curious cases, where it would seem that
the musical intelligence has a direct influence on
the quality of the sound.   There is the well-known
experiment made with laths of wood, suitably
shaped and of various densities : each one falling
separately on the floor simply gives an impression
of noise.   If allowed to fall in a certain order, they
give a very clear impression of the gamut.   We
have to admit either that the mind instantaneously
modifies the sensation (the wave-sound remaining
the same), or else that the ear does not react, like the
apparatus of which the spring has been . released,
but possesses a kind of " judgment."

It seems impossible to explain the very complex
phenomena of audition, if we depart from the
principle that the ear is a mechanism acting
according to purely physical laws of immovable
fixity ; it is quite another thing if we admit a kind
of compenetration of the musical psychological life
and of the auditory organ, and if we consider this
organ as actually at the stage of a possibly un-
finished evolution.

§ 1. Capacity of the Ear for Education

When one thinks that all primitive instruments were made for a small number of notes, and if we recollect the resemblances furnished by the general study of evolution, it is permissible to conjecture that the ear, considered as reacting to certain outside solicitations, began by very limited functional manifestations. It is possible that it was only sensible at first to sounds subject to periodicity, to the fundamental intervals: *i.e.* the fifth and the fourth. This hypothesis seems borne out by the descriptions which have reached us of the primitive lyres and by the history of the scale, at first limited to four notes: *Do, Fa, Sol, Do*. The introduction of the *La* and the *Mi* has been attributed to Terpander, that of the *Si* and *Ré* to Pythagoras.

Among the moderns, the passage from the simple to the compound has been quite as slow; composition in the chromatic style only dates from the epoch when Cyprian de Rore wrote his madrigals (middle of the sixteenth century).

A similar process seems to characterize the history of the notion of colours. Neither in the Koran nor the Bible, any more than in the hymns of the Rig-Veda, is the blue colour of the sky ever mentioned. Red and yellow, a kind of dominants, are the first differentiations effected, because they belong to the longest and most powerful ethereal waves. To Aristotle the rainbow only had three colours; red, green, and blue, and their shades only became specific sensations at a fairly late date.

Acquiring, like the retina, new aptitudes under

the incessant impacts of the molecules of the ether, the ear improved by degrees under the influence of circumstances such as the chase, war, and all the relations of social life. It is at the present day the paramount artistic sense, certainly superior to that of vision, for its impressions have given rise to the language which is most capable of unifying individuals and of creating collective emotions, and has finally reacted on the ear itself.

It is no longer a machine, the study of which belongs only to anatomy and its microscopes, or to physics, but an organism into whose tissues penetrate, every minute, phenomena of a psychical order. The ear has a purely organic memory, similar to that which stores itself up in the fingers of the virtuoso, capable of playing " by heart " the most difficult compositions, while carrying on a conversation on any given subject. It compares, it appreciates, and it judges, quite apart from the intensity of the impact, the distance which separates it from the source of emission. It selects, for one of the marvels of its structure is that it not only hears, but also, that it does not hear certain sounds which, though musical in themselves, would render music impossible were they perceived. It has arrived at such a degree of sensibility that certain conflicts of vibrations are a positive suffering to it. It distinguishes the finest shades ; lastly, if it makes the synthesis of sound, it excels—and that is its superiority over the eye— in the analysis of a group of sounds.

The eye is unable to analyse its impressions. If, for example, we cause to revolve rapidly a disc on which bands of all colours have been superposed, the eye will only see one result : the colour white. On the contrary, sound a perfect chord, and if his ear be at all educated, the listener will distinguish the three notes, their position, and their timbre. While it is difficult for us to admit that we have simultaneous states of consciousness, he will say whether the first note is given by a violin, the second by an alto, and the third by a wind instrument. In the middle of the rendering of a symphony by eighty or a hundred musicians, the conductor, sensitive to a slight in-accuracy of tone, will direct one of his musicians to tune his first string slightly up or down. We may add that the eye only properly catches the waves in front of it. The ear, on the contrary, can equally well receive the waves of sound whether the subject be in front, behind, or at the side of the source of emission.

All this, no doubt, presumes a superior mechanism of which it would be a very feeble explanation to urge that the need of hearing ended in creating the means of hearing ; but it must be admitted that psychical life intermingles with the organs which are its condition, and that the boundaries of physiology cannot be very accurately defined. As between the sonorous body and the receptive appa-ratus there must exist a medium of conduction, such as the air. Thus, in the same way, while passing from the network of nerves and the centres of the brain to the consciousness, the vibrations seem to traverse a medium formed of habits, of localized images and of innate or acquired aptitudes. . . .

Q

CHAPTER II

THE LOCALIZATION OF IMAGES

IF now, we resume the journey the broad lines of which have been indicated above, and study its last stage—the one in which the sound-waves impress themselves on the brain—we note some very curious phenomena, which should be noted here. The attempt has been made to deduce from these phenomena conclusions which they do not warrant. They are in no way incompatible with the theory of musical thought (acting in the same manner as verbal thought, but without concepts) which has been upheld in this book. I have already had to reproach certain scholars with judging music from laboratory experiments, which do not deserve the name of music. We shall see that they do not always abide by the experimental method, and sometimes argue like theologians.

The articulate verbal language and the musical language—the one rendering thought, the other the emotion which is its accompaniment—are closely united, in the embryo state, in the instinctive and natural speech observable in the child, the non-civilized, and the man under some emotion to which he gives free vent; but they are united somewhat in the same way as two persons standing back to back ; the first step forward and they separate, to commence evolutions very different from one another.

The first language was composed of words with a conventional and partly intelligible meaning ; the second is formed of sounds which have been called positive gestures of the muscles, provoked by involuntary reactions and of a universally intelligible meaning. But a moment comes when the logical element of speech and the melodious element are differentiated, bifurcate, and organize themselves separately. This dissociation might have for symbol the structure of the lyre, the two horns of which, forming the base of the instrument after starting from a common point, follow different directions.

First of all, each of the two languages primitively united acquires new functions. Thus, the verbal language, which, in its inception, only had two, audition and articulate emission, adds to these writing and reading ; while the musical language, to audition, writing, reading, and song adds instrumental execution. In the second place, it is thought that each of these functions is rendered possible by the localization in the brain of what may be called, though such a word may be rather inappropriate, groups of distinct *images*. Truth to say, this doctrine of localizations does not present itself with proofs from anatomical observation. It has been recently attacked (together with the theory of Broca) by one of the most distinguished of Charcot's pupils, Dr. Marie ; and, after the rejoinder of Déjerine, the question may still be called an open one. With this reservation, we give a very concise account of a theory of which we must, especially, bear in mind the general principles.

As regards speech, the verbal auditive images are localized, according to the majority of physiologists, in the posterior part of the first temporal lobe, and, according to certain authors, in the first circumvolution of the left temporo-sphenoidal lobe, called " Wernicke's centre " ; the visual images of words are localized in the lower parietal lobe, called " Déjerine's centre," or " Kussmaull's centre " ; the images of articulation in the posterior part of the third left frontal circumvolution, at a point called " Broca's centre." As to the graphic images (the localization of which, it is true, has been rejected by many neurologists), they have, as the seat of their concentration and activity, a place situated at the foot of the second frontal circumvolution, called " Exner's centre."

As regards music, hypothesis no doubt has more than once to be called in, and observation is not so far advanced. For the brain, as for the ear, lengthy researches are still necessary and difficult. Still (except for the graphic centre), the parallelism of the musical and verbal localizations seems very defensible to the greatest experts in these matters. The images of auditive musical sensation would be localized in a centre which forms a specialized function of the general auditive centre ; the visual images necessary for notation would be localized in a centre, itself included in that of sight generally ; the images allowing emission and song would specialize a function of articulate speech ; graphic images, indispensable for guiding the movements which realize writing, would be localized, perhaps, in certain cellular groups of the centre of verbal writing. As for instrumental execution, it would proceed from several functional localizations, the same muscles not being always called into play : for instance, the pianist plays with his hands, the organist with his feet as well as his hands ; the flute player with his hands and his breathing apparatus, etc.

The distinction between these two groups of functions—verbal language and musical language : and, in each group, between the functions of the specializations—is founded on clinical observations. Indeed, it is by closely studying the abnormal, the hysterical, the mentally deranged, the degenerates, and those afflicted with hereditary taints, and by examining very carefully the connexity or the independence of certain disorders, that it has been possible to deduce logically the existence of the several centres, and their total, unequal, or partial synergy. It was first noted that the functions of the musical language did not become disturbed together with those of the verbal language, and that often, if not always, one or the other could be altered or reduced to impotence while the other remained normal ; it had therefore to be recognized that they constituted two physiologically distinct systems.

For the rest, I imagine that, while making use of the lesions (hæmorrhage, softening, etc.) which disease has caused in brains hitherto normal, neurologists consider the proofs from these irregular cases as a last resort.

§ 1. Aphasias and Amusias

The localization, on distinct points and in a separate system, of musical images confirms the independence and originality we have claimed for music. This differentiation of the physiological mechanism, ending in a dualism of autonomy, results from the observation of aphasias and amusias.

We term aphasia the loss of the functions of the verbal language, and " amusia " that of the functions of the musical language. Either one or the other may be total or partial, affecting either the centres of sensorial images (reading) or the centres of images of movement (song, writing, execution). Finally, they may be non-concomitant. Here are a few cases I borrow from Dr. Ingegnieros.*

1st. A young man, aged twenty-five, accustomed to perform a great deal of music, sat down to the piano one evening. He remained motionless, as if suddenly impotent. He could find nothing to play. It seemed to him " that memory had left his brain." He opened a score. He was no longer able to read it. He tried to whistle, to hum the opening bars of his favourite melodics. It was of no avail. The inhibition was complete. The patient had completely lost the language in all its functions : memory, song, reading, and execution. (*Total sensorial and motor amusia.*)

2nd. A young woman, twenty years of age, had an attack of hysteria ; since then, every time she sat down to the piano, she imagined "she was playing on an instrument without strings." She

* *Le langage musical et ses troubles hystériques.* Alcan, 1907.

had preserved the power of singing and execution by simple muscular memory, but neither heard what she sang nor what she played. The loss of musical audition was complete as to all instruments and voices. (*Partial sensorial amusia : deafness.*)

3rd. A woman of twenty-two had an excellent ear for music, read perfectly, could also write music, but phonation (musical) and articulation (of the verbal language) were entirely lost. (*Partial motor amusia, combined with dumbness.*)

4th. A girl of seventeen, through convulsions brought on by disappointment in love, lost the faculty of singing while still able to read, write, hear, and execute music. Concurrently, all the functions of the verbal language had disappeared. (*Partial motor amusia, combined with complete motor aphasia.*)

5th. A young woman became unable to move her fingers at the piano, while still capable of hearing, reading, and writing music. (*Partial motor amusia.*)

Anomalies have also been observed, due not to any lack, but to irregular conditions : such as the exaggeration or the perversion of a function. A young woman of twenty-nine could no longer read a printed text unless she sang it with all the musical inflections of an interminable romance, continuously improvised. The subject of the reading, whether newspaper, letter, scientific work, novel, etc., did not affect the song. Here is the morbid synergy of a function of the sensorial images in the articulate language, with a function of the motor images, become preponderant, in the musical language.

A young Creole was haunted by the memory of a song in an operetta, especially at night, and lost her sleep through it. Here is a predominance, with recoil on the general organism, of the function of the sensorial and motor images.

A young lady violinist of the Institute of Montevideo failed in an examination for which she had worked hard, and this failure brought on convulsions. Ten years after she still held the violin in horror ; and every time she heard it she had a fresh attack. She had to retire from all society life.— Here is a partial exaggeration of the functions of the sensorial images, due to an association of ideas which had become indissoluble.

A man took an aversion to piano playing. By degrees all music, vocal and instrumental, became intolerable to him ; at length, bells, whistles, sirens, and electric bells inspired him with an unconquerable irritation, and hearing a military band pass caused him to faint away.—The same as above : hyperæsthesia of a centre of sensorial images, without association of ideas.

A young woman, of odd tastes, very fond of music, and a fair pianist, divided her répertoire into several groups : red, green, blue, white ; she could only perceive sounds when associated with colours. —Here is a morbid connexity of two groups of different sensorial images.

These examples, which might be multiplied, have enabled a classification of the diseases of the musical language to be made, and at the same time its different functions to be considered as independent. It is plain that in the case of a patient who can

hear words, but not perceive singing, or who can
sing, but has lost the faculty of writing music, one
has the right to assert that these various functions
are diversely localized. They may be tabulated as
follows—

I. Aphasias	*Sensory* (centripetal function)	{ Verbal deafness { „ blindness
	Motor (centrifugal function)	{ Aphasia, properly so called { Agraphia
II. Amusias	*Sensory*	{ Musical deafness { Inability to read music
	Motor	{ Loss of singing power { „ „ writing „ { „ „ power of instru- mental execution

To this last group we should perhaps add the
hypermusias, due to exaggerations of functions,
and the *paramusias*, due to morbid associations
which have become more or less fixed.

Let us now inquire what conclusions may be
drawn from these facts.

From a study of the centres of musical language,
the different types of the musician have been determined, by virtue of a predominance of some of
these centres over others ; and, finally, the musical
intelligence itself, which would seem to be an
aptitude for the development of this special language. Here are some inextricable difficulties,
which certain physiologists have eluded by the use
of vague formulas, unworthy of a scholar, or even,
which is worse, by contradictory ones.

Having thus sought a useful contribution from
physiological teaching, we shall now be compelled
to combat its encroachments.

CHAPTER III

MUSICAL INTELLIGENCE

IN their normal state the centres of musical language are usually synergetic, with a predominance of the activity of one of them, produced by hereditary predisposition, congenital instinct, or education. For instance, the talent of the pianist who is a virtuoso without being a composer presupposes the common activity of *all* the centres, with a predominance of the motor images. The merit of the amateur who possesses an excellent memory for melody (without, at the same time, that of words or figures) presupposes a predominant activity of the sensorial centres, almost invariably linked with a certain aptitude for execution. But to remember music, to decipher it, to write it (materially), are, after all, but secondary operations. Above this is the musical intelligence. Let us see how it is attempted to explain this.

I will briefly examine the theory put forth by Dr. Ingegnieros, because it comprises the most recent theories. If it appeared as a simple contribution to the study of musical phenomena, we should only have to note the results of the experiments it makes known. But, as Pythagoras, after having found the numerical relations expressing certain intervals, claimed to draw from them a

doctrine regarding the plants and the organization
of the universe, so, at the present day, most scholars
find it difficult to resist the temptation of generalizing *à outrance* and of making facts say more than
they really do. Every day they set literary men or
the " æsthetes " the sorry example of a method
which ceases to be scientific by the substitution of
romance for observation.

The musical intelligence, we are told, comprises
four kinds of aptitudes—

" 1st. The individual aptitude for perceiving the
auditory sensations provoked by musical stimula-
tion."—This is self-evident, and amounts to saying
that the musically intelligent have a delicate ear.

" 2ndly. The memory of musical sensations,
comprising the preservation of auditory images, the
power of reproducing them, or the capacity of local-
izing them, and the remembrance of the emotional
states which accompany the stimulations produced
by music."—An excellent observation to which we
eagerly subscribe. Memory is almost always the certain sign of musical intelligence, and it is evident that
it implies the remembrance of the emotional states
provoked by former stimulations. The musician
who, by his fireside, reads an orchestral score as he
would a journal or a book associates the visual
images of the notes with the actual effect, previously
felt and preserved by him, which the instruments
of the orchestra would produce in rendering the particular notes. Deciphering is a perpetual evocation,
a sort of abstract emotion produced by an internal
and silent execution, based on the recollection.

3rdly. " Musical intelligence includes the reproductive imagination."—This is a form of the memory; it is the aptitude for bringing back to the domain of consciousness images which, once perceived, had passed into the unconscious state.

4thly. " Musical intelligence comprises the constructive imagination, or so called musical fancy; that is to say, the aptitude for transforming and combining images without subordinating them to the memory of their original perception."—We may leave out of the question this novel aptitude, seeing that, in order to be musically intelligent, it is in no way necessary to be able to compose. Moreover, it might be said that musical creation, in a great number of cases, and in its elementary form, is a recollection of the images previously stored in the mind. Let us beware of the false analogy here established between the verbal and the musical language. In the case of the former, the normal working of the intelligence comprises the aptitude for creating, or transforming and combining, at the same time as the aptitude for perceiving. What would be, indeed, a person who could hear but not speak ? But, in the case of the musician, his intelligence may be very active, without lapses, and yet be limited to hearing. The verbal language is founded on necessity or utility ; the musical language is æsthetic, an object of luxury. The first develops among individuals acting equally and for the same reason ; the second presupposes a public, an essential distinction between performers and listeners who take no part.

" 5thly. The intelligence of the musician further comprises ' musical ideation ' in its figurative sense, corresponding to what it is agreed to term 'musical ideas,' *i.e.*: a certain co-ordination or series of emotional states associated with an idea by education. It is formed by the three most developed processes of the musical intelligence : (*a*) the *conception*, or the aptitude for comparing, associating, and abstracting the various elements of music and its representative states ; (*b*) the *musical judgment*, or the aptitude for perceiving and interpreting the relations of affinity, difference, quantity, identity, genesis, and development between these elements and these states ; (*c*) *musical logic*, or the aptitude for co-ordinating, subordinating, and connecting the technical and psychological elements of the musical language in a manner analogous to the logic of ordinary verbal thought."*—Here we come to the delicate part of the question, and we must keep close touch with the meaning of the terms employed.

Of the first three operations mentioned—*comparison, association, abstraction*—we may disregard the first two, seeing that they are already implied in the aptitude for being affected by auditory sensations. To perceive (musically) a sound is to connect it with a tonic, which is the same as " comparison and association." As to knowing how to *abstract*, it is certainly one of the essential conditions of musical intelligence if by this it is meant to convey that, given the formula expressive of an emotional state, the musician should be able to appreciate and enjoy this formula *per se*, regardless of the sentiments or the object with which it was originally connected. Thus, a musically intelligent

* Dr. Ingegnieros, *loc. cit.*, pp. 65-8.

person is he who, in an opera, appreciates the
melody and the instrumentation by isolating them
and disregarding the libretto and the scenery.
All history shows that in music progress has taken
place thanks to this operation : viz. music weaned
by degrees from literature, from utilitarian action,
and from visual forms.

But this separation once effected, on what principle does there form in the composer's mind the
independent synthesis of the musical images, and
in that of the listener an intelligent perception of
the same synthesis ?—According to an " ideation,"
we are told, that is to say, " *a certain co-ordination.*" This is very vague and very insufficient.

An " idea " is a simple image, not an organizing
principle, and the words I have underlined might
be applied to no matter what, for everything
whatever can be considered as a *certain* co-
ordination ; it has a *proprium quid.* It is this
proprium quid which must be clearly explained if
we would be scientific. Shall we find it in " the
aptitude for perceiving and interpreting the relations of affinity, difference, quantity, identity, etc.,"
of musical elements ? No, certainly not, for to
possess this aptitude is to know the rules of harmony, and harmony is no more music than verbal
grammar, with its rules of syntax, is poetry.

Shall we find it in the aptitude for grasping the
relation which exists between the musical phrase
and such or such a state of emotion ? Still less is
this the case. First, we have just seen that to be a
real musician one must have the power of abstraction ; secondly, the perception of this relation is

most generally impossible. Take the charming
Sonata of Beethoven (Op. 49) for piano—

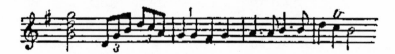

I think I fully appreciate it—which is really not
a difficult matter—but I assert that no one could
declare, without incurring ridicule, what state it
expresses. There certainly is one, but the composer has not enunciated it; probably he could
not have done so, and we have no need to know it.
In the second place, does any one think that to
hear this phrase with intelligence it is enough to
know what is a perfect concord, a fifth, a triplet,
an embroidery, a passing note, a mediant, an imperfect cadence? Is it with such scholarly pedantry
that one listens to the music of a Mozart? Anxious
to arrive at something precise, and manifestly embarrassed, the author I have quoted concludes by
saying that the elements of the musical language
are co-ordinated *in a way analogous to the logic of
the ordinary verbal thought.*

This is a very serious matter. It would simplify
everything were it exact and capable of proof.
Unfortunately, the word "analogy" implies differences as well as resemblances; in this case it is
the *differences* which constitute the specific phenomenon; they must not be mentioned in a vague
formula, which resolves the chief difficulty by
pretermission.

In the same way that there is a logic in the verbal
language, so is there one in the musical language:

this is the very general principle that may be laid
down ; but the use of the word "co-ordination" is
insufficient to make it plain, for it ought to be
stated under what law this co-ordination is effected.
When one confines oneself to recalling "what it is
agreed to call musical ideas," one forgets that,
since the time of Plato, the principal duty of
science is precisely the control or explanation of
conventional judgments ; one forgets, likewise, that
an "idea" is a simple image, and can only form
a synthesis with other ideas thanks to something
which dominates it.

Logical resemblances between the two languages ?
I fail to see any. The identity of certain intervals,
both in instinctive speech and in melody, constitute
a common material, but by no means obliges the intelligence to put it in operation the same way. The
rhythm of a musical phrase can be dissected exactly
like that of a phrase written in irregular verse, and
a certain sonata of Beethoven is constructed on the
same plan as one of Pindar's odes ; but rhythm is
not logic. The proof of this is that, by isolating it,
all interest in the thought is removed. I might,
indeed, reproduce on the drum the rhythm of the
sonata of Beethoven of which the beginning is given
above ; but there would no longer be anything
musical in it.

The means of "expression" (intensity, variations of movement, timbres, *shades*) are the same, but
music can dispense with them ; they are, so to speak,
external to it, and proceed rather from the executant
than from the composer.

There is no indication of the "shades" in certain

works of the greatest masters ; they have, nevertheless, a very clear meaning. To exhaust all
possible hypotheses, I will add that there exists in
music a very important art, which has its counterpart in literature, and which is the art of development. A verbal formula is taken, then on each of its
component words there is constructed, by means of
analysis, a system of words, more or less extended.
The greatest musicians have shown their superiority
in the use of this process ; Brahms has made an
exaggerated use of it. But of two things one :
either this musical " development " is purely
formal, and therefore of moderate value ; or else it
is organic, essential (as it always is in Beethoven),
and, in that case, it simply renews the thought, so
that the explanation we are seeking must again
be foiled by an inexplicable *proprium quid.*

However much we may multiply analyses, unless
we ignore, in a problem of this kind, all that is
artistic, and thus either argue beside the question
or waste time on trifling matters of which we
exaggerate the importance, we cannot escape
the following observation : to be intelligent in
music is to *understand.* Understand what ?—the
thought that a melody *exists.* This is to be capable
of seeing a meaning where concepts do not exist ;
a meaning where there do not exist words ; a logic
where all the processes of verbal dialectics are excluded and replaced by a kind of direct intuition.

That this faculty may be educated, perfected by
the aid of practice and culture, cannot be denied ;
but is not this the case with the intelligence also ?
Aptitude for education is not a characteristic ;

R

before understanding *better*, one must have already some understanding. Thus, before giving skilful attention to a plant, the cleverest horticulturist of Haarlem or Rotterdam must first have the seed from which the plant springs. We must further note that education in the technical language is in no way necessary to the musical intelligence. The crowd is easily moved by eloquence, yet knows nothing of rhetoric. In the same way, the musical thought may be understood by persons totally ignorant of music, not only of harmony and counter-point, but even of the notes of the scale. The active co-operation of all the centres of the language of music is not necessary ; one may possess musical intelligence without being a performer or singer (and *vice versa*), or even without having a good memory.

The parallelism established by physiologists between the localization of the sensory and motor images of the musical and verbal languages enables us to generalize this observation, and even to draw from it an argument as simple as it is decisive, in favour of our theory : there is no necessary relation between the activity of the centres of the verbal language and ordinary thought.

Would one venture to assert that a deep thinker like Pascal or Liebnitz was a man with good ear, an excellent memory, capital " phonation," and a splendid handwriting like a lawyer's clerk ? It is the same with a musically intelligent person.

It is through neglecting this evident fact that a classification of the various degrees of musical intelligence, in great part based on the distinction between the sensory and motor centres, has been made which is inadmissible. The examination of this point is not devoid of interest, for it brings in incidentally some rather curious facts.

§ 1. TONE DEAFNESS AND MUSICAL DEAFNESS— DEGREES OF MUSICAL INTELLIGENCE

This is how physiologists explain and settle the matter—

1st. Starting from the zero absolute, as physicists say, they place on the lowest rung of the ladder the "musical idiots." This idiocy "consists in hearing sounds of different pitch without perceiving a difference." "Not to perceive the difference," says Ferrand,[*] "between two neighbouring notes, and to think one hears the same sound when the performer's finger goes higher or lower when running over the contiguous steps of the musical scale . . . implies a special deafness," termed tone deafness. It is the deafness of the "musical idiot." Examples of musical idiocy : Victor Hugo, who has defined music as "the least disagreeable of all noises"; Andrew Lang, who declares he can only understand a melody when the words are nice; Théophile Gautier, who shared Hugo's opinion; Macaulay, who, according to the testimony of his nephew, was never able (save on one occasion) to distinguish one tune from another ; Cuvier ; the surgeon Desgenettes, who had a deep aversion to music, etc. ; and, Dr. Ingegnieros concludes : "*Musical idiots cannot perceive the pitch of sounds ; they hear noises instead of notes.*"

In this first statement, just given, I see a

* His teaching is adopted by Dr. Ingegnieros, *loc. cit.*, p. 69.

somewhat whimsical literary development, a few real misapprehensions, and an interpretation of facts far from scientific. It is rather amusing to see a Victor Hugo thrust down among the "idiots" of music, but is it sufficiently warranted by a simple witticism—which, moreover, might be taken for an eulogium of musical art? How could one dare to speak of the tone deafness of him who spoke so magnificently of Palestrina, and who wrote—

Gluck est un forêt ; Mozart est une source?

Andrew Lang figures in the same category because he has said : "It is the only art which is forcibly thrust upon us, since we cannot escape from sounds, though we can fly from paintings." Kant has written something similar : "Any one who draws from his pocket a scented handkerchief compels you, whether or no, to smell the perfume, just as, at church, the choir forces its chants upon you." But is this really a sufficient foundation for the diagnosis of "tone deafness"?

The testimonies of this or that writer on persons now deceased ought to be verified, but cannot be so. All this is somewhat "got up," a little "smart," amusing from the pen of a journalist, but inadmissible when said by a clinical authority. Tone deafness is really pathological, and does not exist in the normal organism. If a poet does not appreciate music, it is because he does not understand it, not because of any unlikely disability to tell a third or a fifth from unison. It is antipathy of a purely intellectual nature, similar to that of Lamartine for figures.

2nd. On the next higher rung comes "musical imbecility"; that is to say, the case of those "who can hear music, but do not understand it." Well and good; but does not the fact of "not understanding" imply a meaning to be understood"?

Various little facts are added. Goethe complained to Eckermann that he was not sufficiently sensitive to Mozart's music. Napoleon said that music disturbed his nervous system, and that he preferred listening to the stupidest, because it caused him less pain. Grant hated music; obliged to attend a musical séance in Paris, he considered that time as one of the dreariest in his life. Napoleon III frowned whenever he saw a piano opened. Gambetta regretted the time lost in listening to music, because it produced no impression on him. Zola could never understand the delights of amateurs of music. Stook could never appreciate any other than that of the inevitable *God Save the Queen*. Max Muller did not understand the singing of Jenny Lind, and explained his failing: "I am as refractory to sounds as some others are to colour." Fontenelle placed music among definitely incomprehensible things: "Society, women, music, and acrobats," etc., etc.

Let us admit all these observations, including the frown of Napoleon III interpreted as a sign of "imbecility." None of these cases differ from those classed in the first group; it is, again, musical unintelligence. Such persons do not *understand*, hence their boredom and aversion. If they do not understand, it is no wise because they are unable to connect the formula they hear " with the emotional states they are thought to express " ; the most accomplished musicians could not do so when listening to a fugue or certain sonatas. Neither is it, either, because they are ignorant of the technique. The relations of attraction or inhibition that exist between the notes may be correctly realized and perceived by the aid of phrases which are undeserving of the name of music—

We have here a regular sequence, devoid of meaning. The knowledge of technique is not indispensable to the intelligent hearer. It is a proof, no doubt, of a good education to be aware that in these four groups there is a perfect tonic chord followed by one on the sub-dominant, a third, which is an inversion of the seventh, on the dominant, and, lastly, a return to the tonic ; but this is a proof of scholarship, not a sign of intelligence. In fact, those possessed of the best technique do not listen to music in an analytical spirit. " Understanding " is quite another thing ! And it is quite natural that when one has not understood, music should simply seem a distressing noise.

3rd. A fortiori, we must keep to the same standpoint for judging the two higher forms of musical intelligence : the talent of execution and the genius of creation.

A pianist can only be considered to have " talent " if he has a comprehension served by sound organs, of the musical thought. He must certainly have a centre of acoustic sensations readily impressionable by the most delicate appeals from without, a highly differentiated and very active centre of visual images and of co-ordination, and a synergy of these different aptitudes or faculties. He must possess a good ear, a quick eye, and a sure hand. Memory, audition, reading, impressibility of the nervous system, and muscular movements have for him a very important and almost equivalent rôle. He must have very great energy, not only to play *fortissimo*, but also, and especially (like the singer), to distinguish the half tones of *piano* and *pianissimo ;* energy is further necessary to keep his nerves under restraint, and it is probable that the very difficult and very complex act, supplemented by a number of extra-musical things, of playing, in public a concerto of Bach or of Beethoven, creates habits, varying with each person, which give rise to localizations, which it would be impossible to enumerate in the form of a general law.

But the performer is only deserving of the name of artist when he understands and can bring out the thought contained in the melody he is playing. In this we have the sure criterion which allows us to classify the higher and lower forms of talent.

Lowest in the scale must be placed the pianist who only possesses memory and "fingers" hardly differing from the automatic organs in Dutch brasseries, instruments in which the sensory and motor centres are replaced by clock-work. Above him —and here the variations are numerous—is the pianist who thoroughly feels that in music there is something more than notes, but who renders incorrectly or erroneously the thought of the composer. This is the artist who acts as *traditore* instead of remaining *tradutore;* or he even makes nonsensical mistakes, evidenced by faults of rhythm, unseasonable changes in the rests, wrong "colouring." Or again, what is most common, even in celebrated virtuosi—he carries to the extreme the spirit of analysis ; he overdoes the details ; he wishes to be brilliant, to give an original rendering without noticing that he gradually falls into the ridiculous error of substituting his own thoughts for those of a Beethoven or a Bach, and of thrusting his own personality in front of these great masters' own.

At the highest point of this hierarchy is the pianist who understands the musical thought, identifies himself with it, and reproduces it exactly. An example is Anton Rubinstein. Certainly Rubinstein had, in a very high degree, those aptitudes which are described and explained by physiology ; but, as regards this, it is very important to note that if on certain points (memory, for instance) he was perfection itself, as regards others there were lapses. "In an eminent pianist," says Dr. Ingegnieros, " the centre of co-ordination must be particularly perfect." This was not at all the case with Rubinstein; his playing was not free from faults. An eye-witness told me that at the end of a concert given in Paris, when receiving the congratulations of the audience, he replied to one of his admirers : " A whole piece could be composed with the false notes I struck." And yet, to all who heard him—to those even, mark you, who

were by no means professionals or connoisseurs—
Rubinstein gave the impression of being a genius.
Nothing is more easily explained. When playing
Beethoven's sonatas, Rubinstein understood exactly
the composer's idea and reproduced it faithfully
with so *adequate* a rendering that, in listening to
him, one no longer thought of the presence of the
pianist, but of that of Beethoven himself. In the
presence of so complete an identification, and by a
quite natural illusion, we applied the same qualifi-
cations to the interpreter as to the composer
interpreted. This is the most authentic and striking
case that can be quoted to prove the reality of the
musical thought and to show its effects.

4th. Genius is musical intelligence at its highest
point, but it wholly escapes physiology. It is often
served by moderate or defective organs. It is
incapable of education. It is unconscious and
spontaneous.

It is a power which resembles the primary principles, or fundamental forces, of Nature. Here,
more than anywhere else, it must be confessed, that
if " to know is to comprehend the cause " (Aristotle), or " to demonstrate things in a regular
manner," or again, " to reduce an order of things
known to a systematic whole " (Kant), we know
nothing as to the composition of genius. At least,
we can say from its effects what genius is not.

The classification which I have reproduced and
examined in the preceding pages terminates with
this definition : " Musical genius creates new
forms of expression; or else conceives and realizes,
in an entirely personal manner, forms of expres-

sion already known." A very inexact definition,
which requires fresh light on an essential point :
What are we to understand by "form" in music ?
We shall now point out one of the most grievous
errors which have hitherto vitiated the whole of
musical æsthetics.

We must not content ourselves with words, but
must always keep before our minds the real facts to
which the terms employed relate. Nothing is easier
than to invent new "musical forms," but to think
that this act of invention is necessarily a sign of
genius, is going rather too far.

In 1882, Rimsky Korsakof had the peculiar
whim of employing the bar in eleven time (characterized by the use of eleven crotchets, forming an
indivisible group), certainly a new form ; is it a
mark of genius ? No, only a framework, the value
of which is determined by the contents.*

The Turks have rhythms, *ousouls*, in a consider-
ably larger number of times ; but that alone does
not cause the Western nations to describe them as
musicians of genius.

The composer in the Middle Ages who bethought
himself to repeat a melodious phrase, simultaneously
in the upper fifth or lower fourth (*diaphony, organum*)
certainly made an innovation ; but although this
attempt has been fruitful, he has been looked upon
by nearly all the critics as a barbarous musician
with no ear. An amateur utterly devoid of talent
may write a symphony in which he upsets all rules
as regards plan and style, and runs counter to
all accepted ideas of harmony and counter-point.

* Last scene of his opera, *Sneyorutschka.*

The more ignorant he is, the more the forms he uses will be "novel." Any one who, in an opera, placed the orchestra on the stage in costume, and the singers in the orchestra in evening dress, would evidently produce a novelty.

M. Vincent d'Indy, in his *Istar*, has placed his leading theme at the end of the variations instead of before them; this novelty in no way gives to the work its value, which is quite independent of this whimsical arrangement. Let us also remark that, to the psychologist, a novelty is the more "personal," the worse, the more incorrect, and the more inartistic it is. Nothing can be more original than the scrawls of quite young children. Contemporary musicians who have created "new forms" are legion; but do they all possess genius?

Take, on the other hand, a Schumann, a Bizet, a Cæsar Franck, or a Saint-Saëns composing a melody. This melody has a form constituted by the notes of which it is composed. Can the one be taken apart from the other? Is not the melody (the thought) and the form one and the same thing? And has not the act of invention consisted, in short, in finding out a new form? We approach a problem which has greatly exercised æsthetes :—whether in a sonorous phrase there is a receptacle and a content? Certain critics, after turning this question over and over from all points of view, have declared—which is perfectly correct—that a melody is indissolubly bound up with the form which realizes it; and from this they have concluded—which is wrong— that in music there is nothing else but forms. This is the theory of Hanslick; it is also the generally accepted theory, for no one, to my knowledge, has ventured to affirm the existence of a purely musical thought outside forms of melody.

Without entering into a tedious discussion of *matter* and *form*, which would call to mind Molière as well as Aristotle, I shall simply say that, as regards this point, it is the same with music as with ordinary language.

It is impossible for us to think, even in silent communion with ourselves, without the use of words, and yet we cannot go so far as to say that thought, a natural act of the mind, is identical with a system of artificially acquired signs ; it precedes it as conception precedes birth—in accordance with the classical saying, " Man thinks his words before putting into words his thoughts." There are even cases where it has been possible to note that the one existed without the other. All philosophers have heard of the celebrated Laura Bridgeman, who, though blind, deaf, and dumb, yet had a highly developed intellect. It may be said that all language *presupposes* a thought.

In the same way, in music, the notes of a melody presuppose a thought. The connection between the two is the normal fact, but it also has exceptions. Does not the musician, when composing, sometimes seek for notes—as an author hesitates for words—in order to convey his exact thought ? Beethoven's note-books testify to this. It would even seem that when writing the orchestral score of a melody, or founding on it a series of variations, a certain break occurs between the form and the substance.

I shall therefore conclude that :—Genius is
musical thought raised to its highest power, together
with the sense of beauty, the logic, and the penetrating expression belonging to it. It is the complete and supreme emancipation from all concepts ;
something which, without using words, should
give us the equivalent of the plays of Æschylus
or Shakespeare : all the forces of life, of the imagination, of feeling, and of reason exalted in their full
freedom, but in the pure state, disentangled from
every object and attempting many syntheses as
if for the preparation of a new cosmos. Thus
does musical genius present itself to us in the
adagios of Beethoven's quartets. One can understand that, when listening to these, thinkers like
Schelling and Schopenhauer, carried away by their
metaphysical dreams, should have ascribed to
music a direct hold on First Principles. Between
the verbal thought contained in our practical
language and that of those adagios, the same
difference exists as between the atmosphere of our
cities, laden with dust and smoke, and the pure
ether where glides through infinite space the light
of the stars.

In music, as in poetry, genius is not passion—
which is attainable by any idiot—but thought,
lightning - like and supreme,— dominating everything.

§ 2. Conclusions of the Third Part

To sum up: (1) The musical intelligence has
organs which serve it admirably, but cannot be
said to produce it. The musician finds the means

of *action* in his auditory apparatus and in the
rich organization of his brain ; but when he *thinks*,
he can only think within himself ; the fundamental
error of certain physiologists has consisted in
reasoning like Helmholtz in the first pages of his
book : " there are no external models nor concepts
in music ; *hence, in music, sensation* is everything."
This conclusion is by no means unavoidable. There
is another explanation, which is the one we have
adopted. The exclusion of concepts does not at all
imply that of thought, and may, on the contrary,
favour the acts of a freer and less superficial intel-
lectualism. (2) The " parallelism " of the musical
and the verbal language, treated as localizations in
similar centres, is a quite admissible thesis founded
on many observations, but it in no way interferes
with our own ; it shows us, in a harmony, an
essential differentiation, which is sufficient for us.

Parallel lines neither begin nor end in the same
point.

FOURTH PART

MUSICAL THOUGHT AND THE LAWS OF NATURE

CHAPTER I

MUSIC AND PERIODIC PHENOMENA

§ 1. OUTSIDE THE EAR

WE continue this retrograde journey, of which we have already accomplished several stages. From the psychological phenomenon to the brain centres; from the acoustic nerve and the very minute network in which it terminates to the internal ear—the only absolutely indispensable part of the mechanism of audition; then to the chain of tiny bones, to the membrane of the tympanum, and, by the auditory conduit, to the chamber opening on to the external world.

What are the phenomena produced outside the ear and subject to laws independent of our will, which it is important for us to know in order to have a complete notion of "*music*"? This is the last question we have to deal with. I have no intention of reproducing or summarizing here a treatise on acoustics—for all sound, as we have seen, is not necessarily

musical—but will simply try to indicate a few fundamental phenomena which enable us to perceive an
agreement between the extremes of a series : on the
one hand, the laws which regulate the vibration
of the bodies which produce the sound ; on the
other hand, the unconscious habits of the composer
when writing a sonata or a symphony.

The musician, who thinks in sounds, is in harmony
with social life, and his intelligence is subserved
by an organ of which it appears to understand the
mechanism. We shall now see him in harmony with
objective nature.

It is especially at this point that the method
followed in the present work could be justified, if
necessary. We might first say that sound is a
purely subjective creation of the ear, and that
outside us it has no existence. To it might be
applied the adage : *esse est percipi*. And this fact
will be found linked to what is the very foundation
of our thesis.

By the consciousness we directly grasp what a
melody is ; if we separate ourselves from this feeling, of which the physiological conditions are already
very obscure, either we shall no longer be aware of
anything but modalities, and shall not penetrate
into the essence of things, or else we shall enter the
field of hypotheses—that is to say, the region of
clouds and wrangles.

By the aid of mathematics, philosophers make
measurements. Given a vibrating string, they first
register, by the use of ingenious apparatus, the
number of vibrations per second ; they measure the
length of the wave they produce in the conducting

air and the time taken to reach the auditory
apparatus ; they measure, in decimetres, the length
of the string and the radius of its section ; they
reckon, in kilogrammes, the weight which stretches
it ; they estimate the specific weight of its substance ; and then, having noted that the relation of
these phenomena or properties remains constant
whatever the sharpness or depth of the sound
produced, they sum up these measurements and the
comparison they have made of it in a formula
which becomes a law.

This formula may be transposed into ordinary
language. Example : *The number of vibrations of
the string per second*—that is to say, the pitch of the
sound—*is in inverse ratio to the length and radius
of the string ; it is directly proportional to the weight
which stretches it ; it is inversely proportional to the
square root of the density.* For brevity, each of the
properties figuring in this equation may be expressed by an algebraic sign.

But all this simply describes matters by external
observations and nothing more. If the physicist
does not desire only to study externals and movements, if he wishes to penetrate into the inwardness
of things, the bases of certainty fail him, and he is
reduced to hypotheses. Do not ask him, especially
nowadays, *What* is matter ?

This general remark has for its object to reduce to
their proper proportions the pretensions of certain
authors who, like Helmholtz, have approached the
science of acoustics on the principle that it ought
to give us the secret of the language of
sounds. Of this secret we already know all that

can be known. It is internal observation, it is psychology alone, which has revealed it to us. After having shown the relations of the musical phenomenon to social life, and after having studied its physiological conditions, we have now only to determine its place in nature, and to show that on this outward side, which looks towards the *cosmos*, there are links which connect music with the whole or a part of the whole of the other phenomena.

§ 2. VIBRATIONS—A FIRST AGREEMENT OF THE MUSICAL MIND WITH OBJECTIVE LAWS

Music employs as material, if we may use such a term, sounds—not noises—of a certain kind. Musical sound is produced by periodic vibrations. It is important to note at once that the cell of every musical work, the *sound*, is a type of "composition."

Periodic vibrations occur when, during strictly uniform periods of time, an elastic body, disturbed from its position of equilibrium and set in motion, passes again and again through the same states. The duration of the period is a constant : it is the time which elapses between two successive reproductions of the same state of movement. The sensation of noise is due, on the contrary, to non-periodic movements, producing irregular sounds breaking forth by jerks, and not "compound."

Many efforts, as we have seen, have been made to discover the origins of rhythm : from Plato to Karl Bücher the explanations proposed vary greatly. Have we not here a fact to be strictly reckoned with ? When the musician, in his freest exercise of fancy, employs the uniform frame of the bar; when he introduces symmetry between two parts of a phrase, between two phrases or two strophes or two systems of strophes, he is instinctively obeying a law which is already realized in a single sound. The distinction between mere *noise*, in which numerous auditory sensations are mingled and jostle each other; and a *musical sound* due to the periodicity of the vibrations does not only enable us to say where the domain of music begins, but makes us perceive an initial principle of organization which reverberates through the whole work of the musician.

Is music, then, uniformity, or the regular repetition of identical movements? Certainly not. Is it pure caprice? Not that either. It is both one and the other. It rests always on an opposition and an adaptation: opposition of the creating liberty which delights in the unforeseen, and of the law of rhythm, which demands the regular recurrence of like phenomena; and lastly, adaptation of this tendency to that law. In every musical work there is a conflict at the same time that there is a harmony. Composers at the present day carry the conflict as far as possible, while the classics reduced it to a minimum, but they only exaggerate it to give themselves the pleasure of resolving it. They are in a situation similar to that of the gymnast or dancer who takes the most abnormal positions without, however, emancipating himself from the laws of gravity.

We recognize, therefore, that when Beethoven wrote a symphony he arranged all the parts of it rhythmically, both because a certain order was in-

herent to the nature of his thought and because
this thought itself was unconsciously subject to
the influence of the law which regulates periodic
vibrations.

Here are two facts which will enable us to grasp
in a more exact manner this concord of the subjective work of the composition with that which
is outside the will of the composer.

§ 3. THE HARMONICS

First fact.—This is the phenomenon of multiple
resistance, commonly admitted to be the basis
of our musical system. A string, when a bow is
drawn across it, or when struck by a hammer,
has one total movement and, at the same time, a
great number of partial movements. It subdivides
by itself into very unequal parts, separated by relatively fixed points, termed *nodes*, which produce
independent vibrations, superposed in the sound
wave on the total vibration, somewhat as small
waves are superposed on large ones. The same
thing occurs with the column of air which is made
to vibrate in a tube. The sounds resulting from
this subdivision are as follows—

When we strike a *Do* (a fundamental sound) on
the piano, we produce at the same time sounds of
lesser intensity which enwrap the auditory sensation of the first, and are indicated here by the

crotchets 2, 3, 4, 5, 6, 7, 8. . . . These figures are not only numbers of order, but indicate relations: the octave gives twice as many vibrations as the fundamental note; and the twelfth (*Sol*) gives *three*, while the octave gives *two*, etc. This subdivision of the vibrating string is explained by a celebrated theorem of Fourier, which may be thus formulated: every form of periodic vibration can be decomposed into a certain number of vibrations, of which the durations are a half, a third, a fourth those of the movement given. The calculation enables us to determine the amplitude of the various vibrating fractions, so that a periodic movement not only *can* be subdivided into a certain number of simple divisions, but *must* indeed be divided in one single way.

Calculation was first employed a priori to estimate the divisions of the string. Helmholtz demonstrated that the harmonics were something more than a mathematical fiction; he isolated them and demonstrated their objective existence. I will not here enter into the objections raised against his theory, particularly by M. Guillemin, which, I think, have not yet succeeded in overthrowing his doctrine.

Now, the first harmonics which are superposed on the fundamental sound form the perfect chord: Do, Sol (*Do*), *Mi*. This was termed by Rameau "the first outburst of nature."

Second fact.—If I turn over the leaves of a book of music—opera scores, sonatas, collections of concertos, and symphonies—I note that the perfect concord is the beginning and the end of all compositions (save some rare and deliberate exceptions), and is only departed from to be returned to. *From the very first line it is the framework in which the musician denotes his thought.*

Let the reader call to mind the first bars of compositions familiar to him : in Beethoven, the *eroïca* Symphony, the first pianoforte concerto ; the Sonata Op. 31, No. 2 ; the *Appassionata ;* the Sonatas Op. 2 (No. 1, and Scherzo of No. 2) ; the Sonata Op. 7 ; the *presto* of Op. 10, No. 2 ; the Fantasia Op. 27, No. 2, and its *presto agitato,* etc. ; of Mozart, the Sonatas 3, 5, 6 (*allegro alla turca*), 9, 15, 16, 17, 19. . . . He will see that very beautiful specimens of musical thought have for their formula the perfect concord.* This concord is, as it were, the first outburst of composition.

There is, then, a harmony between these two facts : the one psychological and artistic (the form instinctively given by the musician to his thought), the other objective (law of multiple resonance).

The bringing together of these two verified facts seems to support the theorists who declare that

---

* In order not to bring in musical theory and to keep within the bounds of ordinary experience, I will further instance : Haydn, quartets Op. Nos. 1, 2, and 5 ; Op. 2, Nos. 5 and 6 ; Op. 3, Nos. 2, 3, and 6 ; Op. 9, No. 2 : Op. 17, No. 3 ; Op. 20, No. 6 ; Op. 50, No. 3. The Sonatas Op. 54, No. 2 ; Op. 64, Nos. 1 and 4 ; Op. 74, No. 2. Beethoven, the beginning of the Septet No. 20 ; the Sextets (*Adagio* and *Allegro*) Op. 8b and Op. 71 ; the Quintet (for piano, hautbois, clarinet, horn, bassoon) Op. 16 ; the Quartets 5 (Op. 18, Nos. 5 and 6), 8 (Op. 59, No. 2) ; the Quartet (with piano) Op. 16 ; the serenades Op. 8 and Op. 25. Mozart, the beginning of Sextet in F ♯ major, the Quartets in D ♯ major, in F ♮ major. . . . The first pages of the *Rheingold* (51 bars), wherein R. Wagner endeavours to represent the genesis of all things, are curious in this connection.

the foundation of music rests on an objective law, outside and independent of us. In the eighteenth century Sauveur, Rameau, and d'Alembert had endeavoured to establish the theory of music on this basis. Helmholtz took up and completed their attempt. After stating precisely the doctrine of harmonics, he claimed to deduce from it the elements of a grammar.

This theory, thus set forth, cannot be accepted, and must be essentially modified. It is inexact to say that, if we attribute a paramount part to the perfect chord, it is because this phenomenon is the first to present itself in the vibration of strings or sounding tubes. Indeed, this phenomenon would perhaps escape our notice, among several others which contradict it, had we not already within ourselves the notion of its importance, or an organization (physiological or intellectual) which predisposes us to ascribe to it a predominant rôle. As an excellent musician* has said : the principle of harmony cannot be deduced from an experiment which *supposes to be known*, or valued as they deserve, the laws of this harmony.

In a word, between the mind of the musician and nature there exists a harmony, and not simply a relation between cause and effect.

Amid the enormous complex of the phenomena of the physical world we should not make straight for this fact more than another were there not within us a certain reason for this choice.

Certain very simple observations will make this clear—

1st. The harmonics called forth by the funda-

* M. Dador (*Revue musicale*, année 1905, p. 508).

mental note are not all allies which contribute to the beauty of the principal sound. The exact value of *Si♭* is 7, 11 ; and there is no note, marked sharp or flat, in any scale which represents it absolutely (the *La♯* represents 7, 12); this *Si♭* is not used in music. The notion of the perfect chord, if borrowed, therefore implies a choice, and this choice can only be made in obedience to the very feeling of harmony which exists within, and not outside us.

2nd. The instruments capable of employment in music do not all give harmonics, or rather partial sounds in consonance with the fundamental note, as do the strings and the tubes. Circular plates, and distended membranes, have very numerous accessory sounds, very contiguous to the base and greatly dissonant from it. As regards elastic rods, the partial sounds are, on the contrary, very distant, but quite as dissonant. Thus, representing by 1 the number of vibrations of the fundamental sound (designated by *Do*), the following are the partial sounds of a freely swinging rod—

	No. of vibrations.	In ordinary notation.
First sound (fundamental)	1	Do_0
Second sound	2·7576	$Fa♯_1 + 0·2$ (instead of the 8ve)
Third sound	5·4041	$Fa_2 - 0·1$ (,, ,, 12th)
Fourth sound	13·3444	$La_3 - 0·1$ (,, ,, dble. 8ve)

Rameau and the majority of the theorists of the eighteenth century considered as an object of worship everything which was " natural." But these organic dissonances of rods, membranes, and plates are as " natural " as the consonances of tubes and strings. Then comes this question :

Why, while we are using these two groups of instruments in our orchestra, do we attribute to the one a very secondary, and to the other an exceptionally important part ?   Why do we consider as still barbarian musicians those savages who only know how to strike stretched skins or metal objects ? What is the cause, if it be not musical feeling, of the distinction we draw between systems both equally springing from nature ?   To the physicist the realm of dissonance is even greater than that of the other !

3rd. We will also remark that to say that the perfect chord is the "first outburst of nature" is to ignore the first harmonic at the octave of the fundamental sound, or to consider it as identical with this latter. Now this identification can have but a subjective foundation ; objectively, it would be as inadmissible as the equation $2-1$. The ear separates 2 into $1+1$, and draws from the paradox $2=1$, which, from the musical point of view, is not false.

We thus see that it is not possible to assert that our system has a strictly scientific basis.

The harmony of two terms does not consist in their identity ; it presupposes differences, with certain points in common and an adaptation. After comparing the two facts above stated, we do not subordinate the second to the first : we place them on the same level. Between the two there is a harmony which the metaphysicians of the seventeenth century would have termed "pre-established" ; but we content ourselves with noting the fact.

We could insist much further on this similitude
which we have indicated.

§ 4. MUSICAL SOUNDS AND COLOURS

The objective analogy of natural phenomena has
for parallel or consequence the correlation established
between the two realms of sensation ; in other words,
our organs do not react in a manner absolutely
independent of outside influences ; the actions of the
one reverberate not infrequently on the other, and
there results from this a more or less important or
regular synergy, which may be considered as the
image within us of the unity around us.

Thus, in many cases, visual sensations are accompanied by auditory ones and reciprocally. The
fact does not happen continuously, and any attempt
to regard it as a law is condemned to fail ; but,
even as an exception, it has interest, for the
connexity of certain facts supposes a relationship
between the causes which produce them.

We will point this out by taking, for a brief
comparison, two given realms :—music and light.
The two senses to which they correspond, the eye
and the ear, alone receive impressions which
systematize themselves into a work of art ; smell,
taste, and feeling, though susceptible of the highest
education and in no way limited to a utilitarian part,
have not given rise to creations of a truly æsthetic
character.

To show the analogy between sound and light,
music and colours, will be to realize, on an
essential point, the programme of harmony we
have traced out.

1st. In the diagram of vibrations* the phenomena of light occupy, like the musical sounds, seven octaves, if we include those which, situated in the regions of the infra-red and ultra-violet, are not decomposable by the eye ; but visible light, decomposable by the colours of the prism, comprises but one octave, placed between the 48th and the 49th (of the series of 55 octaves of vibrations, which represent the phenomena known to us), viz. : *red, orange, yellow, green, blue, indigo, violet.* Even this octave (9 : 15) is incomplete. It is only by forcing nature a little that one could arrive, by comparing the wave-lengths, at establishing the following octave : 0·0008 mm. for the red, and 0·0004 mm. for the violet, situate on the opposite side. We may say that the violet has a tendency towards the repetition of the red. However this may be, the region of discernible light and of colour is much smaller than that of sounds (whence it follows that blindness is a slighter ill than deafness).

Let us now point out the similarities.

2nd. Do the simple elements which form ordinary light form one organized series by a law similar to that of the harmonics which constitute the fundamental sound ?

There is a difficulty in comparing clear and well-defined matters, such as musical sounds, to others without a fixed beginning or end, like the colours of the spectrum. Thus the red commences at 400

* A complete scale of ether-waves compiled by Prof. Lebedeff is given in Prof. Bruno Kölbe's *Introduction to Electricity* (Eng. ed.), Kegan Paul & Co., London, 1908, p. 383.—ED.

trillions of vibrations per second, and extends as far
as 460 trillions.   It is the same with the others.
But by selecting a suitable point in these diminu-
tions or accelerations of tones, it is possible to construct chords of light on the same basis as musical
chords.

Taking red at the limit of the spectrum, yellow
at the (approximate) limit of the orange, and green
at that of blue, we obtain the ratios 8 : 10 : 12,
which are those of the three notes of the major
perfect chord *Do-Mi-Sol.*

Taking at their extreme limit the three colours
which terminate the series of colours easily discernible by the eye—orange, green, violet—we get the
ratios 10 : 12 : 16, representing the chord of sixth.
By taking the terms of comparison in the middle
region of the spectrum, we should still more easily
find a counterpart to the chord of sixth and fourth.
We may state the following equation—

$$\frac{586 \text{ (green)}}{488 \text{ (red)}} = \frac{703 \text{ (violet)}}{586 \text{ (green)}} = \frac{5}{6} \text{ (minor third)}.$$

We must not lay too great stress (as M. de Hartmann has done in his *Esthétique*) on the identity of
these two series of constructions.   But we have
other points of comparison.

3rd. The teaching as to the auditory and visual
sensations at first passed through a similar period
of error.   It is known at the present time that
sound and light are nothing else but the perception
of a particular mode of movement ;   but in former
times it was thought that the impressions on the ear
were due to a particular agent called *sound,* having

a real and objective existence; and this metaphysical conception, coupled with a vicious circle
(due to the Pythagoreans and reaffirmed by the
Stoics), has for counterpart the primitive hypothesis, according to which the sensation of light
was produced by "*luminous* corpuscles." Let us
remark, in passing, that this last. lasted much
longer than the other. It is only since the seventeenth century (Descartes and Huyghens) that the
undulation theory has displaced that of emission.
Now, Plato, Aristotle, and Theophrastus among the
ancients had already perceived the real nature of
sound.*

4th. Are the two senses of hearing and of sight
formed by the same evolution and by a similar
process? This is what the facts of history would
seem to affirm. The ancient poets only speak of a
very small number of colours, and the history of
painting offers facts parallel to these literary testimonies. We know, from Pliny, that the pictures of
the ancients were painted in one unique red tone, the
cinnabar or minium of Ephesus (then red ochre, or a
particular kind called *Sinopid*). Little by little the
palette of the painter was enriched by fresh resources. At the present day the Papal manufac-
tory of the Vatican, which is the most important
of all existing mosaic establishments, possesses
28,000 stones of different shades.

These facts have as their equivalents, in music,
the primitive and scanty constitution of the scale,
reduced to the fundamental intervals, and ending,

---

* See the fragment of a lost treatise by Theophrastus (édit.
Wimmer, III, p. 32, in Diels' *Doxographi græci*, 1879, p. 525, 18).

later on, in a chromatism of the twelve semi-tones ; harmony, at first restricted to the exclusive use of unison, soon enriched by the octave, the fifth, and the fourth, and then making use of dissonances ; lastly, the evolution of the orchestra, starting from such humble origins and afterwards arriving at the formidable display of its present forces.

5th. Every day we see confounded the two orders of sensation and the two arts which correspond to them, which doubtless is wrong from a purely artistic point of view, but testifies to an instinct which evidently has its rise in natural analogies.

It is well known that artists daily employ musical terms when talking of painting, and *vice versa.* Eugène Fromentin speaks as follows of the *Assumption* of Rubens : " His palette . . . *resounds* in the few dominant notes, yellow, red, black, grey." Th. Sylvestre says à propos of Delacroix : " He makes the red resound like war trumpets, and draws from the violet *mournful moans.*" Taine, Charles Blanc, M. Sully Prudhomme, and a thousand others have employed a similar language. Nietzsche has uttered the following paradoxical judgment upon Wagner, giving it, it is true, the value of a criticism : " Wagner as a musician should be classed amongst the painters ; as a poet, among the musicians."

A priest of Western Flanders, the Abbé de Lescluze, has attempted to reduce to a system what had hitherto passed as an instinctive approximation or a simple oratorical phrase. According to him, a painter like Memling " plays a different melody " on each of his canvases. What characterizes each painter or each school is the use of a particular scale of colour, given by a simple number and by its multiples. There is the Spanish *gamut*, made up of multiples of 5, and having orange as its tonic ; the scale of Jordaëns, multiples of 9, with red as tonic ; the gamut of Rembrandt, the Italian, the Japanese, etc.

6th. We will give some more precise observations.

In the first place it was observed that certain persons always associated the idea of a colour with that of sound (a morbid phenomenon called *coloured audition*); nothing more was needed for a new path to be opened out to the researches of physiologists and to their attempts to establish systems. In 1892 a bibliography of this course of study, drawn up by an American (Mr. Krohn), contained no less than eighty-five articles. Since then some important works have enriched this list ; I will mention only that of M. Flournoy, professor of experimental psychology at the University of Geneva : *Les phénomènes de Synopsie.** It contains a great number of curious facts, and the author has the merit of great prudence in drawing conclusions.

M. Flournoy's method is as follows : He questions men, women, and children.—When an impression strikes your ear, do you, at the same time, see something, and if so, what ? Since when has this happened to you ? Has it varied ? etc.—And he has noted that, with many persons, seeing and hearing are inseparable acts.

Never to perceive a sound without associating it with colour is termed "having photisms." There

* Paris, Alcan, 1893.

are alphabetical photisms. To certain persons *a* is white ; *i* is red ; *o*, bright yellow ; *u*, green, etc. There is a photism of names. To various persons *Cecilia* is bright yellow ; *Susannah*, chrome yellow ; *Mary*, pearl - grey ; *Alice*, cherry - red ; *Henry*, myrtle-green ; *Lucy*, intense blue ; *Edmund*, dark blue ; *John*, grey-blue ; *Leo*, golden yellow. Lastly there are musical photisms, produced by the notes of the scale, by tones, instruments, and by the music of such and such a composer. With one person, the fact of making a note sharp or flat simply modifies slightly its tint : *Mi* is dark blue and *Mi*♭ light blue ; *Fa*♮ is light violet and *Fa* ♯ is amethyst or sapphire blue. With another person an operation of this nature completely changes the colour : *Si*♯ is green and *Si*♭ lilac.

As regards the colours suggested by the work of a composer taken as a whole, the associations are very different and often contradictory ; there is nothing astonishing in this, seeing that it is no longer a question of a physiological phenomenon, but of a work of art freely interpreted. The single symptom of agreement occurs in the case of Gounod, whose music gave the impression of violet colour to one person and of blue to another.

7th. Above all these verbal statements, we may set the example given by a large number of eminent composers who likewise seem to have possessed " photisms " or to have sought for them, for they have been greatly enamoured of what the Germans call *Tonmalerei*, music painting : Kuhnau, Haydn, Weber, Félicien David, R. Wagner, Liszt, Berlioz, Saint-Saëns, Massenet . . . and how many more

. . . among the old masters and among our contemporaries, have given, or endeavoured to represent, colour by means of the orchestra?

In Part III of the Introduction to the *Creation*,
Haydn clearly intends to represent the fresh morning
tints when he employs flutes in conjunction with
stringed instruments ; in *Harold in Italy* Berlioz
is certainly painting the twilight when he marks
the *Prière des pèlerins* by the persistent note
of the horn. To render his landscapes sonorous,
the musician often turns to account a simple
analogy established between the shades of the
same colour and the various tones which form a group
in the instruments of the orchestra. Thus green
comprises delicate green, Veronese green, emerald,
and black-green ; in equal relation are found, in a
quite different series, the violin, the alto, the violoncello, and the double bass. Blue comprises cobalt,
ultramarine, Prussian blue . . . ; the hautbois, the
cor anglais, the bassoon form a series of similar
shades. Between the various yellows (Naples, ochre,
terra-cotta . . .) there exist differences corresponding to those which separate the fife, the flute,
the clarionet . . . By this it is easy to perceive
that music treats the objective colour, taken as
a model, as it treats feeling : by the aid of a
system of equivalences it only reproduces its dynamics.

8th. This equivalence takes place on another
point which has greatly exercised the æsthetes :
namely, timbre.*

* On these questions see the excellent exposition of M. Lechalas
in his *Études d'Esthétique*, p. 169 *et sqq.* Alcan.

T

Between the two orders of phenomena which
we have compared, there appears, at first, a singular
difference. In music, the conditions of tone seem
to be the exact opposite to what they are for light.
A sound owes its "colour" to the number of
harmonics by which it is accompanied, to their
intensity in relation to the fundamental note,
and to their relative pitch : thus the sounds
accompanied by the first six harmonics, with an
average intensity, are full and "furnished," as organ
makers term it, and have an agreeable tone ; those
sounds accompanied only by the alternate harmonics are of a poor and nasal character, and have
a disagreeable tone ; the sounds which are accompanied by the higher harmonics, very clear at the
start from the sixth or seventh, are sharp and harsh.
As to the simple non-decomposable sounds, such as
those of the diapasons associated with resonant
pipes, they are dull and devoid of tone, like phantom sounds. In a word, the compound has colour,
the component parts none (indeed, all simple
sounds are like one another).

In white light it is exactly the reverse ; the
compound has no colour, the simple components
are alone differentiated : *violet, indigo, blue,* etc.
This inversion of facts is, perhaps, only due to the
imperfect presentation that we make of them, and
to the difficulty we have in defining the word *tone,*
when we are no longer dealing with acoustics. We
shall confine ourselves to noting a few facts.
White light is not the only one which exists : the
stars send us light with different shades which
constitute their "tones"; and in the same way

that those different shades are due to the chemical constituents of the stars, it is not to be doubted that the quality of the harmonics, and the form of compound vibration resulting therefrom, are due to the molecular nature of the vibrating body.

Without looking so far away : in the paintings of Rubens, Rembrandt, Raphael, and Velasquez there are identical colours—red, black, green, etc.— but with a different "tone," that is to say, with a particular physiognomy obtained by the aid of certain component elements which constitute the manner or the originality of each artist, because the choice and the proportions of these elements destined to produce a complete impression are the artist's secret. The process is the same in the matter of instrumentation.

Delacroix (according to a remark of Ch. Blanc) at times obtained from a colour an exquisite effect by mixing together the commonest tones ; likewise one is astonished to find a composer like Berlioz often associate instruments which seem "as if they ought not to go well together " (this is the parallel drawn by M. Camille Saint-Saëns), and yet draw from them a charming tone. So that, in both these cases, the theory of tone finds it application.

Must we conclude from all this that the musician is a kind of painter, and that, as has been proposed by an engineer of the present day (M. L. Favre*), our orchestras might be subjected to a radical transformation, to render them more intelligible, by constantly associating visible colours with the tones produced ?   Nothing is further from my

* L. Favre, La Musique des Couleurs. Paris, Schleicher.

thought. Such confusions are illegitimate and dangerous. To reduce music to a mental imagery is inartistic. But it is one thing to misunderstand the insurmountable frontier between two arts by assimilating their practical effects, and another to note the close relationship—secret and unperceived by the hearer—of the materials which they employ.

There are many things which we enjoy without being conscious of them. Such are the degrees of civilization reached by our ancestors since the beginning; the social organization of which we form part; and our adaptation to the cosmos. Yet it is owing to these three aids that present man stands upright and lives for a brief space! In the same way, in music, the resemblance of sound to colour is one of those profound phenomena which appertain to the realm of the unconscious. It contributes to the creation of the indecision and the disturbance of musical emotion in the average listener, who does not listen with the ear of a contrapuntist, and gives way artlessly to the charm of a composition. It reveals to us the harmony of two different worlds ; and the pleasure we find in such a feeling would vanish, if this harmony, instead of being diffused over our sensibility, took the shape of clearly defined images.

§ 5. The Place of Music among Periodic Phenomena

In nature everything is vibration ; this broad view of things has given rise to a kind of axiom propounded by modern science. As music is the art of combining and systematizing vibrations, we need not confine ourselves to comparing it with light and may seek to discover what place it holds in the series of universal phenomena.

Here is a pendulum making one oscillation per second : we will imagine this oscillation to increase in rapidity—in which case it transforms itself into vibrations, that is to say, movements, which we can neither see nor count—and we will class the phenomena which result for 55 octaves, 1, 2, 4, 8, 16, etc., by doubling the number of vibrations up to 55 times. In reality, there is nothing in the phenomena of which we are about to speak which corresponds to the purely physiological effect from which has been drawn the definition of the musical octave ; but we may use this word here without ascribing any real value to it ; it is a simple means of estimating the field we have to go over.

At 16 vibrations per second, with a wave-length of about 20 metres,* our pendulum would commence to produce acoustic sensations, the field of which would extend, in our supposed diagram, from 16 to 30,000 vibrations per second. In this first region, which has for limits, on the one side, very deep and heavy sounds, and on the other shrill whistles—is enclosed the field of musical sounds, comprising about seven octaves, from the fifth to the twelfth.

From 30,000 vibrations per second to 10 millions appear the high frequency currents (Kelvin), which are quite another phenomenon : to wit, the intensity of an electric current, subject to periodical vibrations in a wire. This region, moreover, overlaps the preceding one, for alternators are constructed

---

* By a wave-length in the air is meant the amount of space traversed by the sound during one complete vibration.

which yield currents of which the frequency is of the order of 80 to 100 periods per second, that is to say, are comparable to the deep notes of the musical scale.

From 10 millions of vibrations per second to 100,000 millions the phenomena produced by our pendulum would be the Hertzian oscillations the lower limit of which cannot be fixed, for they also may be slow.

From 100,000 millions to 3,700,000 millions we have an unexplored interval.

From 3,700,000 millions, and for about six octaves, *dark heat.*

From 375,000,000,000,000 (ultra-red of the spectrum) to 750,000,000,000,000 (ultra-violet), *light.*

Beyond that come the two octaves of the *actinic rays*, which act upon photographic plates and excite thermo-electric batteries.

After an unexplored interval one would arrive at the *N*-rays of M. Blondlot (30,000,000,000,000,000 vibrations per second), of which, however, the existence is, rightly or wrongly, contested by several physicists.*

These phenomena differ very widely one from the other ; they can, however, be made the object of a comparison based on certain analogies. As was the case when dealing with verbal language, musical language, and the localization of images,

---

* For all this, see Bruno Kölbe, *op. cit.* Why M. Combarieu should attribute the discovery of high frequency currents (he evidently means the oscillatory discharge of a Leyden jar) to Lord Kelvin, I do not know.—ED.

we note resemblances with essential differentiations. Here, the vibrations are perceptible, can be registered, and are produced in air; there, they are the object of a double hypothesis concerning their existence and the conducting medium (ether). Here they are perpendicular to the line which represents the direction of propagation, and are called transversal; there, they follow the direction of propagation, and are called longitudinal. Certain vibrations are intramolecular (electricity), others are on the periphery. There is, however, one characteristic—vibration itself—common to all the generating causes and in certain cases to the modes of transmission. Here are a few facts which tend to justify the comparison we have set up.

There is, and we should not forget it, enormous differences between heat and sound. One passes through a vacuum, the other cannot; what produces the acoustic sensation is the vibration of a mass of molecules, relatively slow and transmitted at a speed of some hundreds of metres per second; what makes heat is an *individual* and very precipitate movement of each molecule from the focus of emission, reproducing itself many trillions of times and transmitted (solar heat) at a speed of 300,000 kilometres per second.* And yet these two orders of phenomena are related; they offer three great identical facts: (1) in the first place, an accumulation of a certain force, alike in the body heated and in the body vibrating; (2) dissemination at a distance by synchronous vibrations (that is to say, with periods of like duration, backwards and

* The author seems here to confuse heat and light.—ED.

forwards) transmitted by the ether or the air ;
and (3) a partial capture of this *vis viva* in every
direction by bodies which become heated or give
forth sounds.

On the other hand, heat and light have been
closely approximated ; after it had been noted
that they were subject to the same variations of
weakness or intensity each time the vibration
itself was modified, it became possible to consider
them as two phenomena due to one unique vibratory
movement possessing two connected properties, the
one luminous, the other calorific, and producing two
different effects. Lastly, and of this there can be no
doubt, the luminous and the electrical oscillations,
projected in the same medium, relate to one
single phenomenon.

Thus, after having observed the properties
common to electricity and light, to light and
radiant heat, to heat and to sound (*exceptis
excipiendis !*), it is difficult not to acknowledge a
certain unity in things, ·with special laws for very
different modalities.

This unity the mathematical physicist continually
finds inscribed of itself in the formulas he uses,
and in which it seems as if the phenomena he puts
into words mutually exchange their language.
When he meets with the same equation in the
theory of attraction, in that of the movements of
liquids, in that of the electric potential, in that of
magnetism, and in that of the propagation of heat,
etc. . . . it is difficult, unless one is blind, not to
see that the most opposite phenomena, having no
apparent relationship, are yet connected by a secret

internal analogy, that of the principle which governs them.

Music has its place in this harmony. It is not an exception, a miracle, it forms part of a concert in which one can define its field. Its originality consists in belonging, at the same time, to two different worlds, and in subjecting to the conditions of objective life, to the laws of acoustics and of numbers, that flow of force which proceeds from the depths of feeling. . . .

We can, therefore, extend to all phenomena the observations made above with regard to sounds and colours. As a rule, physicists are not fond of generalizing ; they study, especially, the restricted systems that observation can reach and declare that they know nothing of the Universe, taken as a whole. They willingly leave to philosophers the work of constructing theories which go beyond the range of experiment. Yet one idea disengages itself from their labours. If everything is vibration, everything is energy. Energy is not merely a force superposed on matter and which, distinct from it, animates it by virtue of a fundamental law ; it is identical with the things of reality and would suffice to explain everything. " On this hypothesis matter would only be the capacity for kinetic energy, its pretended impenetrability energy of volume, and its weight energy of position in the particular form which presents itself in universal gravitation ; nay, space itself would only be known to us by the expenditure of energy necessary to penetrate it.*

Lucien Poincaré, *La Physique moderne, son évolution*, p. 67 *sq.*, Eng. ed. (Kegan Paul & Co., London, 1907).

Even were this idea somewhat insufficient to constitute a complete and thoroughly solid doctrine, it would be quite capable of explaining certain characteristics of musical emotion.

Now music, as we have seen, unable as it is to " imitate " any given passion, generalizes and confines itself to reproducing the *dynamics* of psychological life. But these dynamics we do not regard as being the exclusive image of feeling ; the concepts once put aside, we interpret these dynamics as a new and involuntary generalization ; unconsciously, we assimilate them to those of natural phenomena. Of the nature which adds itself to our internal being, we know nothing or next to nothing, and if by chance we do know something, we certainly do not think of it when we are listening to a symphony : but this ignorance is exactly a condition of the psychical state created by music. It amazes us, disturbs us, and fills us with delight as if, unknown to us, it placed us in the heart of things and put us in communion with the principle of them : hence that emotion, in which those unconscious phenomena, ignorance and illusion, play so great a part, tends to take us outside the bounds of our personality, by making us feel beyond the petty things of the ego, through a prism of brilliant images—Life !

CHAPTER II

MUSIC AND MATHEMATICS

IT is not possible to study the phenomena of nature without bringing in the numbers which measure them. In the course of this study we come across a question—a sort of annexe to the subject examined in the preceding chapter—which occupies a very large place in the history of music, and appears, in the eyes of many persons, to be surrounded with mysteries difficult to unravel : What part do mathematics take in the theory of the musical art ? By what right are they brought into it ? What services do they render ? Let us at once comfort the reader by assuring him that, if he wish to be informed on this subject, it will only require a little attention and curiosity on his part.

At the outset of his celebrated lecture at Bonn, Helmholtz stated that he had always been struck by the relations between the musical art and mathematics. This is an idea which is as old as science itself, and has given rise to theories, sometimes excellent and at others inadmissible, according to the manner in which the same facts were presented.

Pythagoras, who is considered by our Western tradition as the greatest of all inventors in this province, discovered the numerical ratios which expressed the two fundamental intervals: $\frac{3}{2}$ for the fifth, $\frac{4}{3}$ for the fourth, $\frac{2}{1}$ for the octave. To be historically exact, we should say $\frac{2}{3}$, $\frac{1}{2}$, etc.; for the ancients, instead of counting the vibrations, measured the length of the vibrating strings, which is in an inverse ratio. But this matters little. Delighted with his discovery—which was, besides, an admirable one—and yielding to the temptation to generalize common to nearly all scholars, he first began to assimilate numbers with musical sounds, and then with the whole of reality. He elaborated from his discovery a theory both astronomical and cosmogonic. He imagined that, in nature, numbers were the substance of things, and that the quaternary number, the *tetractys*, 1, 2, 3, 4, was the "source of eternal nature" (*Vers dorés de Pythagore*, 47).*

I will give an idea of his point of view by stating that, had he known the phenomenon of multiple resonance, he would not have said : " The ratio of the first harmonic to the fundamental is $\frac{2}{1}$ because it is placed at the octave." He would have said instead, "that the first harmonic is placed at the octave because it must be in the ratio $\frac{2}{1}$ to the fundamental sound, and that this ratio pre-existed before all the rest." Numbers are being itself; the music in which they are realized is but an epiphenomenon. One sees at once that this fact, the numerical ratios of sounds, may become singularly strange, according to the manner in which it is pre-

---

* It is, of course, excessively improbable that the Golden Verses, a Neo-Platonic production, contain anything of Pythagoras.—ED.

sented, and that a thesis of abstruse metaphysics
may itself be substituted for the most inoffensive
observation.

The Chinese held not very dissimilar views. They
said that 3 was the sky, 2 the earth, and $\frac{3}{2}$ the
harmony of the world!

These ideas, though they were disputed by the
Eleatic philosophers (Parmenides, Zeno, fifth and
sixth centuries B.C.), long persisted in the mind of
the Greeks. Traces of them are often found in
Plato and Aristotle. "Numbers are the ideas (i.e.
things) and the sources of reality.—The soul is a
number which has movement." Discarding its
metaphysical pretensions, this system was handed
down to the Middle Ages by Boethius, and for centuries it tyrannized over music, forbidding, in the
name of the arithmeticians, certain advances which
popular instinct would of itself certainly have
realized.

In modern times, Descartes, who when defining
matter by its extent spoke as strange a language as
Pythagoras, Euler, and many others after them,
have attributed to numbers a very important part
in musical theory. I will mention the original and
brilliant—but somewhat empty—saying of Leibnitz : "Music is an unconscious arithmetical exercise." In his *Introduction to Philosophy*,* the
German philosopher Herbart writes, not without
some peevishness : "There are allegations whose
authority is due to audacity alone ; for instance,
it is claimed that numbers and their ratios (which

* *Lehrbuch zur Einleitung in die Philosophie,* Hartenstein's
complete edition (1850-2), I, p. 151, and II, pp. 114-6.

give the sole and unique means of distinguishing consonance from dissonance) are not the true elements of the *Beautiful* in music ! "

What must we think of all this ? Why into the theory of musical art are there brought, with the ratios of numbers, square-roots and logarithms ? In what way can this support or contradict the theory upheld in this present work ?

§ 1. Mathematics as a Means of Simplification and Analysis

Mathematics has no right to supreme power, but it has great claims to the gratitude of musicians.

1st. *It serves—and it is an infinitely valuable service—to convey in plain language that which has been created by the musical instinct.*

The order of facts is as follows : (1) The popular singer—who can neither read, write, nor cypher—invents melodies formed of certain intervals ; (2) the scholar studies these melodies, arranges in a certain order the notes of which they are composed, deduces from them the *scale*, and by empirical observations (comparison of the length of the vibrating strings which produce the sounds) he succeeds in determining the numerical relations representing the musical intervals : $\frac{1}{2}$ for the octave, and $\frac{2}{3}$ for the fifth, relations which, as soon as it becomes possible to count the vibrations, must be reversed and become $\frac{2}{1}$, $\frac{3}{2}$.

In propounding these relations, the mathematician has accomplished two things : he has summarized some real facts, for which he substitutes, for the greater facility of analysis, a very concise formula ;

in the second place, he has connected them with an objective law, independent of all music (law of the lengths of the strings).

This last act and the discovery it implies do not allow him to restrict himself to the part of an observer taking measurements : he has—or thinks he has—a principle to which everything may be referred ; the interval of the fifth will now enable him, not to build up an abstract system, created all of one piece by arithmetic, but to see more clearly into the phenomena of real music ; it is thus that he arrives at the constitution of the scale called " Pythagorean," which already is a mixed work, founded on observation, but attributes to *one* of the facts noted a preponderating importance—

$$1 \tfrac{9}{8}, \ \tfrac{81}{64}, \ \tfrac{4}{3}, \ \tfrac{3}{2}, \ \tfrac{27}{16}, \ \tfrac{243}{128} \ 2.$$

When two groups of vibrations are in the ratio of 1 to $\tfrac{9}{8}$, there is between the two sounds an interval of a major tone, *Do—Ré ;* if in the ratio of 1 to $\tfrac{24}{64}$, there is an interval of a third, etc. All these ratios are obtained from the single datum : $\tfrac{3}{2}$.

§ 2. Mathematics Suggest the Idea of Necessary Corrections

2nd. *By placing before our eyes, by means of perfectly clear symbolical substitutes, musical facts, to the direct observation of which we should sacrifice an enormous amount of time, the mathematician shows us, at one glance, the corrections of which these musical facts are susceptible.*

We will remark that, if *observation* supplies the primary basis, we cannot rely solely upon it to establish a musical system. In these days, when education is carried to such a pitch, how rare are the singers whose voices are always in tune! While observing what is done by musicians, we should rectify their habits, and not be the dupe of their mistakes, nor take a fault for a primary fact; in a word, put order into what is undetermined. Without this, it would be impossible to form the scale or, rather, to give a settled foundation to musical grammar. The mathematician, therefore, becomes dogmatic after having been a simple observer; he sets up and organizes musical facts after measuring them; he is forced to take up this new part, for the language in which he obliges the phenomena to express themselves is so clear and striking that it of itself suggests the idea of certain improvements.

Here is the interval of the third, valued in the Pythagorean scale at the ratio 81 : 64. This measure is deduced from a general principle (the fifth), and, at the same time, it has been possible to deduce it from certain usages amongst musicians. But we shall see immediately that it is not a very happy one.

Two simultaneous sounds give rise to a third sound, the number of vibrations of which is determined by the difference between the two first. In this case, between 81 and 64, it would be sound 17. Now, 17 has for its octave 34, and for its double octave 68, which is higher than 64. The two sounds of the Pythagorean third therefore give rise to a sound which is dissonant in relation to them, and for this reason this third is contrary to the harmony. It is too great.

In the scale called the physicists', in which the

system of Pythagoras has been modified, this third has been reduced to the ratio 5 : 4. In this the sound produced is 1, which has for its octave 2 and 4, and consequently strengthens one of the two elements composing the third.

This new third, likewise, is given by experiment as well as being discovered by theory. The remarks of MM. Mercadier and Cornu have, in fact, proved that musicians use the third 81 : 64 in monody, and the 5 : 4 in polyphony.

The slightest modification in so delicate a system as the scale is pregnant with consequences. If, from an excessive longing for unity, we adopt the second third to the exclusion of the first, the whole of our scale is in disorder, although this change seems insignificant. If we reduce the interval *Do—Mi*, we are obliged to reduce at the same operation the two other thirds, *Fa—La* and *Sol—Si*. Further, to lessen *Do—Mi* necessarily enlarges *Mi—Fa*, and the same occurs between *Si* and *Do* by the modification of *Sol—Si*. Lastly, the sharps and flats likewise feel the effects of these alterations. In the scale of the physicists, the *Do*♯ is lower than the *Ré*♭; in the Pythagorean system, on the contrary, it is higher. We are therefore confronted by the following question : Admitting a change in one part of the scale, to which of the other parts must we look for compensation ?

Mathematics has created the difficulty ; by its aid we shall find the solution.

A third scale has been constructed, named the "temperamental," which, instead of subjecting this or that interval to the necessary alteration, applies

this alteration to *all* the intervals of the scale,
divided into twelve uniform semi-tones. Here,
again, it is calculation which gives us the formulas,
and that in the most simple way.

Let us represent by a the tonic as our starting
point. The octave should be $2a$. Between these two
points we have to place 12 equal semi-tones.

The first degree above the tonic will be obtained
by multiplying this tonic by an unknown quantity.
This obligation of *multiplying* instead of adding
was unknown to the ancients, and need not
surprise us. To state that *Ré*♮ is to *Do* in the
ratio $\frac{9}{8}$ is to say that *Ré* ♮=the $\frac{9}{8}$ of *Do*. To find
Ré we must therefore take the $\frac{9}{8}$ of *Do*, that is,
multiply *Do* by $\frac{9}{8}$.

Let q be the constant interval to be inserted
12 times in the new scale. The first degree after a
will be aq; the next $aq \times q$, or aq^2; then $aq \times q \times q$,
or aq^3, etc., which will give us—

$$a, aq, aq^2, aq^3, aq^4, aq^5, aq^6 \ldots 2a.$$

If, instead of taking each value, always formed
of the same elements a and q, but with different
exponents, we take these exponents alone (0, 1, 2,
3, 4, 5, 6 . . .), we obtain an arithmetical progression instead of a geometrical one ; and if q is
known, it will be sufficient, in order to determine
any note in the scale, that we know the corresponding exponent. This is what is called finding a
number by means of its *logarithm*.

The base we require here is obtained as follows :
to go from a to $2a$, it being a question of ratios,
expressed in fractions, we have had to proceed by
multiplication, and not by addition ; consequently,

to obtain the degree-type of our scale, which comprises twelve uniform intervals, we have not to divide the *difference* $2a - a = a$ by 12, but to take the twelfth root of the *quotient* $2a : a = 2$. The fundamental formula of the temperamental scale is therefore $\sqrt[12]{2}$, the value of the chromatic semi-tone.

The following table gives the intervals of the twelve degrees of the temperamental scale to about $1/10^6$. Side by side are the values of the notes of the Pythagorean and physicists' scales—

Temperamental Scale.	Scale of Pythagoras.	Scale of Physicists.
$Do \ = 1$	$1 = 1$	1
$Do \ \sharp = 1 \cdot 059463$		
$Ré \ = 1 \cdot 122462$	$\frac{9}{8} = 1 \cdot 125$	$\frac{9}{8} = 1 \cdot 125$
$Ré \ \sharp = 1 \cdot 189207$		
$Mi \ = 1 \cdot 259921$	$\frac{81}{64} = 1 \cdot 265625$	$\frac{5}{4} = 1 \cdot 25$
$Fa \ = 1 \cdot 334840$	$\frac{4}{3} = 1 \cdot 333 \ldots$	$\frac{4}{3} = 1 \cdot 3333 \ldots$
$Fa \ \sharp = 1 \cdot 414214$		
$Sol \ = 1 \cdot 498307$	$\frac{3}{2} = 1 \cdot 5$	$\frac{3}{2} = 1 \cdot 5$
$Sol \ \sharp = 1 \cdot 587401$		
$La \ = 1 \cdot 681793$	$\frac{27}{16} = 1 \cdot 6875$	$\frac{5}{3} = 1 \cdot 6666 \ldots$
$La \ \sharp = 1 \cdot 781797$		
$Si \ = 1 \cdot 887749$	$\frac{243}{128} = 1 \cdot 8984375$	$\frac{15}{8} = 1 \cdot 875$
$Do \ = 2$		2

Thus arithmetic, it will be seen, after having been *ancilla cantus*, becomes *magistra cantus*, in the sense that it succeeds by degrees in disengaging from the facts the principle which governs them.

In music it is not always, as in physics, the sole language used ; the composer might even be unacquainted with it : feeling, imagination, and pure thought might fully suffice him. If, however, we do not rely on instinct alone and demand a doctrine, arithmetic presents itself first, since the musical construction is formed out of measurable quantities. It is immensely convenient—eliminating all the complex peculiarities of things and only retaining their form, and it places before the eyes of the theorist symbols which save him from loss of time, and on which he can work as on the realities themselves.

It has been objected that, on the one hand, numbers and numerical ratios reject *all approximate calculations ;* that, on the other hand, in practical music everything is but approximation, perfect and absolute exactness never having been obtained ; and that, consequently, all connection between the language of figures and that of sounds is vain. This objection would have the sole effect of demonstrating the utility of mathematics : they furnish means, more certain than the ear, of appreciating the errors themselves ; and the system they allow us to set up, if never strictly followed by the virtuosi, is a necessary ideal which they should seek to attain as nearly as possible.

This observation applies, above all, to the symphony, in which several instruments which need a common base of agreement come in. To adopt as a normal pitch a sound created by 870 vibrations per second, and make it the principle of this base, is to recognize that music cannot be socialized without the aid of arithmetic.

Finally, the musical instrument maker finds himself in the same position as the physicist, as regards method and means of labour ; without the formulas

which mathematics has constructed once for all
from a study of the facts, he would only succeed,
after a long course of experiments, in fixing the
spot where the tube must be bored for making a
flute, or the point on the distended string where the
hammer should strike in a piano. The extent of
each instrument is fixed by acoustic laws ; the composer who writes for the trombone, the horn, the
flute, the double bass, etc., must know accurately
this compass ; he is, therefore, in the act of creation,
ruled by objective laws which can be expressed by
numerical formulas, which he must master if he
would not resign himself to the use of simple
receipts.

§ 3. Mathematics as a Means of Discovering Important Analogies

3rd. *By causing reality to speak a language in very
general use, mathematics enables us to perceive curious analogies between music and phenomena very far
removed from it.*

It has been said that the great book of nature
" is written in the language of mathematics ' '
(Galileo). And, certainly, while bearing in min d
that writing is not thought, we may say the sam e
of a musical work, which can be entirely expressed-
by numbers and their ratios. Now, one of the
great advantages of the expression of fundamental intervals by numerical ratios is that it
allows us to make very easy comparisons between
separate phenomena, and suggests to us analogies
which, without them, might have remained un-
noticed.

It is a fact singularly worthy of notice that a fundamental sound emitted by a stretched string and the first five partial sounds accompanying it should be towards one another as the numbers 1, 2, 3, 4, 5, 6, that these first harmonics should give the perfect chord, and that the simplicity of the ratios which constitute them should cease at the next harmonic, which is very dissonant in relation to the base and out of use. Is there in this a peculiarity special to music? or is it, indeed, the manifestation of a general law?

It is understood that one cannot tell precisely when a ratio ceases to be simple; but, in practice this difficulty does not exist. If, when playing the piano, my right hand has to strike a certain number of semi-quavers taken from the series 1–6, while my left hand plays a certain but different number of quavers in the same series, I experience no great difficulty, because the ratio of the two movements will appear simple to me. But if, on the contrary, I have to produce five sounds with one hand, and a lesser number with the other, it will be difficult to manage. Thus is it, with a great show of reason, that consonance has been considered to be due to simple ratios.

This was the opinion of Pythagoras and Aristotle, as also that of Descartes, who only admitted in musical constitution the numbers 2 and 3, and rejected the number 5 as creating a rhythm perfected with difficulty. His error was rectified two hundred years later, in 1818, by M. Gallin, when he stated that the quinary rhythm could be as easily perceived *in any rather quick movement* as the binary or ternary rhythm. In 1739, in his *Essais d'une nouvelle Théorie musicale*, Euler took up the Cartesian theory and developed ideas which may be summed up as follows: "No assembly of sounds can please us save when we can discover the law of their arrangement. The more plainly we see the order which reigns in the object constructed, the more we find it simple and perfect."

Among the moderns, one of the most convinced partisans of this system was M. Meerens, who regards the numbers 2, 3, 5 as always giving out musical sounds, and places in these numbers alone the principle of melody, of consonance, and of time and rhythm.

M. de Hartmann* thought to establish very important considerations on this fact, that the simple ratios, so much discussed in musical theory, also regulate the series of colours. M. Hugo Goldschmidt, professor of natural science at the University of Heidelberg, has written a recent work to affirm that the law is the same in the phenomena of crystallization. In a curious work, *The Magic of Numbers* (1882, in German), Hellenbach asserted that "the Universe is constructed so as to realize as much as possible the law of simple and rational numbers."

This last affirmation will perhaps seem on a par with the idea of Kepler, that, when creating the world and regulating the order of the heavens, God had in His mind the five regular polyhedrons of geometry! But, without having such soaring dogmatic ambitions, we only need to read and compare

* In his *Philosophy of the Beautiful*, 1867, in German.

in order to perceive, on certain points, an identity
between the laws of music and those of chemistry.
The comparison of these two orders of phenomena
was already patent to the Greeks, who called by
the name of *mixture* and *combination* (κρᾶσις and
μίξις)—without distinguishing between the two—
every emission of simultaneous sounds in simple
ratios, and compared consonance to the "mixture"
of wine with honey.

Let us recall some of the laws discovered at the
beginning of the nineteenth century—

"*When two or several bodies are united in several
proportions, the weights of one of these bodies which
unites it to an equal weight of the other are in direct
proportion to each other.*" (Law of Multiple Proportions, or Dalton's Law, 1808.) For instance,
oxygen forms with nitrogen six different compounds.
In these the weights of oxygen, combined with a
like weight of nitrogen equal to 7, are respectively
equal to 4, 8, 12, 16, 20, 24, or, between themselves,
resemble our harmonics 1, 2, 3, 4, 5, 6.

"*The weights according to which the different
bodies are united to the same weight of the same substance represent the ratios according to which these
weights unite among themselves, or are the simple
multiples of these ratios.*" (Law of Proportional
Numbers, ascribed to Berzelius, 1810.)

"*When two gases combine, the volumes of the component gases are in direct proportion to each other;
(2) the volume of the combination, measured in the
gaseous state, in the same conditions of temperature
and pressure, is in direct proportion to the sum of the
volumes of the components.*" (Laws of the com-

bination of the volume of gas, ascribed to Gay-Lussac, 1810.)

Thus the volumes of hydrogen and of oxygen which combine to form water are in the simple ratio, 2 to 1. This is the ratio which expresses the octave in music.

CHAPTER III

MUSIC AND LIVING BEINGS

THERE is one last realm I wish to explore.

We have just compared music to the phenomena, which we were unable to term "material" in the old sense of the word, now that the ideas of energy and vibration have penetrated into the intra-molecular world itself ; at all events, we cannot confuse them with living beings. Is it possible to stretch as far as the latter the parallel sketched out above ? If so, where are we to search for the second term of our comparison ? Shall it be in the mind and the thought of the musician ? or in the various kinds of compositions—symphony, opera, religious chants—considered as organized beings ? or, again, in the concrete and personal musical work ? Without going too closely into the question, I would point out a few similarities which will serve to make plainer the part of the unconscious which enters into musical emotion, and the harmonies of which it is composed.

1st. Living beings are capable of assimilation and are organized ; (2nd) they evolve ; (3rd) they reproduce their species, decline, and die.

Such are the three general ideas round which a few musical facts may be grouped.

§ 1. Assimilation and the Musical Mind

In his *Leçons sur les Phénomènes de la vie Communs aux Animaux et aux Végétaux* (1878), Claude Bernard makes the following declaration : " Relinquishing the attempt to define the indefinable, we will simply endeavour to characterize living beings in relation to matter." Thus, we do not define life ; nor the *essence* of musical thought, which is a form of life. We may generalize, and say that all *essential* definition is impossible ; if, by chance, any definition of this kind were given to us by a superman, we should not comprehend it.

There are persons who, not satisfied with the surface measurements given by physicists, want to know " of what consists " or " of what is made," intrinsically, such and such a phenomenon. It is doubtful whether they know clearly what they are asking. However much I may cudgel my brains, I am unable to conceive a force *in itself*. We are only cognizant of effects and mechanism ; and we must not be more exacting with regard to the musician than to the physicist or to the biologist. There is but one way of knowing life or artistic thought direct ; it is the inward sense, or consciousness.

All living bodies are distinguished from material bodies by one fundamental property, *i.e.*, assimilation. At every moment, on every point of the matter of which they are made, there occur losses and gains, a breaking down and a building up, which imply the assimilation of two substances. The musical mind also has the unceasing and invisible activity of "elementary life," and is placed, at whatever moment we take of general or individual history, between a conservative heredity and revolutionary forces. It may react in an infinity of ways—to its advantage or the contrary—by the contact and penetration of two kinds of influence, viz.: those proceeding from its environments, which it transposes or transforms; and those which are derived directly from ancient or modern music. By an assimilation, nearly always unconscious, the mind of the musician forms itself, like that of the man of letters, by (musical) reading, by the examples of the masters, by imitation and by observation. Conversely to matter, it is not used up, but fortifies and develops itself by the exercise of its activity. Like living beings, it nourishes itself with aliments which have to be suitable and digestible to assure its growth, or otherwise they may give it disease, poison it, and kill it.

The characteristics connected with the faculty of assimilation are, in the case of living beings, complexity and organization. The microscope reveals the fact that they are not homogeneous, but that their existence results from a mixture of various substances reacting on each other. We know, likewise, the very complex elements which analysis discovers in the formation of the musical mind :— physiological aptitudes of the ear, memory, sentiment, faculty of abstraction, purely intellectual activity, and imagination ; hereditary patrimony and acquired culture ; unconscious application of the law of numbers and creative spontaneity ; social life and objective life penetrating into personal life. . . . And if we examine a symphony, and borrow the methods and the terminology of the biologists, we shall have no difficulty in demonstrating the same complexity.

The co-ordination of the mechanism of life in a superior living being is admirable. Biologists relinquish all idea of describing it completely ; they are compelled to divide it into partial activities or functions, which they can only distinguish in a very conventional way, because they are so closely bound together. Admirable, likewise, is the unity of musical thought creating such a complete work as a quatuor or a symphony of Beethoven.

Of such an organism we may say, with Claude Bernard : it is a " special arrangement which gives birth to the immanent properties of living matter." A fugue starts with a subject which is a cell subjected to dichotomy. *All* the elements of which a symphony is composed react on each other. Two forms only seem to escape this general law ; but they are very inferior forms which prove the rule : one, the *rhapsody*, limits itself to juxtapositions without construction or development ; the other, the *pot-pourri*, of which the sole object is to please the ear.

The opera itself, when it is in truth a lyrical drama, obeys this law of co-ordination and unity. The *Leitmotive*, or "conducting themes," have only been one of the means employed to *organize* a very vast composition, to preserve it from the inartistic fault of indefinite juxtaposition, and to arrange its parts in a coherent whole.

We may even draw from this a rule of criticism : a musical work should form one complete and unbroken whole. In the same way that we do not—except in the case of hydras !—make extracts or " chosen portions " of living beings, so should it be impossible to cut in two a fine composition without altering its character ; and every time that, from an opera, a symphony, or any poem, we are able to take a few pages without lessening their value, to play them apart, it is, except in special and rare cases, a certain sign that the work is only of moderate value.

§ 2. Musical Evolution and Living Beings

The second characteristic of living beings, the most remarkable of all, according to Claude Bernard, is evolution. Every being is so perfectly adapted to its conditions of existence that from the first we doubt whether such admirable instruments can have been suddenly produced in their state of perfection. Thus, a machine, with all its improvements, could not have been invented by one single man (Darwin). Music offers us ample material for here continuing our parallel.

While obeying an instinct which escapes our analysis, and is even impossible for us to conceive, the musician, as we have already seen in a special chapter, feeds himself on everything which his social environment sends him. Now, this external environment changes, and therefore the internal conditions of musical life change also.

Music necessarily renews itself in order to adapt itself to circumstances, which also are incessantly renewed. The formation of a musician's talent, influenced both by the principle of heredity and by quantitative or qualitative acquirements from out-

side, brings clearly to mind the formation of a living
being.   In lieu of studying it in history, it can be
viewed in the individual, who repeats and often
exemplifies the evolution of the species.   The musical
mind of the child who has just learnt his notes, their
places on the keyboard, and the elements of the
grammar, only knows the parasitical life.   When he
has reached exercises in harmony, he still resembles,
docilely listening to his master's word, the embryo
which in the maternal womb assimilates nutritive
matter.   He develops, as the biologists say, by
epigenesis ; that is to say, by the addition of new
to pre-existing parts.

After having placed notes one atop of the other, in
order to construct chords, he passes on to the study
of counter-point ; and it is for him a new life, a
kind of metamorphosis, like that of a tadpole
which, first adapted for the aquatic life of ponds,
afterwards fits himself for life on land. He eliminates
from his mind certain now useless ideas ;   henceforth left to himself, his evolution continues un-
ceasingly, either continuing the line of heredity—or
the mysterious impulsion of nature—or adapting
himself (*necessarily*, but as far as in him lies) to
outside conditions.   It is thus that Bach absorbed
the art of the Italians, that of the French, that of
the Germans who had preceded or were contempo-
raneous with him, before he opened the era of
modern music.   Thus did Beethoven imitate Mozart
before he wrote the sonata dedicated to the Archduke Rodolph ; thus did Wagner imitate Meyerbeer
before writing the tetralogy ; and thus did Verdi,
like so many others, modify late in life his æsthe-

tics in order to adapt himself to the Wagnerian fashion, then supreme.

To understand and properly judge a composer the critic should, therefore, replace him in the historical concatenation of which he is one of the links.

These " variations "—in the sense given to the word by naturalists—are almost always a conquest of some higher form of life ; but they may be wandering or arrested by malady or fatigue or even retrograde, that is to say, they may suddenly reproduce, in the middle of their upward progress, the lower and obsolete type of some ancestor. We have examples of this in the symphony and opera of the present day. One reservation only, and that a very important one, must be added to the indication of these analogies.

The living being must either change or remain passive when adapting itself to the conditions of existence. Either in a direct way (Lamarck), or after the struggle for life and hereditary transmission (Darwin), he is subject to what G. Saint-Hilaire, in 1828, termed the " ambient world," and what we now call the " environment." There is in the South of France an olive tree adapted to the climate ; take it to the Champ de Mars in Paris, and it will perish. The musical or literary work which has a success in Norway, because it is there in harmony with the social life, may, similarly, be struck by a kind of death if transferred to Paris ; but it is possible also that it might transform the " environment " and not be transformed by it. In a word, music, up to a certain degree, is an educating force.

For the study of musical evolution a more definite object than the musical mind might be taken : the orchestra, for instance, comparable at the present day to some gigantic and powerful animal.

The succession of the various embryonic stages shows that the living being is at first indeterminate. It does not possess all its organs at once : some are wanting or are merely rudimentary. The individual is formed by degrees, passing from the simple to the compound, from the homogeneous to the heterogeneous.

The orchestra experienced, at first, the indeterminate stage. I refer to those "Recueils" of the sixteenth century—songs, four-part dances—which are to be *sung* or *played*, or both one *and* the other, but without giving a precise indication of the instruments in the composer's mind : "For all kinds of instruments" sometimes says the sub-title.

In the seventeenth and eighteenth centuries a specialization of the functions begins to appear, but all the orchestral parts are not written down ; some are *ad libitum*. The chief care of the composer, after fixing on the type of instrument to accompany the singer, is to establish a bass. Each note of this bass ought to form a support for a chord, but he confines himself to representing them by ciphers ; and it is the pianist, placed in the centre of the orchestra, who, guided by these indications, does all the rest. It is something like a substance without any settled texture, but able to give birth to new cells.

One of the creators of opera, Caccini, announces at the beginning of his *Eurydice* (1600) that he has marked *in the bass* the intervals of the fourth, sixth,

x

and seventh, the major and minor thirds, but that "for the middle voices, necessary in certain places, he leaves them to the judgment and taste of the executant." Glück himself, who represents a more mature period, does not always take the trouble to note all that the orchestra has to say, or to name distinctly the instrument to which he gives the word. "It will hardly be believed," remarks Mlle. Pelletan in her edition of *Iphigénie en Aulide*, "that the copyist had, in many cases, to himself compose the scores of the wind instruments from those of the stringed." Glück at times writes the scores of the first violins on the line of the seconds; he writes on the upper double octave of the basses those of the altos, which should be in unison; or, again, he forgets the tone of the horns; he writes a part without indicating whether it is for the flute, the hautbois, or the clarionet; he writes on the line of the double basses a few important notes for the bassoon, etc.

Such an orchestra may well be compared to a new-born child whose frame and organs are not fully formed. At the present day, as we are aware, nothing of the kind happens. The composer leaves no detail uncertain ; the slightest shades of rendering are minutely indicated. The orchestra has reached the adult age, in possession of all its organs, which are clearly differentiated.

The ever-increasing number of the forces which the orchestra utilizes is also a type of evolution.

We know from various documents that the orchestra of J. S. Bach was composed of sixteen voices and scarcely twenty instrumentalists. That of Handel, on the same plane, reached thirty-two performers. Burney, writing in 1770, informs us that in the church of Padua there were forty musicians, of whom sixteen were singers. These specific cases enable us to imagine the ordinary usage. For secular music the orchestra does not appear to have exceeded, in the eighteenth century, fifty in number, and was nearly always below this figure. To-day it has increased with the size of the halls, as has the number of the audiences, and the richness of the scenery. Wagner needed 110 musicians; Berlioz wanted 800 ! . . .

From a more technical point of view, again, the evolution of the orchestra is interesting. Formerly— at the period anterior to Glück's best operas— instruments were not employed, as now, in one great mass; they were divided into types coming in one after the other. For accompanying the voices, and for each item in his Mass in *Si* minor, Bach selects the instrument which he deems most suitable; and during the whole piece this instrument remains the chief one, often without any other support than the bass. Thus, the *Corno da caccia*, (hunting horn) which accompanies the *quoniam* of this mass, only appears in this one piece; it is the same with the *Viol d'amore*, the hautbois, and the bassoon, the cornets (*Zinken*), the trombones, the trumpets, and other instruments which, in turn and not simultaneously, are put in prominence. When one calls to mind the fullness of the modern orchestra, one sees that evolution has taken place not only in the direction of power, brilliancy, richness, and colour, but also of that unity which allows the living being, endowed with responsible faculties, to become conscious of all that he is.

I will add that in the musical world, as with living beings, it is difficult not to recognize a "struggle for life." Among the composers who write, the virtuosi who perform, the masters who teach, the instrument makers who manufacture—among the forms of art themselves, whether in the secular or in the religious world—competition is as sharp as it is continuous. At all epochs there has been a conflict of talents unequally adapted : conflicts of schools, conflicts of theories, conflicts of kinds. The symphony has supplanted religious music ; and the opera is now killing the symphony. In music, as in all else, the strongest triumph, only to recommence the struggle, and to be overcome in their turn. Thus is evolution produced.

§ 3. Generation and Music

The third characteristic which distinguishes living beings is generation, with which we may link everything relating to anomalies, decay, and death.

In nature, as in music, generation may be studied under two forms—

1st. Living beings are distinguished from material bodies by the faculty they have, after having been engendered, to generate in their turn. *Omne vivum ex vivo* (Harvey). The belief in spontaneous generation is now classed among errors championed by nobody. A musical work is a spontaneous creation, but this spontaneity could not exist had it not proceeded, and, as it were, been called forth by a more or less distant heredity. A masterpiece, sym-

phonical or lyrical, is never an isolated fact.   If
preceded by a line of ancestors, to it succeeds a line
of descendants.   Hence we see that compositions
cannot be likened to living beings, except in the
case of compositions of a superior order.

All the evolution of polyphonic song earlier than
the sixteenth century culminates in Palestrina.
Nor did Bach invent anything.   Never was work
more evidently prepared by his forerunners than
his.   Every great artist proceeds from a previous
one, and in his turn generates others.   To Peri (end
of the sixteenth century), who confined himself to
recitatives and choruses of three or four voices
generally accompanied by a figured bass, succeeds
Monteverde, to him Lulli, to Lulli Rameau and
Glück : the chain continues with Mozart, Weber,
Meyerbeer, and ends without a break in the author
of *Tristan und Isolde*.   The composer raises up heirs
by his example, by his teaching, by the disciples
directly formed by him, and by the school or
opinion he has created.

2nd.   A second form of generation may be mentioned here.   The transmission of talents and
qualities does not always occur between individuals
of pure race, in a straight line which represents the
heredity of the characteristics of the race.   Among
living beings, unions are formed between persons
near to one another, or greatly differentiated.

I shall venture a few reflections here on the
analogies between musical and plant life.

The fruit served up at our table, the flowers with
which we like to decorate our rooms, nearly all the
comestible or ornamental species we utilize are the

produce of art, cultivation, and selection, in fact of the art of *grafting*. Cultivation from seed is thought insufficient.

In the arts something similar occurs. First, in literature, Nisard has already remarked that the law under which French poetry was developed was that of *imitation*, which is nothing else but *grafting*. Corneille grafted the genius of Latin on to that of French, and as the first introduced specific modifications into the second, there resulted an intermediate type. Racine did the same with Greek, etc. The same law seems to hold good in music.

In fact, we are only acquainted with different sorts of music which have developed because a foreign art has been united with them. In the East, Korean and Chinese music were grafted on the Japanese. This last had itself borrowed from that of the Hindus. Egyptian music grafted itself at the outset on the music of the Assyrians and Hebrews, as later did the Persian on Arab music. Among the Greeks, as attested by the names of certain modes, Oriental music was grafted on to the national music.

Among the moderns the art of those Netherlanders, who from 1450 to 1600 were the recognized models, successively imparted its sap first to the French, and then to the Italian genius. Italian art, which from 1600 to about 1700 was the most brilliant of all, interpenetrated the German genius, and this latter, which from the eighteenth century downwards held the supremacy, was grafted on to the art of nearly all the other countries of Europe.

One very side we see nothing but crossings, changes, transmissions, and interpenetrations. Phenomena of this kind might be, above all, studied in France, where musical eclecticism has been very great, and where the combination of very different hereditary patrimonies with unequal coefficients, distributing its effects over a large number of descendants, produces at the present day a remarkable polymorphism.

The results of cross unions are the most vigorous, because the already adapted average type will always be present (Le Dantec).

This is the point when the comparison becomes more interesting and may even give rise to practical conclusions.

Naturalists warn us that certain species cannot be grafted. There must be selection, else the labour is in vain. The mistake made by the ancients, by Virgil and Pliny, was endeavouring to make the vine grow on the olive tree, and holly on the rose tree. These are what are called "heteroclitical" grafts. A contemporary of Buffon, Duhamel du Monceau, has proved them to be impossible. To arrive at any result, the operations must be carried out with plants as nearly related as possible, and with a close botanical affinity. It is the same with the transfusion of blood. If blood from a different species is injected into an invalid, not only is the patient not fortified thereby, but may die through the toxic effect of the serum from species not related, and especially through the globulicide action.

Many musicians have fallen into an error of this species. If the grafting of the Italian on the French genius has produced a charming musician, such as Gounod, it is because it brought together two

kindred races'; but is not the visible check of certain
attempts at the acclimatization, in France, of other
forms of musical art due to a contrary circumstance ?

The analogy just pointed out may be carried
further. Modern naturalists inform us that the
principle which excludes heteroclitical graftings *is
only in part true* (Dastre) : it applies to the apple
and pear trees, but not to the almond and the peach,
the plum and the apricot trees, which are genera
further removed from each other. It has been found
possible to fix the olive on the lilac and on the ash
tree. Recently, M. Daniel has succeeded in joining
the lilac to the maple. Thus there are exceptions.
But even to this extent, and precisely on account of
these exceptions, somewhat indeterminate in number, the principle is applicable to musical works.

We have French composers who, by miracles of
skill, have succeeded in producing exotic music ;
but these are exceptional works, always presenting anomalies and gaps. Bach may have gained
much by imitating Italian genius, but we may
be allowed to urge that, at times, the same operation was less favourable to Handel.

As in a plant resulting from too risky a graft
the size of the tree and the exuberance of the foliage
are greatly sacrificed to the size of the fruit, so in
musical works which aspire to bring together
mannerisms of feeling, of thought, and of expression
too different from one another, there are evident
inequalities, shocking incongruities, and something
strange and deformed. Thus, in the operas of
Handel the ornate at times resembles an excessive
vegetation, which jars on the mind.

Living beings do not always procreate healthy, well-constituted individuals of normal organization. Sometimes they produce beings of a doubtful character, and even monsters. The study of anomalies takes a large place in natural history; musical works also offer to it ample and interesting matter.

In the first place, there are among living beings Protean kinds (Darwin), that is to say, genera very complex and as it were shunning analysis. By some they are considered true species, by others simple varieties. There is something similar in music. The madrigal, the oratorio, the symphony with its programme are often difficult to classify. This undecided character recently allowed the *Damnation of Faust*, by Berlioz, to be put on the stage as a real opera, and at the same time produced energetic protests against this attempt. Contemporary opera is called, in turn, "dramatic action," "lyrical comedy," "musical romance," etc. It is Protean, polymorphous.

The illegitimate pairing of two individuals of different species produces monsters, and as these monsters seem to be characterized by the juxtaposition, in all parts of their being, of two molecules which do not interpenetrate each other, they are usually sterile.

In music also there are monsters : they may have an ephemeral success and create a passing infatuation, but they never found a lasting school. They are sterile. I will quote two examples.

In the sixteenth century some composers, such as Claude de Jeune and Mauduit, imitating the eccentricities of certain poets of that period, bethought themselves of writing melodies in the fashion of antiquity, by measuring French words into shorts and longs, like the Sapphic and Alcaic Odes of Horace. It was coupling two principles which could stand side by side, but not combine. Monsters only were produced ; they have been sterile.

In the seventeenth century some well-meaning minds thought they would create the religious opera, edifying and spiritual : such were *Il Santo Alesio* of Laudi (1634), *Philotea, id est anima Deo cara*, a sacred comedy (1643). It was joining together two principles which cannot usefully unite ; so these works remain isolated in history.

Finally, species once extinct never reappear (Darwin). In music also, in which there is continuous evolution, we may speak of " extinct species." At the present day many kinds once held in honour have disappeared from use. Is it impossible that they should return ? The whim of a composer, no doubt, could restore to them a semblance of life ; nothing prevents the writing now (1907) of one of those dances so beloved during the ancient regime : *allemande, loure, canaries*, etc. etc. The musician may even go back to the Middle Ages and amuse himself by writing a diaphony or an organum, a "conduct" or a "hocquet." But naturalists point out a fact which is a warning : archæological resurrections cannot have for more than a moment any but a phantom life. They would no longer find among us conditions favourable to their existence.

Thus the essential laws of organized matter are

rediscovered in art.   The musical work appears, develops, and perpetuates itself like the living being :
escaping, like it, all complete and qualitative definition, it is in a like manner an organism formed
of   complex   elements   brought   into   unity ;   it
evolves,   for   numerous   reasons,   of   which   many
escape our notice (for the *primum movens* remains
unknown), but one of which is the struggle for life,
and the resulting selection.   Like the animal and
the plant, it can and must improve by the cross-
breeding of individuals belonging to species not too
distant.   Like them, finally, it has the gift of transmitting life after receiving it.

CONCLUSION

AFTER so many incursions into fields where I must, at times, have shown more curiosity than actual knowledge or clearness, it is time to conclude.

In order to define music, we have taken as starting-point musical feeling, which has revealed to us that a melody, when really deserving the name, is a thought *sui generis*, without concepts, but as significant to the musician as is, to the literary man, a thought formed without concepts. From musical feeling we passed on to the study of sensation and of the physiological mechanism; there, two routes branched off which we have successively followed : on the one side, social life; on the other, objective nature. We have shown the relations of music to both.

Music is refractory to all analysis which wishes to explain its essence; it appears isolated amid the arts of painting and poetry. But if it be so, it is solely because it has connections, deep, and not superficial, with the individual, social, and cosmic life. The mystery which surrounds it is in no way due to its nature or its organization, it proceeds from life itself, which it expresses with deep penetration and in the most general form. It issues from a universal and deep-seated instinct of humanity; it is feeling and imagination; and it obeys those laws which rule things and living beings. If a part of its secret is hidden from us, it is that the secret of nature is unfathomable; even did we know it, we should be unable to express it in words.

We think, however, that we have established a clear principle founded on observation, and supplying in practice a sure criterion, by enunciating the following definition : *Music is the art of thinking in sounds.* If this be not granted, it will be impossible to understand a quartet of Beethoven, or any other musical composition; a phrase can no longer be distinguished from a simple, regular sequence of sounds; it cannot be explained in what way *Au clair de la lune* differs from an adagio of one of the great masters. Our definition embraces all the facts and sacrifices none. The composer of music-hall waltzes is a man who thinks in sounds as does a Bach or a Handel, only his thought is weak, superficial, trivial, poor, and as far from that of Handel or Bach as that of an ordinary writer differs from the thought of a Leibnitz, a Pascal, or a Bossuet. The Hottentot, who has only three or four notes in his melodies, also thinks in sounds, only his thought is (from our point of view) blurred, incomplete, and barbarous.

Many minds fashioned by classical education are loth to admit that thought is possible without the aid of words. Yet it is a fact which must strike an observer. I have endeavoured not to multiply the already very numerous points of view I have had to take up in this work, by examining the real value of verbal language as the expression of deep psychical life, but I will sum up my opinion in a few words : the *essential* nature of things (moral or material) cannot be defined ; now verbal language, formed

of very clear concepts, only acts by means of definitions. It, therefore, deforms all it touches.

Music, on the contrary, liberated from literary
formalism and only borrowing from reality its
most general dynamics, is more able to pass through
the surface of things and to penetrate, more or less,
into their inmost being. This causes it to be a very
realistic and very valuable art, for, without it, many
far-off phases of moral life would remain closed to
us. But music is also a work of great imagination.
It is not too much to say that it gives a plastic form
to immaterial realities ; without neglecting fundamental laws, it creates possible ones. It is flexible,
diverse, and unequal ; it is free, it has wings, like
thought ; in a word, it does what it will.

At every stage of our investigation—physiology,
sociology, acoustics, mathematics — we have met
with a system which claimed to stay us by forcing
upon us its own explanation. But we simply, while
keeping on our road, stored up " contributions," and
it is indispensable thus to set things right.

The student of acoustics who sought to explain
musical art by that science alone would achieve
very poor results. One might as well, in order to
understand the poetry of Lamartine, simply study
his manuscripts, note their caligraphic mannerisms,
and interpret them after the manner of the graphologists. Sounds considered as mere matter certainly play, in a symphony, a more important part
than the caligraphic style or the voice of the
reciter does in poetry ; but, however pure, agreeable, and regularly connected they may be, they do
not, of themselves, constitute music.

The theory we are upholding—which, after all, only notes an evident fact, which we are unable to define fully---has no need whatever to call in metaphysical conceptions or to appeal to a vague mysticism. Musical thought is a form widely differentiated from our intellectual activity; but, by showing us its universality, history enables us to connect it with a primordial and persistent instinct of humanity, which is, no doubt, very apt for the dialectic of concepts, but has always required feeling, belief, and imagination for its existence.

We also know that the work of the musician, entirely permeated by social influences, is organized in accordance with general principles which overpass it and govern many other phenomena. We have discovered the same laws at various stages in life. We have, therefore, the right to draw conclusions as to the sentiment of one grand ensemble in which everything is connected by secret links.

In an article on music, in which all the conceptions of the Western world are again met with,* the Chinese Se-Ma-T'sien says : "Music *comes from within us*—music is *that which unifies.*" This twofold formula, in agreement with what has been said in former pages as to primitive magic and German philosophers, sums up the ruling thought of this book.

In a celebrated poem in his *Feuilles d'Automne (Ce qu'on entend sur la montagne)*, Victor Hugo contrasts the voices of nature with those of humanity. Nature gives out a grand, peaceful and joyous music, and the world, floating in space, is wrapped

* *Mémoires historiques de Se-Ma-T'sien*, translated, with notes, by Ed. Chavannes, Professor at the Collège de France. Leroux, 1889, Vol. III.

in harmony.   Humanity, on the contrary, gives
forth a sound which grates, like one produced
by a brazen bow on an iron lyre ; it is no longer a
symphony, but there are shrieks ! A contrast easy to
note, if in humanity we only view the conflicts of
interests, mean passions, political storms, and social
events, in fact, the superstructure, but if we penetrate to the permanent and universal base, there is
no longer a dissonance, and there is a concert which
should appeal to the poet's ear.

Without suspecting it we live, as guests of the
Cosmos, in the midst of a sublime harmony ; and
it is not possible for perfect accord not to exist
between what is within us and what is all around us.
The grandest function of music, by enlarging the
ego and freeing it from all surface divagations, is to
replace us in this harmony of which we have never
the full consciousness, but to which we are insensible,
because it is in us, and because without it we should
not be.   A *Lied* of Schumann, a nocturne of Chopin,
and a symphony of Beethoven, quite pure and without " programme," have the privilege of emancipating us and plunging us again into the midst of
universal harmony.   An art such as this, in spite of
the technical knowledge with which it has been enriched, is full of simplicity : it expresses, exalts,
and magnifies the feeling of life which aspires to a
higher state ; and it is marvellous that so many
things so coarsely indicated by analysis should be
contained in a passing breath of air. . . .

INDEX OF NAMES, WORKS, Etc.

INDEX OF SUBJECTS

A. A. S.

WILLIAM BRENDON AND SON, LTD.
PRINTERS, PLYMOUTH

THE
International
Scientific Series

Edited by F. LEGGE.

Each Book complete in One
Vol. Crown 8vo. cloth, 5s.,
unless otherwise described.

KEGAN PAUL, TRENCH, TRÜBNER,
AND CO. LTD.
Dryden House, Gerrard Street, London, W.

NEW VOLUMES

IN THE

INTERNATIONAL SCIENTIFIC SERIES.

The contents of this new important volume in the series are: Introductory Chapter dealing with methods of finding atomic weights; Historical Survey, including Prout's work, Dobereiner's Triads, Pettenkofer, Gladstone, Cooke and Dumas, Newland's Octaves, The Telluric Helix of de Chancourtois, The Periodic Law of Mendeléeff, Lothar Meyer's Atomic Volume Curve.

Carnelley's work on the melting and boiling points of the elements and their halogen compounds, Sir Wm. Crooke's Spiral, Johnstone Stoney's Logarithmic Spiral.

The properties of the elements as periodic functions of their atomic weights, illustrated with numerous diagrams

The various attempts to obtain a formula for the calculation of the atomic weights of the elements.

The atom considered from the standpoint of the periodic law.

The places of the Argon group, and of the Radio-active substances in the periodic table.

NEW EDITION IN PREPARATION.

XV. **LIGHT AND PHOTOGRAPHY.** By Dr. H. VOGEL and A. E.
GARRETT. Revised and brought up-to-date by A. E. GARRETT
Illustrated.

Will contain among other things chapters on the following :—

I.—Historical Survey including Work of Wedgewood and Davy
The Camera Obscura, The Daguerreotype, Talbot's Lichtpaus Paper,
The work of Nièpce de St. Victor, Archer's negative process, the wet
plate, &c.

II.—The chemical action of light including Pseudo-photographic
impressions.

III. Lenses—Single lens, Portrait lens, Telephoto lens, &c.

IV.—Plates and Films.

V.—Photographic papers, and the preparation of photographic
prints. Photography with chromium compounds.

VI.—Camera appliances.

VII.—Photographic Art: (*a*) Perspective; (*b*) Composition of
pictures; (*c*) Scientific and Technical.

VIII.—Book illustration: (*a*) Collotype; (*b*) Photo-lithography
(*c*) Half tone process; (*d*) The three colour process.

IX. Astronomical photography.

X. Röntgen Ray photography.

XI. Micro-photography.

XII. Colour photography.

XIII. Photo-telegraphy.

XIV. The kinematograph.

NEW VOLUMES IN PREPARATION.

EVOLUTION OF PURPOSIVE LIVING MATTER. By N. C.
MACNAMARA, F.R.C.S.

CHRYSTALS. By Dr. A. E. H. TUTTON.

PRACTICAL ARCHÆOLOGY. By Prof. GARSTANG.

A HISTORY OF BIRDS. By H. O. FORBES, LL.D., F.R.G.S., F.R.A.I.,
Reader in Ethnography in the University of Liverpool.

THE MODERN SCIENCE OF LANGUAGE. By HENRY CANTLEY
WYLD.

THE

INTERNATIONAL SCIENTIFIC SERIES.

Edited by F. LEGGE.

Each Book Complete in One Volume. Crown 8vo. cloth, 5s.
unless otherwise described.

Printed in the United Kingdom by
Lightning Source UK Ltd., Milton Keynes
141736UK00001B/49/P